WEST'S LAW SCHOOL ADVISORY BOARD

OIL AND GAS LAW
IN A NUTSHELL
FIFTH EDITION

By

JOHN S. LOWE

George W. Hutchison Professor of Energy Law,
Southern Methodist University

WEST®

A Thomson Reuters business

Mat #40657645

1st reprint—2010

To my best friend (and wife),

Jacquelyn Taft Lowe

*

PREFACE

The first oil well in the United States was drilled in 1859 to a depth of 69 feet. In the century and a half since then, the United States and the rest of the world have developed economies that are based on oil and gas as their major fuel sources. Approximately 40 percent of U.S. energy used comes from oil and another 25 percent from natural gas. On a worldwide basis, oil is equally important. Natural gas is of lesser relative importance, but a major and growing source of energy, as well as petrochemicals.

The end of the petroleum age is in sight. We have discovered the easiest, the largest, and the most productive of the world's oil and gas deposits. Present reserves and likely resources cannot sustain growing world demand for more than a few generations. We have used more than half of the probable oil and gas resources of the United States, and those remaining we probably will exhaust over the next fifty years or so.

It does not follow, however, that oil and gas law is waning in importance in the United States. The oil and gas resources that remain are likely to become more and more valuable. For this reason, commercial and property lawyers, as well as people who work in the oil and gas industry, need to understand the legal principles that control oil and gas development in this country.

This book focuses upon the legal rules that govern development of privately owned mineral rights. I have chosen that focus because most mineral rights in the United States are owned privately, though the federal and state governments own hundreds of millions of acres—approximately 30 percent of all mineral rights. Also, the rules for governmentally owned resources in the United States tend to be based on those for private lands.

Because of the value of oil and gas resources, there are numerous secondary sources and research materials available. Those that I have used in preparing this book include Eugene Kuntz, THE LAW OF OIL AND GAS (Lexis/Nexis); Howard Williams and Charles Meyers, OIL AND GAS LAW (Lexis/Nexis); Ernest Brown, THE LAW OF OIL AND GAS LEASES (Lexis/Nexis); Richard W. Hemingway's OIL AND GAS LAW AND TAXATION (West); W. R. Summers, THE LAW OF OIL AND GAS (West); and Maurice Merrill, COVENANTS IMPLIED IN OIL AND GAS LEASES (Thomas Law Book). In addition, I have used many of the cases included in John Lowe, Owen Anderson, Ernest Smith and David Pierce, CASES AND MATERIALS ON OIL AND GAS LAW (West), and Richard Maxwell, Patrick Martin and Bruce Kramer, CASES ON OIL AND GAS (Foundation), as illustrations.

I acknowledge the support of the many research assistants at The University of Tulsa and Southern Methodist University who have helped me research and prepare various editions of this book—

some now nearly as gray-haired as I am. These include Nugent "DJ" Beaty, Ashley Songer, A. Z. Scott Goldberg, Ann Lane, Laura A. Hudock, Matthew T. McLain, Jamey Seely, Richard K. Vangelisti, Dona K. Broyles, Gregory N. Fiske, Laurie A. Patterson, David Keehn, James Arlington, Kenneth L. Wire, David P. Page, Jeffrey R. Fiske, Arthur H. Adams, Tommy H. Butler, Michael F. Miller, Joseph G. Staskal, Curtis L. Craig, Michael D. Cooke, Steve E. McCain, Harley W. Thomas, Laura E. Frossard, Mark S. Rains, Thomas J. Wagner, Charles E. Molloy, and Robert W. Kennard. Special thanks are due to Larry D. Vredenburgh, Ph.D., an independent geologic consultant, for help with my initial drafts of Chapter 1, to Dr. Norman J. Hyne, Associate Professor of Geology at the University of Tulsa, who provided the first diagrams for Chapter 1, to Dr. Joseph F. Fusco, formerly Director of Instructional Media at the University of Tulsa, and to John Taft Lowe, Kathryn June, and the St. Michael School, Dallas, for their help with graphics, to Professor John Dzienkowski, James A. Hogue, Sr., Esq. and Professor Peter D. Maxfield for their comments on tax matters, to Bryan A. Garner and Jeffrey Newman for their help with my Glossary, and to Professor Owen L. Anderson, his wife, Kathie [PhD], and Maria M. Seidler, Esq., for their general review. I alone am responsible for any defects in analysis or errors in statements.

The Hutchison Endowment at SMU's Dedman Law School financially supported my work on this 5th edition, for which I am grateful. Accolades are

PREFACE

also due to my dean, John B. Attanasio, for his continuing encouragement. Finally, I thank my wife, Jacquelyn Taft Lowe, for tolerating the domestic disruption caused by this project—I completed this 5th edition as we traveled through New Zealand, Australia, Angola, Malawi, and Scotland, during what we had planned as a working vacation, and on our sailboat, *Lone Star*, on the coast of Maine.

JOHN S. LOWE

Dallas, Texas
July 2009

OUTLINE

PART III. OIL AND GAS LEASING

*

TABLE OF CASES

References are to Pages

TABLE OF CASES

TABLE OF CASES

TABLE OF CASES

TABLE OF CASES

*

OIL AND GAS LAW

IN A NUTSHELL

FIFTH EDITION

*

PART I

THE NATURE AND PROTECTION OF OIL AND GAS RIGHTS

CHAPTER 1

THE FORMATION AND PRODUCTION OF OIL AND GAS

Oil and gas are the liquid and gaseous forms of petroleum, a chemically complex substance composed of hydrogen and carbon with trace amounts of oxygen, nitrogen, and sulphur. Petroleum occurs in gaseous, liquid, and solid states, depending upon its physical composition, temperature and pressure.

A. FORMATION OF OIL AND GAS

Petroleum is found in sedimentary rocks formed by ancient seas. The generally accepted theory for petroleum's origin is that sediment from rivers and remains of marine plants and animals simultaneously accumulated on sea floors, forming layer upon layer of sediment and organic residue. As layers were buried deeper and deeper, they were compressed and subjected to increasing pressure from the overlaying sediment. Increased pressure generated heat which acted upon the sediment for tens to hundreds of millions of years, transforming the organic material into crude oil and natural gas.

Originally, sediment deposits on the sea floor were nearly horizontal. But millions of years of deformation of the earth's crust have left the layers folded and faulted, forming traps where petroleum might accumulate. These *anomalies*, as geologists call them, are of limited size and can occur from depths of several hundred feet to tens of thousands of feet. People in the oil and gas industry try to locate anomalies by mapping, rock evaluation, and seismic studies.

All sedimentary rocks contain pore spaces between the sediment particles. To be a good source for petroleum, sedimentary rocks must be both *porous* and *permeable*. When the amount of pore space is relatively large, geologists say that there is "high porosity," meaning that the rock contains a relatively large area within which oil and gas might accumulate. Geologists describe rocks in which the pore spaces are well-interconnected, as highly "permeable." High permeability is as important to oil and gas production as high porosity, because permeability permits petroleum, which is lighter than water, to float upwards through the original seawater contained in the pores of permeable rocks to collect and to flow towards a borehole.

Layers of permeable rocks are often bounded by layers of impermeable rocks. When the rock layers form a dome-like shape, they form a petroleum *trap*. A petroleum "reservoir" is created when the pores of the rock in the trap contain sufficient quantities of oil or gas and the permeability is high enough to permit profitable production. As the following diagram shows, it is reservoirs that the oil industry seeks to locate by drilling operations.

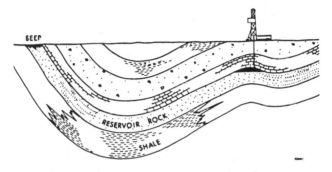

B. DRILLING FOR OIL AND GAS

An anomaly can only be *tested* by drilling a well. No technology is sure to detect petroleum in rocks thousands of feet below the earth's surface without drilling. Two types of drilling rigs are used—the rotary rig and the cable-tool rig. The cable-tool rig, an older style, rarely used today, pulverizes the rock by raising a heavy bit and letting it fall. Th cable-tool technique is limited in application and cannot be used below depths of a few thousand feet, but it is inexpensive.

Most wells, both onshore and offshore, are drilled by the rotary technique. A typical rotary-drilling rig consists of a derrick structure, a string of pipe, a drill bit, circulating fluid, and a derrick-floor rotary turntable, as the following drawing shows.

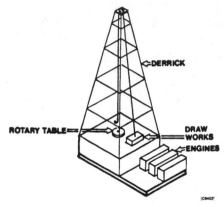

The derrick structure is assembled over the drill site. The drill bit is screwed into the bottom of a thirty-foot length of pipe which passes through the rotary table. The circulating fluid (a mixture of chemicals called "mud,") or air is forced down the inside of the pipe, out through the jets in the bit, and back to the surface, where the cycle is repeated. As the turntable rotates, so does the drill pipe, which forces the drill bit to abrade the rock into matchhead-size pieces, which the circulating fluid carries to the surface. A drawing of a rotary-drill bit follows.

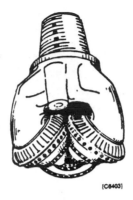

[C8403]

Each time the rig drills a thirty-foot depth of hole, the crew adds a new length of drill pipe. At a depth of fifteen thousand feet the continuous *drill string* would consist of 500 pieces of pipe screwed together end-to-end. Most wells are drilled *vertically*—from a surface location on the leased land to a formation below it. Modern technology, however, permits the drilling of *directional* or *horizontal* wells. When the well reaches the total depth recommended, the driller evaluates the data in drilling and the owners decide to (1) plug and abandon, if there are no indications of petroleum in the rock, or (2) "set pipe," if petroleum is present.

C. PRODUCING OIL AND GAS

If it appears that a well has located commercial quantities of oil or gas, the drilling crew places a continuous *string* of production-casing pipe (thirty-foot lengths screwed together) in the hole. Cement is forced around the outside of the pipe, sealing off the space between the rock wall and the pipe exterior. This process is called "setting pipe." A perforating *gun* is lowered down the hole through the pipe to the depth of the potential petroleum-bearing rock. The gun contains explosives that penetrate the casing, cement, and several inches of rock. Perforation allows the petroleum in the rock to drain into the well bore. Sometimes it is necessary to *stimulate* the well by forcing fluids into the rock to fracture it or to inject acid to dissolve away some of the rock. Both procedures will improve permeability.

If the natural pressure within the rocks is high, the pressure will force oil to flow to the surface. If the pressure is low, the well owner will install pumping equipment to lift the oil to the surface; generally the familiar "horsehead" pumping jack is required. Gas will normally flow, controlled by a system of valves and gauges at the top of the well called a "Christmas tree."

Because crude oil, natural gas, and salt water are commonly produced simultaneously, the producer must flow the fluids produced through a *separator* to remove the natural gas and perhaps through a *heater-treater* to separate oil and water. The oil is then stored, piped, or trucked to the refinery, and the gas put into a pipeline. The diagram that follows shows a typical production configuration.

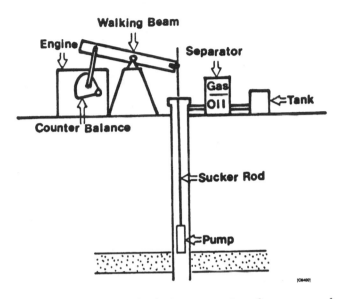

After some period of time, ranging from several months to many years, the natural or *primary* pressure in the reservoir rocks may drop to such a level that petroleum will no longer flow into the well bore. At that time, the operating company will consider artificially enhancing the reservoir pressure by injecting water or gas into the reservoir; this is commonly called *secondary recovery*. In more advanced *tertiary* or *enhanced* recovery projects, fire flooding, which heats oil in place in the rock to lower its viscosity and increase reservoir pressure, or complex chemical techniques are used.

CHAPTER 2

OWNERSHIP OF OIL AND GAS RIGHTS

A. THE AD COELUM DOCTRINE

In most of the world, the state retains ownership of valuable minerals. In the United States, private ownership is the norm, though public ownership is an important factor. The federal government owns nearly 30 percent of U.S. mineral rights—about 25 percent of domestic production of both oil and gas come from federally owned property—and the states own tens of millions of acres of minerals. Today and historically, however, transactions involving privately owned minerals dominate.

Oil and gas law is an example of the development of a new body of law by modification of existing common law concepts. In 1859, when Edwin L. Drake drilled the first oil well at Titusville, Pennsylvania to a depth of 69 feet, the prevailing principle of mineral ownership in the United States was *cujus est solum, ejus est usque ad coelum et ad inferos,* commonly referred to as the *"ad coelum"* doctrine. Translated, that meant that the owner of the bundle of legal rights that we call "ownership" of property, owned everything from the heavens above the surface of his land to the core of the earth beneath it. Professor Cribbett called this doctrine the "heaven to hell" principle.

Early in the history of oil and gas development it became apparent that the *ad coelum* doctrine, which works well with "hard" minerals, was inappropriate to govern extraction of petroleum. Oil and gas are fugacious; they may move from place to place within sedimentary rock. In addition, oil and gas are fungible; it is difficult to determine whether a given MCF of gas or barrel of oil produced has been drawn from under one tract of land or another. Adherence to the *ad coelum* principle would have hamstrung the development of an industry potentially important to America's continued economic development. Mineral owners would have been discouraged from drilling by the fear of liability for drainage from their neighbors' properties. Further, application of the *ad coelum* principle would have conflicted with *laissez faire*, the prevalent political and economic theory of the era, which emphasized a policy of rewarding the diligent worker to the ultimate benefit of society. It is not surprising, then, that the rule of capture was developed to modify the *ad coelum* doctrine.

B. THE RULE OF CAPTURE

The rule of capture may be stated as follows:

There is no liability for capturing oil and gas that drains from another's lands to a well on one's own land. The owner of mineral rights in a tract of land acquires title to the oil and gas produced from wells drilled on the land, though part of the oil and gas may have migrated from adjoining lands.

Some courts that have applied the rule of capture have relied upon analogy to the common law of wild animals, which reasons that the only way to gain ownership of wild things, *ferae naturae,* is to capture them. Others, *like Kelly v. Ohio Oil Co.,* 49 N.E. 399 (Ohio 1897), have treated the rule of capture as following from an owner's absolute right to use land; "whatever gets into the well belongs to the owner of the well, no matter where it comes from."

Professor Kuntz described the rule of capture as a "rule of convenience." What he meant was that the rule developed from courts' recognition of society's need for energy resources, rather than from the logic of precedent. The rule of capture substantially departs from the principle of the *ad coelum* doctrine. The best way to understand it is to view it as judicial policy-making to encourage development of oil and gas resources.

The rule of capture is an unusual rule of law because it is a rule of nonliability. It gives a mineral owner the shield of a positive legal principle as he or she drills and produces wells. So long as a mineral owner conducts operations without trespassing or interfering with the rights of neighboring owners to drill to the same formation under their lands, a mineral owner will not be liable. All the oil or gas the well produces will belong to the mineral owner, even if it drains from beneath others' lands. An extreme example of application of the nonliablity principle is *Coastal Oil & Gas Corp. v. Garza Energy Trust*, 268 S.W.3d 1 (Tex.2008). There the lessee, Coastal, planned and executed a fracture job designed to extend beyond its lease lines. The Garza Trust, a leasehold royalty owner, sued. A jury found that the fracture and invasion of propellants across the lease lines constituted trespass, and awarded compensatory and punitive damages. The Texas Supreme Court, however, held that because the trust's royalty interest was nonpossessory, the trust had to show that it had actually been damaged, and because of the rule of capture, it could not do so.

C. LIMITS TO THE RULE OF CAPTURE

The rule of capture is not a perfect shield to liability, however. There are inherent limitations, limitations imposed by the doctrine of correlative rights, and statutory limitations to the rule. All are consistent with the underlying rationale of the rule of capture.

1. INHERENT LIMITATIONS

The rationale of the rule of capture inherently limits the rule. As has been noted, the rule of capture developed from recognition by the courts that mechanical application of the *ad coelum* doctrine would deprive society of important energy resources. The rule of capture was developed to encourage development of oil and gas resources for the benefit of society. Its purpose limits the scope of its protection.

a. Escaped Hydrocarbons

The inherent limitation of the rule of capture has been demonstrated by several cases that have raised the issue of the right of a mineral interest owner to capture oil or gas previously produced by another. Several cases distinguish between gas as it exists in its natural state and gas that is captured elsewhere and injected into storage. Gas in its natural state is subject to capture, but once captured, gas remains the property of whoever captured it until it is abandoned. In *Champlin Exploration, Inc. v. Western Bridge & Steel Co., Inc.*, 597 P.2d 1215 (Okl. 1979), the Oklahoma Supreme Court held that the rule of capture did not protect a mineral-interest owner that dug trenches on its premises and pumped out refined hydrocarbons that had leaked from a nearby refinery and drained into the trenches.

Similar results have been reached by the few courts that have considered situations in which natural gas produced and injected into a storage reservoir escapes and is recaptured in a well drilled on a tract not subject to the storage rights. Generally, courts have reasoned that oil or gas becomes personal property when produced, so that ownership is not lost by mere loss of possession. See, for example, *Pacific Gas & Electric Co. v. Zuckerman*, 189 Cal.App.3d 1113, 234 Cal.Rptr. 630 (Cal.App. 1987), and *Texas American Energy Corporation v.*

Citizens Fidelity Bank and Trust Company, 736 S.W.2d 25 (Ky.1987). The result in these cases is consistent with the purpose underlying the rule of capture—to encourage development of the resource; holding that the rule transfers title to escaped hydrocarbons that are recaptured by another would add nothing to society's energy supplies. These cases are also consistent with the common-law rule that a wild animal that is either (1) domesticated or (2) removed from its natural habitat does not revert to the wild if it escapes.

b.　Drainage by Enhanced-recovery Operations

Courts have also recognized limitations to the rule of capture in situations in which capture has been brought about by secondary-recovery operations, procedures that improve the productive capacity of the reservoir by injecting fluids to increase the pressure differential or to move oil and gas in place to the borehole. Here, courts have generally recognized that permitting a lessee to sweep oil and gas from under the property of a neighbor by use of water-flooding techniques is beyond the scope of the rule of capture. A few courts, including courts in Oklahoma and Arkansas, have held that the mineral owner conducting secondary recovery operations is liable to adjoining mineral owners that are drained of oil and gas on a theory of nuisance or trespass. Others, including the Nebraska Supreme Court in *Baumgartner v. Gulf Oil Corp.*, 168 N.W.2d 510 (Neb.1969), the Fifth Circuit in *Tide*

Water Associated Oil Co. v. Stott, 159 F.2d 174 (5th Cir.Tex.1946), and the Texas Supreme Court in *Railroad Commission v. Manziel*, 361 S.W.2d 560 (Tex. 1962), have rejected liability for nuisance or trespass where the drained party has refused what the court has considered a "fair" proposal to participate in an enhanced-recovery program, and the state conservation agency has approved the project as necessary to prevent waste and maximize production. Professors Williams and Meyers have described the finding of nonliability for displacement as a "negative rule of capture." Though such decisions find no liability, they recognize that the rule of capture will not excuse all drainage.

The rule of capture should be applied to protect mineral interest owners engaged in secondary and tertiary-recovery operations, at least where those operations are necessary to maximize ultimate production. All oil and gas reservoirs contain reserves that can be produced by primary-recovery techniques and those which can be produced only through the use of secondary or tertiary-recovery techniques. Use of enhanced-recovery techniques to sweep away reserves that an adjoining property owner could produce by primary recovery techniques should not be protected by the rule of capture, however. Those reserves would have been produced anyway; application of enhanced-recovery techniques merely speeds up their production and permits one mineral interest owner rather than another to produce them. On the other hand, when a conservation agency finds that enhanced-recovery techniques permit production of oil and gas that could not be produced by primary-production techniques, society's interest in maximizing production of its resources dictates that the activity be protected by the rule of capture. A requirement that the drained owner be offered an opportunity to participate in the unit operation on a fair basis should be imposed, however, to prevent enhanced recovery from being used as a weapon against other owners' correlative rights.

2. DOCTRINE OF CORRELATIVE RIGHTS

The doctrine of correlative rights is another limitation to the rule of capture. It is illustrated by the classic case of *Elliff v. Texon Drilling Co.*, 210 S.W.2d 558 (Tex.1948). There Texon's negligence permitted one of its wells on property adjoining Elliff's land to blow out and burn, causing drainage of large quantities of oil and gas from Elliff's property. When Elliff sued for damages for the lost oil and gas, Texon raised the rule of capture as a defense. The Texas Supreme Court rejected the defense on the basis of the *correlative-rights doctrine*: an owner who exercises the right to capture oil and gas is subject to the concomitant duty to exercise the right without negligence or waste. Each common owner has a right to protection from negligent damage to the producing formation. Because Texon was wasting hydrocarbons rather than selling or using them, the rule of capture did not shield it from liability.

The correlative-rights doctrine is a corollary to the rule of capture and follows from its logic. The rule of capture was adopted to benefit the public interest in plentiful energy by encouraging development of oil and gas resources. Activity inconsistent with that purpose is not protected by the rule of capture. Waste or wasteful-production techniques will bring liability, as will negligent damage to the ability of the producing formation to produce for others. Positively stated, the correlative-rights doctrine provides that each owner of minerals in a common source of supply has the right to a fair chance to produce oil and gas from the reservoir substantially in the proportion that the quantity of recoverable oil and gas under his or her land bears to the quantity in the reservoir.

3. CONSERVATION LAWS

Neither the common-law doctrine of correlative rights nor the inherent limitations discussed above have provided sufficient limits to the rule of capture. The problem can be illustrated if you imagine that you own a tract of 640 acres that you are advised can be efficiently drained by a single well located anywhere on the tract. If the rule of capture and the doctrine of correlative rights are the legal rules applicable, where will you drill your well? And, will you drill a single well or several?

The answer to the first question is that, if you are astute, you will drill your first well as close to the boundary of your tract as you can, rather than in the center. Your motivation will be to use the rule of capture to drain oil and gas from your neighbor's land as well as from your own. Even if you are not motivated by greed for the oil and gas under your neighbor's land (as you ought to be if you are a reasonable economic person), you will drill your first well close to the boundary line to protect yourself against drainage from a well drilled on your neighbor's property.

Furthermore, whether your motive is greed or a desire for protection, you will probably drill not one but several wells along your boundary. If you do not, you will not gain the maximum advantage from the rule of capture and you will leave yourself exposed to your neighbors who drill on their properties close to your boundary.

a. Economic and Physical Waste

What is wrong with the scenario outlined? The problem is that it leads to physical and economic waste. The economic waste is easy to see. Because your neighbors will have the same legal rights and economic motivation as you, over a period of time your neighbors and you will drill more wells than are necessary to drain your land efficiently. Each owner will drill the number of wells he or she judges necessary to maximize benefits or to protect his or her land. Each owner will be pressed by economics to drill as many wells as the most active neighbor. If one does not, that owner will be at a disadvantage. The process will be economically wasteful because it will be more costly than necessary since more wells will be drilled than are required to drain the field efficiently.

Economic waste from over-drilling is likely to lead to physical waste. Once wells are drilled, each owner will feel compelled to produce them as fast as possible to drain the reservoir before his or her neighbors, to increase the chances of recovering the costs of drilling and to maximize profits. Short-term overproduction from the reservoir is likely to result in long-term total recovery of a percentage of the oil and gas originally in place that is *less* than what might be achieved by slower production. The natural expansion of oil and gas toward the lower pressure in the borehole will be dissipated among many boreholes with the result that some of the oil and gas in place will be left in the formation. In addition, overproduction of oil and gas is likely to push down the price for product. In the early years of the oil and gas industry, that happened often. When the price dropped below the point that operating revenues exceeded operating costs, producers plugged and abandoned their wells, and the remaining oil and gas was "locked in" the formation.

The correlative-rights doctrine does not prevent the economic and physical waste inherent in the rule of capture. The correlative-rights doctrine gives an individual rights against another owner who negligently or wastefully uses the rule of capture. But over-drilling is not negligent or wasteful from the viewpoint of the individual. Drilling as many wells as fast as possible to take advantage of the rule of capture and to protect against its ravages is prudent from each individual's viewpoint. What is harmful is the sum of these prudent individual actions.

The economic and physical waste inherent in the rule of capture is an example of a common problem of communal ownership. When each owner has the right to act in a way that will benefit himself, while imposing costs on another that the actor does not have to take into account, economists say that *external costs* are present. *See* Garrett Hardin, "The Tragedy of the Commons," 162 *Science* 1243 (1968). Where there are external costs, the group of owners will act contrary to its best interests—by over-drilling—even though each individual owner acts in a self-interested way.

b. Function of Oil and Gas Conservation Laws

States began developing petroleum conservation laws as the problems of unrestrained application of the rule of capture became apparent, exercising their police powers to internalize the external costs of the rule of capture. Petroleum conservation laws limit the rule of capture, virtually transforming it to a "fair share" doctrine. Thus, *Wronski v. Sun Oil Co.*, 279 N.W.2d 564 (Mich.App.1979), held Sun liable for conversion where it produced oil in excess of the rate of production authorized by the state conservation agency. The Michigan appellate court refused to give Sun the protection of the rule of capture because Sun had violated the state's conservation law. The court noted that the protection of the rule of capture was limited by valid conservation orders. Today, conservation laws are the keystone of the legal structure governing oil and gas development.

(1) Purpose

The primary purpose of oil and gas conservation statutes is to avoid physical and economic waste of oil and gas resources. Oil and gas conservation laws are concerned not only with saving resources, but with encouraging their rational development. Rational development prevents waste because it maximizes ultimate recovery. Thus, oil and gas conservation laws seek to further the public's interest in conservation *and* rational development. They also seek to protect owners' correlative rights by providing a structure to make it possible for each owner to get his or her fair share of the oil or gas present.

(2) Well–Spacing Rules

A typical oil and gas conservation statute consists of a series of provisions that seek to balance public interest and private rights. The most important of those provisions are well-spacing rules. Spacing rules prevent over-drilling by limiting the number of wells that can be drilled in a given area. Since the primary problem with the rule of capture is that greed and the need for protection from drainage lead owners of oil and gas rights to drill wells too close together, an important step toward controlling the problem is to require that wells be located far enough from boundary lines and from one another so that excessive drainage will not occur.

A recurring issue in well spacing cases is whether the conservation agency may act to prevent economic waste as well as physical waste in setting spacing rules. Generally, conservation agencies consider economic considerations relevant to the size of spacing units; if an operator believes that a well will not "pay out," the operator will not drill, and the conservation law will not achieve its purpose of rational development. The terms of the authorizing statute control, of course. Thus, in *Larsen v. Oil and Gas Conservation Commission*, 569 P.2d 87 (Wyo.1977), the Wyoming Supreme Court held that the Wyoming legislature had not given the conservation agency the authority to consider economics in determining the appropriate size of spacing units; subsequently, the Wyoming legislature amended the law to grant the agency power.

The most important consideration in determining the location of spacing units is the location of the pool of oil or gas being drilled. Courts generally hold that a conservation agency may not permit spacing units to extend beyond the limits of an oil or gas pool because that would allow owners of nonproductive portions of the unit to confiscate the fair share of the owners of productive portions of the unit.

They give substantial deference to the finding of the administrative agency that oil or gas lies under the spacing unit, however, and that determination is often made before drilling takes place.

(3) Well Spacing Exceptions

At best, well spacing rules are "rule of thumb" attempts to prevent drainage from one tract to another. Well spacing rules are based on the assumption that oil and gas reservoirs are homogenous, so that drainage will be radial. The theory is that a uniform spacing pattern will result in *compensatory drainage,* as the following diagram illustrates:

Compensated Drainage Theory For 80 Acre (Rectangular) Spacing

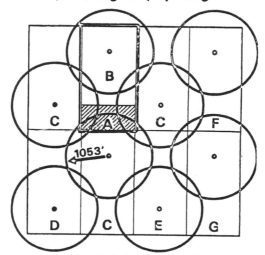

Shown Is A Section Of Land

ASSUMPTION:
Lacking Reservoir Knowledge,
Must Assume "Radial"
Drainage For Each Well.

FACT:
πr^2; Radius Of Drainage For
80 Acres Is 1053 Feet.

Field Spacing Order Requires
Wells Be Located In C NE/4 And
C SW/4 Of Each Quarter Section.

Each Spacing Unit Is A
"Stand-Up" Unit.

CONCLUSION:
When Competitive Develop
ment Finished, Correlative
Rights Of Each Owner (A,B,
C,D,E,F, & G) Are Protected.

Courtesy of Rocky Mtn. Min. L. Found.
from Giles, "The Tech. Under....," O&G Cons. Inst. (1985)

In fact, a reservoir is rarely homogenous and drainage is rarely perfectly radial. In addition, wells are drilled into a reservoir at different times and produced at different rates.

Exceptions to the well-spacing scheme are often necessary. Exceptions may be justified either (1) to protect the correlative rights of owners against drainage or (2) to prevent waste of oil and gas. The following diagram illustrates both:

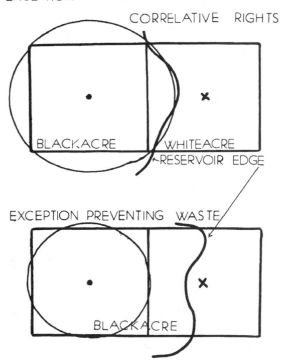

EXCEPTION PROTECTING

CORRELATIVE RIGHTS

BLACKACRE WHITEACRE

RESERVOIR EDGE

EXCEPTION PREVENTING WASTE

BLACKACRE

There is a well on Blackacre that engineering data suggests is draining a portion of Whiteacre. Under the spacing rules that apply, the owner of Whiteacre's mineral rights should protect against drainage by drilling on Whiteacre at the location marked "X." Suppose, however, that a "fault" (illustrated by the heavy curved line running north and south across the west part of Whiteacre) breaks the reservoir in the west half of Whiteacre, so that a well drilled at Whiteacre's "legal location" will not produce the oil and gas to the west of the fault. Unless an exception is made to the spacing rules, Whiteacre will be drained by Blackacre, and the correlative rights of the mineral owner of Whiteacre will be damaged. Courts and conservation agencies have generally permitted a well to be drilled on Whiteacre to offset drainage in these circumstances on the theory that the spacing rules would be an unconstitutional taking of property otherwise. See *Pattie v. Oil & Gas Conservation Commission*, 402 P.2d 596 (Mont.1965).

The second circumstance in which a well-spacing exception is justified is to prevent waste of oil or gas. Consider the second part of the preceding diagram. Suppose that the Blackacre well does not drain Whiteacre, but that a fault runs north and south across the west part of Whiteacre so that a well drilled at the "legal location" under the spacing rules will not produce the oil or gas under the west part of Whiteacre. Unless the conservation agency allows a well-spacing exception, the oil and gas under the west part of Whiteacre will not be produced by either mineral owner.

Economic waste is also a legitimate target of well-spacing exceptions. Thus, in *Exxon Corp. v. Railroad Commission*, 571 S.W.2d 497 (Tex.1978), the Texas Supreme Court upheld an order permitting a producer to recomplete a producing well to a shallower formation, though the conservation rules would not permit drilling a new well in that location to the shallower formation, where the producer showed that drilling at a "legal location" would not have been economically feasible.

(4) Production Regulation

Oil and gas conservation laws also regulate production to prevent waste and protect correlative rights. *Production allowables* are one kind of production regulation. Production allowable rules, sometimes called *prorationing rules*, put daily, weekly or monthly limits on production of oil and gas to prevent overproduction. When the limits are imposed to prevent overly-fast production of a reservoir (in excess of the scientifically-determined maximum efficient rate) the process is called *MER prorationing*. When production allowables are used to prevent wide fluctuations in the price of oil, as was the practice of some of the southwestern producing states prior to the rise of OPEC in the 1970s, the process may be referred to as *market demand prorationing*. The conservation agency may give a well drilled on a spacing exception a reduced production allowable to prevent drainage; as the court noted in *Chevron Oil Co. v. Oil and Gas Conservation Commission*, 435 P.2d 781 (Mont. 1967), "correlative rights are not a one-way street." Production allowables may be supported by *ratable-taking rules,* which require purchasers to take in patterns that minimize drainage from one tract to another. Application of ratable-taking rules against an intrastate pipe line was barred, however, by the U.S. Supreme Court in *Transcontinental Gas Pipe Line Corp. v. State Oil and Gas Board*, 474 U.S. 409 (1986), on the ground that the federal statutes that regulate natural gas have preempted the field.

Gas-oil ratio rules and *water-oil ratio rules* also prevent waste and protect correlative rights. When there is substantial demand for oil, but little demand for natural gas, producers may wish to flare (burn off) natural gas so that they can produce oil. Flaring may lower the reservoir pressure so that oil will be trapped in the formation forever. A similar problem may arise when an operator drills a well into the gas cap of an oil reservoir, as occurred in *Denver Producing & Refining Co. v. State*, 184 P.2d 961 (Okl.1947). Gas-oil ratios and water-oil ratios require that well operators cease production when they exceed appropriate production ratios of gas to oil or water to oil. These rules prevent waste of petroleum by helping to maintain the reservoir pressure that makes production possible.

Conservation law provisions for compulsory unitization or encouraging voluntary unitization may also set limits on production. *Unitization* refers to the joint operation of some or all of the wells over a producing formation to maximize the production from the unit rather than from any individual well. Unit operations may substantially increase the percentage of oil and gas recovered in the long run. In most instances, unitization could not be successful without the help of compulsory-unitization laws because many landowners and producers see a short-term advantage to individual production.

(5) The Small–Tract Problem

Conservation laws or regulations aimed at maximizing ultimate production and preventing physical and economic waste sometimes interfere with mineral owners' correlative rights. When that happens, there is a constitutional "taking" problem.

The classic example of the conflict between the goals of preventing waste and protecting correlative rights is the small-tract problem, which arises when a mineral owner owns mineral rights in a tract too small or the wrong shape to conform to applicable spacing rules. Even if the reservoir underlies the entire spacing unit, the correlative rights of the small tract mineral owner will be destroyed unless the owner is allowed to drill or to share in the production from the well drilled on the spacing unit.

Granting a well-spacing exception to the mineral owner is the usual solution to the small tract problem in Texas. Use of well-spacing exceptions to protect the correlative rights of small tract owners raises the further question, however, of how much the exception-tract owner can produce. Until the early 1960s the Railroad Commission (the Texas oil and gas conservation agency) granted exception-tract wells a production allowable sufficient to permit them to recover their costs plus a reasonable profit, on the theory that such a rule was necessary to avoid a taking. In *Halbouty v. Railroad Commission*, 357 S.W.2d 364 (Tex.1962), the Texas Supreme Court recognized that this practice was a license for small-tract owners to drain other properties and that it seriously conflicted with well-spacing rules. Now, Texas sets production allowables for exception-tract wells to permit owners to recover the oil and gas under their property—their "fair share" of the oil—whether or not production would be profitable. That limitation is universal among states that allow well-spacing exceptions.

An alternative, adopted in most states, is to provide in the conservation law for *compulsory* or *forced pooling*. Forced-pooling laws give a mineral owner whose correlative rights are threatened by drainage a legal right to share in the production of the well that causes the drainage. Forced-pooling statutes may also be used by mineral owners who want to develop their properties to compel recalcitrant owners to participate in drilling or give up their rights in return for fair compensation. Typically, forced-pooled owners are given the choice of (1) agreeing to participate in drilling and pay their share of the costs, (2) agreeing to give up their operating rights in return for a bonus payment and royalty determined appropriate by the state conservation agency, or (3) electing to be "carried" for drilling and completion costs. Electing to be carried means that the other owners will advance costs of drilling and completion, but the carried party will receive only a royalty on production until the parties advancing the costs have recovered some multiple of their investment, after which the carried party will "back in" to a share of the working interest in addition to or in place of the royalty.

D. THEORIES OF OWNERSHIP OF OIL AND GAS

1. NON-OWNERSHIP AND OWNERSHIP–IN–PLACE THEORIES

The judges who developed the rule of capture were willing to apply a rule other than the *ad coelum* doctrine, but they sought to justify departing from precedent by distinguishing ownership of oil and gas from other substances found in the earth. The earliest courts to face the problem, such as *People's Gas Co. v. Tyner*, 31 N.E. 59 (Ind.1892), analogized the rule of capture to the law of wild animals. They held that an owner of oil and gas rights did not own oil or gas until it had been controlled by capture in a well. Until capture, the owner of oil and gas rights had only an exclusive right to explore for, develop and produce oil and gas from the premises subject to his rights. On this basis, many cases, such as *Pacific Gas & Electric Co. v. Zuckerman*, 189 Cal.App.3d 1113, 234 Cal. Rptr. 630 (Cal.App.1987), have characterized oil and gas rights as a *profit a prendre,* a right to go on the land and take some part of the land or a product of it.

Other courts took an approach closer to the *ad coelum* principle. They rationalized that since oil and gas were a part of the soil, the owner of the land owned oil and gas in place, in addition to the exclusive right to explore for, develop, and produce. Ownership was limited, however, by the fugacious nature of oil and gas; the ownership right to a particular barrel of oil or MCF of gas would be terminated if the oil and gas migrated to the land of another. These courts characterized oil and gas rights as a *fee simple absolute* estate in the land, and the right to individual molecules of oil and gas as a determinable interest that terminates automatically upon capture by another.

The first rule is often referred to as the "non-ownership" theory. It is followed in Oklahoma, Louisiana, California, and Wyoming, as well as several other less-prolific oil producing states. The second approach, often referred to as the "ownership-in-place" theory, is the majority rule and has been adopted by Texas, New Mexico, Colorado, and Kansas, among others. The courts in some states have never addressed the issue, while those in others have addressed it inconsistently.

The rule of capture underlies both theories of ownership. It is inherent in the non-ownership theory; ownership of oil and gas can be obtained in a non-ownership-theory state only by capture. The rule of capture is a caveat to the ownership-in-place theory; in an ownership-in-place-theory state, the owner of oil and gas rights owns the right to oil and gas in place, subject to the right of others to divest his or her ownership by capture.

2. SIGNIFICANCE OF THE THEORIES OF OWNERSHIP

a. The Corporeal/Incorporeal Distinction

The primary significance of the ownership theory embraced has followed from the recognition or non-recognition of the owner's present right of possession of oil and gas in the ground. At common law, rights to land are classified as *corporeal* or *incorporeal*, according to whether they carry the right of physical possession. If an interest in land includes the right of possession of the land, it is classified as a corporeal ("of substance") right. On the other hand, if an interest includes only the right to use the land, it is classified as incorporeal ("not of substance"). By this analysis, rights to oil and gas are incorporeal in states embracing the non-ownership theory and corporeal in those that have adopted the ownership-in-place theory.

(1) Abandonment of Oil and Gas Interests

Incorporeal rights can be abandoned at common law, while corporeal rights cannot. The distinction has been applied in disputes over oil and gas rights. In the classic case of *Gerhard v. Stephens*, 442 P.2d 692 (Cal.1968), the successors in interest to two corporations that had been dissolved in 1915 sued to quiet title to oil and gas rights leased by Stephens to Shell in 1956 and thereafter profitably developed. The California Supreme Court held that oil and gas rights were subject to abandonment in California, noting that an earlier case had rejected ownership-in-place theory as the law of California. The court reasoned that oil and gas rights were a *profit a prendre,* an incorporeal right subject to loss by abandonment. By the analysis of *Gerhard v. Stephens,* oil and gas mineral rights, leasehold rights, and royalties are all subject to abandonment in a state following the non-ownership theory. By definition, no owner of any oil and gas right can have the right to present possession of the oil and gas in place in a non-ownership theory state.

Even in states following the ownership-in-place theory, some oil and gas interests may be abandoned. An oil and gas mineral right is an estate in the oil and gas in place. As such, its holder has a present right of possession, and the right may not be abandoned, as the Arkansas Supreme Court held in *Bodcaw Lumber Co. v. Goode,* 254 S.W. 345 (Ark.1923). A leasehold interest, on the other hand, may be either a grant of the lessor's right to use the land to search, develop, and produce *and* the lessor's present right of possession in place, or it may be a grant only of the right to search, develop, and produce. Courts in some states that subscribe to the ownership-in-place theory take the position that whether the interest created in a lease is corporeal or incorporeal depends upon whether or not the granting clause describes the minerals in place.

Other courts, including those in Texas, have held that a lease ordinarily severs all of the grantor's mineral rights, including the present right to possession, whatever the language used in the grant. A royalty interest, a right to a share of oil and gas produced free of costs of production, should always be classified as an incorporeal right, regardless of the theory of ownership of the jurisdiction. A royalty is a right to oil and gas if and when it is produced; there is no present right of possession.

Courts rarely find that oil and gas rights have been abandoned even in non-ownership theory states. The reason is that abandonment requires a showing both of an extended period of non-use and an intent to abandon. Because oil and gas rights are the kind of property interest that one ordinarily may hold for an extended period without development, and because development is the only way to use them, it is difficult to find evidence that an owner intended to abandon them. Courts have uniformly held that non-use by itself does not establish the requisite intent, though the length of the non-use may be considered in determining the intent. The California courts alone have been willing to consider the length of the non-use in conjunction with the existence of economic conditions that would make future use of the right unlikely to find the requisite intent.

(2) Forms of Action to Protect Oil and Gas Rights

Classification of oil and gas rights as corporeal or incorporeal may determine the forms of action available to protect rights. Some forms of action, including trespass, ejectment, and compulsory partition, were said by the common law courts to be available only to those who owned possessory interests in property. Courts in some states have recognized that distinction and have said that only holders of corporeal rights are entitled to possessory remedies. In those states, if the ownership-in-place theory has been adopted, then the owner of oil and gas rights is entitled to the possessory remedies. Conversely, if the non-ownership theory has been adopted, the owner is not entitled.

In as many jurisdictions as not, however, the courts have ignored the distinction between corporeal and incorporeal rights as a prerequisite to maintenance of a possessory action, either by treating oil and gas rights as *sui generis* or by finding that codification of common law remedies has modified their application. Even in those states that have maintained the common-law distinction, the substantive rights of oil and gas owners have been protected by other remedies. For example, where the possessory action of ejectment is unavailable, a mineral owner may maintain an action to quiet title.

b. Classification of Oil and Gas Rights as Real Property or Personal Property

Other important distinctions involving the nature of rights to oil and gas have *not* followed from the ownership theory adopted by the jurisdiction. Classifying oil and gas rights as real property or personal property is one such distinction, though occasional cases have suggested otherwise.

Whether an interest in oil and gas is classified as realty or personalty may be important for a variety of reasons. Intestate or testamentary rights may turn on the distinction. So may tax liabilities, though taxing statutes usually are specific in coverage.

No correlation exists between the ownership theory embraced by a jurisdiction and classification of oil and gas interests as real property or personal property. The distinction between the ownership theories is whether or not the owner has a present possessory right to the oil and gas in place. The distinction between real property and personal property at common law turns on the duration of the interest rather than its possessory quality. If the interest's duration is that of a freehold estate— a life estate or a fee estate—it is real property; otherwise it is personalty. By the logic of the common law, any oil and gas interest—whether a mineral right, a leasehold right, or a royalty—is an interest in land. Whether that interest is classified as real estate or personal property ought to depend upon its duration. Interests that are for "life or longer" should be classified as real property. Interests with a lesser duration should be classified as personal property. Therefore, most oil and gas rights created (e.g., "for ten years and so long thereafter as oil and gas are produced ...") are logically real property because they are potentially perpetual. Of course, oil and gas, themselves, become personal property when they are severed from the land by production.

Whether a particular jurisdiction has classified oil and gas rights as real property or personal property is generally determined by statutory interpretation rather than by application of common-law principles. Thus, in many states, perpetual mineral interests are not "real property" for purposes of the taxing statutes or the judgment lien statutes, although they would be so classified by application of the common-law standard.

c. Practical Impact of the Theory of Ownership

The theory of ownership embraced by a particular state is likely to be more important to law professors than to mineral owners. The theory selected determines the nature of the rights that are associated with ownership. Which theory applies may be crucial in specific fact situations. On a day-to-day basis, however, the similarities in the rights of mineral owners in non-ownership and ownership-in-place theory states are far greater and far more important than the differences.

CHAPTER 3

KINDS OF OIL AND GAS
INTERESTS

Oil and gas interests are generally created and
conveyed like real property interests, but the names
given to the interests created may be unfamiliar
even to those familiar with real property transactions. Also, the characteristics of certain interests
are peculiar to oil and gas law. In this chapter we
will consider commonly-encountered oil and gas interests and their characteristics.

A. FEE INTEREST

People working in the oil and gas industry frequently talk about the "fee interest" in property.
By this term they generally mean ownership of both
the surface and the mineral rights in fee simple
absolute. Technically, using "fee interest" in that
way is incorrect. The word "fee" in property law
describes an estate or interest of inheritance, one
that may be passed from generation to generation.
It indicates the potential infinite *duration* of an
estate or interest rather than the ownership rights
it encompasses. An interest in the surface or minerals alone may be held "in fee." In the oil and gas
industry, however, the term "fee interest" is often

used to describe the whole "bundle of sticks" of rights in real property.

B. MINERAL INTEREST

It is axiomatic in Anglo–American law that an owner of property rights can transfer property rights in whole or in part. Where an owner transfers less than the whole bundle of property rights he or she owns, we say that rights have been "*severed*."

Mineral rights are often severed from the surface rights in land in the United States. Sometimes, mineral rights are severed by a reservation in a deed transferring the surface. On other occasions, severance is by a direct grant of the mineral interest out of the fee simple absolute; a typical mineral deed is included in the Appendix. A severance may also divide ownership of various kinds of minerals.

1. MINERAL INTEREST INCLUDES RIGHT TO USE THE SURFACE

A mineral interest is more than just ownership of minerals. Whether the mineral interest is severed from the surface by grant or by reservation, the mineral interest includes an implied easement to use the surface in such ways and to such an extent as is reasonably necessary to obtain the minerals under the property. Of necessity, mineral ownership implies a right to use the land surface over the minerals because mineral ownership would be valueless without access to the minerals. Courts recognize an implied easement burdening the surface and benefitting the minerals on the basis either that it is the intention of the parties to the severance or that there is a public policy in favor of making property economically useful. The mineral interest owner's easement to use the surface is limited by a standard of reasonableness and an obligation to accommodate the uses of the surface owner, if possible.

The right to use the land surface is so central to the ownership of mineral interests in oil and gas that most definitions of mineral rights are phrased in terms of surface use. A common definition follows:

> The mineral interest in oil and gas is the right to search for, develop, and produce oil and gas from the described premises and, in states that have adopted the ownership-in-place theory, the present right to possess the oil and gas in place under the property.

As a practical matter, the mineral interest's right to present possession of the oil and gas in place that some states recognize matters little. The only certain method of determining whether oil or gas is present is to drill a well to test the property. Therefore, the easement for surface use holds the real economic value of the mineral interest.

2. CHARACTERISTICS OF MINERAL–INTEREST OWNERSHIP

The economic reality, as well as the essential similarity of mineral ownership from state to state, can be seen from the incidents of mineral-interest ownership as they relate to oil and gas. Mineral interests possess the following incidents in addition to the right of surface use in all states, regardless of the ownership theory the state embraces:

a. *The right to profits and the obligation for costs*— From the right to search, develop, and produce minerals from land there follows the right to profits and the duty to pay costs incurred in use. The mineral interest is profit-sharing and cost-bearing.

b. *The right to lease or sell the mineral interest*—a mineral-interest owner has the right to transfer the rights that he or she owns to search, develop, and produce to another. The right to lease is often referred to as the *executive right*.

c. *The right to benefits under an oil and gas lease*— because a mineral-interest owner has the right to develop or transfer, an owner also has the right to whatever benefits are provided to the lessor under the terms of a lease that transfers the right to develop. Typically, these benefits include the right to any payments made to induce the signing of the lease (bonus), any payments for maintaining the lease without development (delay rentals) or production (shut-in royalty), and any share of production allocated to the lessor (royalty).

Just as the owner of a fee interest may convey or reserve the mineral interest separately from the remainder of the property, so may the owner of the mineral interest separately convey or reserve some but not all of the incidents of mineral ownership; they are part of the "bundle of sticks" of mineral ownership. O, the owner of the mineral interest in Blackacre, might convey to A the mineral interest, reserving the right to lease the property, the right to one half of any bonus, and the right to one quarter of any royalties. In that event, both O and A would have something less than a "true" mineral interest. The flexibility afforded property owners in carving out unusual groupings of rights frequently leads to interpretative problems, some of which we will consider in Chapter 7.

3. LOUISIANA'S MINERAL SERVITUDE

Under Louisiana's civil law regime, an owner of land does not own fugacious minerals, so oil and gas rights cannot be severed from surface rights. A *mineral servitude* may be imposed upon land in Louisiana, however, giving its holder the right to search for, develop and produce oil and gas. A mineral servitude creates rights similar to those of a severed mineral-interest owner in a common-law state.

A mineral servitude is subject to *prescription for nonuse.* The Louisiana Mineral Code provides that a mineral servitude will be extinguished by nonuse for 10 years. To interrupt running of the prescription period, one must conduct operations for discovery or production on the land or property pooled with it. Operations need not be successful, but there must be a good-faith attempt to discover and produce.

C. LEASEHOLD INTEREST

A *leasehold interest* is the right to the mineral interest granted by an oil and gas lease. Whether a leasehold interest includes all the incidents of the mineral interest depends upon the precise wording of the granting clause as well as upon the interpretation given by the courts of the various states; for example, a lease of "oil, gas, and other hydrocarbons" would not include non-hydrocarbon minerals like sulphur. In addition, the lessor typically retains a possibility of reverter of the mineral rights (if the lease terminates) and a royalty interest in production.

The leasehold interest is frequently called the *working interest* and sometimes the *operating interest,* because it is usually the leasehold owner that works or operates the property. In fact, a fee owner and an unleased mineral-interest owner also have the right to work property for minerals.

D. SURFACE INTEREST

The *surface interest* is what remains of the bundle of rights of land ownership after the mineral interest has been severed. Just as the mineral interest constitutes somewhat more than ownership of the minerals themselves, the surface interest's rights are both broader and narrower than to the surface of the land. The surface interest is more than the right to the surface of the land; it describes all rights that are not included in the mineral interest. Therefore, the surface interest has rights to many substances (such as potable ground water) and to many uses (such as use of geologic formations for storage of natural gas) that are not commonly thought of as part of the land surface.

On the other hand, a severed surface owner's right to use the land surface is not absolute. As Chapter 8 discusses in conjunction with the lease granting clause, the surface interest's ownership of the land surface is subject to the implied easement of a mineral-interest owner or an oil and gas lessee to use as much of the surface when, where, and in such ways as are reasonably necessary to search for, develop, and produce the minerals. In legal terms, the surface owner's right to the surface is encumbered by and *servient* to the easement of the mineral interest owner.

Disputes between surface owners and mineral-interest owners or lessees are common in oil and gas development. A major cause of conflict is a lack of understanding by many surface owners of the nature of their interest. Generally, purchasers of land from which the mineral interest has been severed understand that as surface interest owners they have no right to develop, to lease, or to share in the proceeds of leases. Severed surface owners often do not understand, however, that their rights to the surface are servient to the rights of the mineral-interest owner or lessee, who does not need permission from the surface owner to use the land surface for oil and gas development.

E. ROYALTY INTEREST

Royalty interests are among the most commonly-encountered oil and gas interests. A *royalty* is a share of production, or the value or proceeds of production, free of the costs of production, when and if there is oil and gas production on the property. Oil and gas royalties are usually expressed as fractions (e.g., 1/8 of production) or percentages (e.g., sixteen and two-thirds percent of production), but royalty interests for other minerals are often stated as a stipulated amount of money (e.g., $4.00 per long ton).

1. KINDS OF ROYALTY INTERESTS

Several kinds of royalty interests exist. A *landowner's royalty* or *lessor's royalty* is the interest in production retained by the lessor in the royalty clause of the oil and gas lease. It is the mineral-interest owner's compensation under the lease for production. An *overriding royalty* is a royalty interest the lessee carves out of the leasehold interest. Overriding royalties are frequently used to compensate landmen, lawyers, geologists, or others who have helped to structure a drilling venture. Since an overriding royalty interest is a creature of an oil and gas lease, it ends when the lease from which it is carved terminates. A *nonparticipating royalty* is a royalty carved out of the mineral interest, entitling its holder to a stated share of production without regard to the terms of any lease, though it is frequently measured by a leasehold royalty; e.g., O conveys to A 1/2 of any royalty provided by any present or future lease on Blackacre. Mineral interest owners who sell their rights often retain nonparticipating royalties. A *term royalty* is a royalty for a stated term, which may be fixed (e.g., for 25 years) or defeasible (e.g., for 25 years and so long thereafter as there is production from the premises). A *perpetual royalty* is a royalty that may extend forever; it is not limited in time. In Louisiana, a *mineral royalty* is similar to a defeasible term royalty in a common-law state; it is subject to prescription for nonuse and will terminate in ten years if production does not occur.

2. CHARACTERISTICS OF ROYALTY INTERESTS

All of the various kinds of royalty interests have four things in common that distinguish royalty interests from mineral interests:

a. *Royalty does not have the right of surface use*—a royalty is a right to a share of production, not a right to produce. Therefore, a royalty-interest owner has no easement for surface use except, perhaps, to go onto the property to collect the royalty share of production.

b. *Royalty is not profit-sharing or cost-bearing*—a royalty is a share of production free of the costs of production. A royalty is paid even if producing is a money-losing venture, and a royalty interest pays no production costs.

c. *Royalty does not have the right to lease*—royalty-interest owners have no right to grant an oil and gas lease because they have no right to search, develop, or produce from the land. Sometimes leasehold-royalty owners, who retain a possibility of reverter of the mineral rights from their lease, will grant the future interest in a "top lease," as is discussed in Chapter 7. Sometimes nonparticipating-royalty owners ratify oil and gas leases so that they can share in benefits under the lease pooling clause, as is discussed in Chapter 7. But a royalty-interest owner cannot give another the right to drill or produce.

d. *Royalty does not share in lease benefits*—since royalty-interest owners have no right to lease, they generally have no right to share in lease benefits, such as bonus, delay rentals or royalties. The leasehold royalty is the exception, but it is created by a lease and specifically given lease benefits.

Confusion often arises whether an interest created may properly be termed a "royalty" as I have defined it here. The term is often used imprecisely by parties to conveyances, as Chapter 7 discusses in conjunction with the mineral/royalty distinction. Disputes arise frequently about how royalty should be calculated, as well, as Chapter 10 discusses.

F. PRODUCTION PAYMENT

A production payment, sometimes called an "oil payment," is a share of production, or value or proceeds, from property, free of costs of production, that terminates when an agreed sum has been paid. Production payments are used in the oil and gas industry for a variety of purposes associated with lease acquisition and the financing of development, and often take the place of mortgages of producing property. Production payments are similar to a royalty interest that terminates when a specified amount has been paid. An example might be "1/5 of the oil and gas produced and saved from said land until the market value at the well of such production shall aggregate One Million Dollars ($1,000,-000.00)." It is important to be precise in defining how production is to be valued.

G. NET PROFITS INTEREST

A net-profits interest is another oil and gas interest closely related to a royalty interest. Like a royalty, a net-profits interest is expressed as a fraction or percentage of production. Like a royalty, it is non-operating. A net-profits interest is different from a royalty interest, however, in that it is payable only if there is a net profit.

Defining how to determine when a net profit has been made is crucial when one creates net-profits interests. Sometimes "net profits" are defined so that costs of exploration, drilling and completing are taken into account, as well as operating costs. Sometimes only operating expenses are considered. Whatever the meaning the parties intend, it is important that the parties define net profits carefully and completely because reference to a "net-profits interest" in and of itself is ambiguous.

The industry sometimes uses net-profits interests in addition to or in place of royalty interests as an incentive for a mineral-interest owner to grant a lease or as compensation for services. One bargaining for a net-profits interest may be able to negotiate a higher percentage net-profits interest than a royalty interest, because the net-profits interest will cost the paying party only if there is a profit, while a royalty interest is payable even where expenses exceed revenues.

H. CARRIED INTEREST

A carried interest is a fractional interest, usually created from an oil and gas lease, free of some or all costs. Often, the interest is carried "to the casing point," the point at which the well has been drilled to the desired depth and a decision must be made whether or not to place production pipe, called "casing," in the hole and proceed to complete the well for production. An interest carried to the casing point is free only of the costs of drilling and testing preparatory to completion. An interest carried to the casing point is still liable for its share of the costs of completing, equipping, and producing the well. Such a carried interest is very much like a leasehold interest except that it is free of the costs of drilling. In contrast, an interest may be "carried to the tanks or pipeline," which probably means that it is free of all costs of completing and equipping the well, as well as of drilling costs. One may argue, however, that "carried to the tanks or pipeline" means that the interest is free of all costs of operation too. If so, the carried interest is tantamount to a royalty.

To complicate matters even more, a carried interest may be (but is not always) subject to the right of the parties paying the costs attributable to the carried interest to recover those costs or even some multiple of them. A common provision in operating agreements is that an owner who does not wish to participate in the drilling of additional wells may elect to be carried for the costs of drilling and completing the additional wells. If an owner makes that election, however, the agreement provides that he or she will receive none of the proceeds of the production until the parties who put up the money to "carry" the interest receive some multiple of the costs they have expended for the carried interest; usually the multiple ranges from 100% to 500%.

Using the term "carried interest," like "net-profits interest" and "production payment," is more an art than a science. By its very nature, "carried interest" is imprecise and capable of infinite variations. Therefore, "carried interest" can be relied on only as a general description, and one must define the term fully in the agreement.

I. OTHER INTERESTS

Owners of mineral rights are free to create their own hybrid interests and frequently do. What we have considered in this Chapter are the most common, however. Frequently lawyers and courts will deal with hybrid interests by comparing and contrasting them to more common interests.

CHAPTER 4

PROTECTION OF OIL AND GAS RIGHTS

As Chapter 2 discusses, the rule of capture protects an oil-and-gas developer against liability for drainage from neighboring lands. The rule of capture does not protect a trespasser, however, whether the trespass is to the surface of the property or to the subsurface. Where an operator drills upon land to which the operator does not own or lease the mineral rights or drills at an angle into the subsurface of property to which the operator does not own or lease the mineral rights, the law will impose liability by the same principles that protect interests in real property.

Owners of mineral interests and leasehold interests whose rights are infringed may receive compensation for (A) damage to the lease value of the interest, (B) slander of title, (C) assumpsit, and (D) conversion and ejectment. Owners typically choose one of the first three measures where the value of their mineral rights has been damaged by the trespass. Owners typically favor conversion and ejectment where the trespass has resulted in the profitable production of oil and gas.

A. DAMAGE TO LEASE VALUE

Permitting an owner to recover for damage to the lease value of his or her mineral interest is an application of the tort of interference with prospective advantage. Drilling an oil and gas well is the only sure way of "proving" a property. Drilling a dry hole or a poor well may "condemn" a property or a formation for oil and gas development by proving that commercially profitable amounts of oil and gas are not present. When that happens as a result of a trespass, the law permits a mineral owner to recover from the trespasser the damages the trespass has done to the lease value of the property.

The classic case illustrating the remedy of damage to the lease value of property is *Humble Oil and Refining Co. v. Kishi*, 276 S.W. 190 (Tex.Com.App. 1925). There, Humble held a lease dated December 23, 1919, but signed and acknowledged by its lessor on January 29, 1920. The lease term was for three years with provisions that it could be extended by commencement of drilling operations leading to production. Humble argued that the lease extended for three years from the date it was signed and acknowledged. Shortly before the end of January 1923, Humble commenced drilling operations and drilled a dry hole. The court determined subsequently that the term of the lease ran for three years from its date, so that the lease had expired before Humble commenced its operations. The court awarded the mineral owner damages for the bonus value of the right to lease, although there had been no offer from another purchaser.

1. RATIONALE OF THE REMEDY

In *Martel v. Hall Oil Co.*, 253 P. 862 (Wyo.1927), the Supreme Court of Wyoming rejected a claim for damage to the lease value from a trespasser who had drilled a dry hole, reasoning that there was no real damage to the true owner where a dry hole was drilled because the property was worthless for oil and gas development in the first place. The court's conclusion ignores economic realities. When property is leased, the lessee customarily pays the lessor a bonus, a payment for executing the lease. The amount of the bonus reflects the potential risks and rewards, as well as the competition for leases in the area at the time. The market mechanism takes into account the risk that there will be no oil and gas under the property leased when it sets the bonus price. All property has some economic value for lease purposes, and there is a real loss to the true owner when a trespasser's actions "condemn" the property.

2. MEASURE OF DAMAGES

An interesting question is how damages should be measured—at what point in time is the lease value of the property determined? To understand the issue, it is helpful to note that the value of property for leasing generally increases as drilling progresses, at least until there are indications that a dry

hole will result. Should damages for destruction of
the lease value of the property by the trespasser be
measured by the value of the property when the
trespass begins or by peak value just before it
becomes apparent that no oil and gas will be found?
Damages should be the difference between the peak
value of the property and its value after condemnation, because trespass is a continuing tortious act.
Thus, the potential liability is sizable.

B. SLANDER OF TITLE

Trespassers to oil and gas interests may also face
liability in tort for slander of the owner's title.
Slander of title is malicious publication of false
statements that are injurious to the plaintiff's title
to property, or to the quality of the title. Generally,
courts state the elements of proof of slander of title
to be (1) a false claim of title, (2) asserted with
malicious intent, (3) that causes pecuniary damage.
Where an owner meets these elements of proof, a
trespasser may be held liable for the amount of the
damage suffered by the owner.

1. FALSE CLAIM

An owner can meet the first element of proof,
that there has been a publication of a false claim to
the property, merely by showing that the trespasser
occupies the property. An owner can prove a false
claim also by showing that the trespasser recorded
an oil and gas lease purporting to cover the owner's
interest in the premises, or, as in the classic case in

the area, *Kidd v. Hoggett*, 331 S.W.2d 515 (Tex.Civ. App.1959), that the lessee of an expired lease has refused to release it.

2. MALICIOUS INTENT

To prove malice, the owner does not necessarily have to show that the wrongdoer acted with evil intent, but only that the slander was deliberate conduct without reasonable cause. Reasonable cause is present where the slanderer had a good-faith belief in the superiority of slanderer's own claims, particularly when the slanderer is acting upon advice of a lawyer. A good-faith belief will not protect against liability for recklessness, however, and the courts tend to define good faith restrictively. Frequently, courts infer malice from the improbability of the slanderer's assertions of good faith.

3. SPECIFIC DAMAGES

In contrast to the remedy for damage to the lease value, slander of title requires a showing of actual loss. Proof of specific damage for slander of title to a mineral property usually consists of showing a loss of contract or opportunity to sell or lease. The owner must provide the names of those who have refused to deal with the owner because of the cloud on title or explain why that is not possible.

C. ASSUMPSIT

Assumpsit is an equitable action brought to enforce an implied contract. In the context of a trespass to oil and gas interests, the owner sues for payment for the right of entry that the trespasser should have obtained.

Assumpsit is often the remedy sought when trespass occurs in the course of a geophysical search. In *Phillips Petroleum Co. v. Cowden*, 241 F.2d 586 (5th Cir.Tex.1957), a geophysical search company working for Phillips obtained permission from the severed surface owner and conducted a seismic survey. The Fifth Circuit Court of Appeals held that the right to conduct seismic surveys belonged to the mineral owners and awarded them the reasonable market value of the use made of their property. Assumpsit is also a favored remedy when a trespasser has drilled a dry hole, because it will permit the owner to claim the lease bonus that the trespasser should have paid.

Where a trespasser enters property in reliance upon a grant of the right from another and that grant contains a warranty, a trespasser theoretically should be able to recover damages the trespasser might have to pay the true owner from the person who improperly granted the right. Thus, if an oil company's lease is no good, the oil company should be able to recover from its lessor. As a practical matter, however, oil companies draw back from suits for breach of warranty for fear that suits will discourage other mineral owners from dealing with them. Furthermore, recovery for breach of warranty is generally limited to the amount of compensation paid, plus interest, which may be a pittance compared to the damages awarded to the true owner who sues in assumpsit.

D. EJECTMENT AND CONVERSION

The final remedies for an owner who has suffered trespass are to eject the trespasser and demand compensation for the conversion of oil and gas production. The measure of damages depends upon whether the court finds that the trespass was in bad faith or good faith.

1. BAD–FAITH TRESPASS

The law of trespass against oil and gas rights is an application of the rules that apply to real property. If an oil and gas trespasser is found to have acted in bad faith, the trespasser is permitted no set off for expenses incurred or benefits conferred. Improvements upon the property and all income from them belong to the owner. Furthermore, unless the owner demands it, the trespasser will not be permitted to plug and abandon a well capable of commercial production; that would be waste. Most courts, such as the Alaska Supreme Court in *Alaska Placer Co. v. Lee*, 553 P.2d 54 (Alaska 1976), presume bad-faith trespass because trespass is *prima facie* wilful and the facts as to motivation are within the control of the trespasser. Some courts, such as the Oklahoma Supreme Court in *Edwards v. Lach-man*, 534 P.2d 670 (Okl.1974), place the burden of proving bad-faith trespass upon the owner.

2.   GOOD–FAITH TRESPASS

If a court finds that a trespasser has committed trespass in good faith—and the courts usually find good-faith trespass—equity will permit the trespasser to recover from production actual costs or their reasonable value, whichever is less. Thus, if the trespasser exercised superior business and technical judgment and obtained a producing well at a rock-bottom price, the trespasser will be permitted to recover only actual expenditures. But if with the benefit of hindsight the trier of fact determines that expenditures were not wisely made, the good-faith trespasser will be permitted to recover only that portion of the cost deemed prudent. The effect of the rule is to remove all possibility of economic benefit for the trespasser.

In considering whether costs incurred by good-faith trespassers are reasonable, courts generally discuss whether the expenditures benefit the true owner. The rationale of the analysis is that even a good-faith trespasser should be able to recover from the owner only those expenditures which would otherwise unjustly enrich the owner.

The "benefit" test is difficult to apply. In a broad sense, even a dry hole benefits the true owner; it will, at the least, show where not to drill. Because of the uncertainty of the benefit test and because of a perceived policy that oil and gas development should be encouraged, most commentators and some courts have suggested that a good-faith trespasser should be able to offset all expenditures incurred in exercise of good-faith business judgment. When good-faith business judgment is the test, a trespasser is treated much like a cotenant who drills without the agreement of other cotenants.

E. CONCLUSION

Because of the nature of the remedies, damage to lease value, slander of title and assumpsit are claims that owners generally assert when a trespass has damaged the economic value of the property. Where a trespasser discovers oil or gas in commercial quantities, particularly where oil and gas have been produced for a substantial period in large quantities, conversion and ejectment are likely to be the owner's preferred remedies. In appropriate circumstances, any of the remedies discussed may impose a heavy burden on a trespasser, and provide an important negative incentive for the oil industry to respect the property rights of others.

*

PART II

CONVEYING OIL AND GAS RIGHTS

CHAPTER 5

CREATION AND TRANSFER OF OIL AND GAS INTERESTS

Oil and gas interests may be created or transferred by conveyance, inheritance, judicial action, or adverse possession. In this chapter we will analyze the basic principles of creating and transferring oil and gas interests.

A. BY CONVEYANCE

A *conveyance* is a transfer of ownership by a presently-operative instrument intended to pass ownership of an interest in land to a transferee. Oil and gas conveyances are usually subject to the same formalities as real property conveyances. Courts typically require five formalities. They are (1) a writing, (2) words of grant, (3) an adequate description, (4) designation of the parties who are grantor and grantee, and (5) proper execution.

1. WRITING

The Statute of Frauds seeks to avoid fraud and perjury with respect to real property (and certain contracts) by requiring that there be a writing signed by the party to be charged with the interest created. Oil and gas interests are treated as real property under the Statute of Frauds. They must be created and conveyed in writing.

Even an informal writing such as a letter may satisfy the Statute of Frauds, but oil and gas interests generally are created and transferred by formal and recordable legal documents entitled "deed" or "lease." Oil and gas conveyances look very much like their real-property counterparts. Sample mineral and royalty conveyances are included in the Appendix.

a. Deeds

There are two general types of deeds in use in the United States to convey oil and gas interests. The basic distinction between them is the presence of covenants or warranties of title.

(1) Warranty Deed

A warranty deed grants the property described with covenants (promises) of the grantor as to title. A warranty deed may contain up to six overlapping covenants by the grantor as to title: seisin, right to convey, no encumbrances, warranty, quiet enjoyment and further assurances. Generally, covenants of title obligate the grantor to protect the grantee and those who take from the grantee against conflicting claims to the interest granted.

Warranties may be specified in deeds or, in some states, may be incorporated by reference (e.g., "I grant with general warranty covenants....") or implied from the use of certain granting language (e.g., "I grant, bargain, sell, and convey the following described land...."). A warranty deed that contains all six covenants of title is sometimes called a "full" or "general" warranty deed. A deed is also sometimes called a "general" warranty deed if it includes a promise to protect the grantee against the claims of "all persons whatsoever" or similar language. A warranty deed that contains fewer than all of the covenants of title or that limits the scope of the warranties to protection against persons claiming "by, through, or under the grantor or his heirs" may be called a "special" or "limited" warranty deed.

(2) Quitclaim Deed

A quitclaim deed contains no covenants of title. The grantor grants whatever interest he or she may have to the grantee, but without any guarantee that the grantor has any interest to grant. Whatever rights the grantor has to the property described, the grantor "quits" or releases to the grantee.

Deeds without covenants of title will usually be entitled "Quitclaim" and use that word in the granting clause (e.g., "The grantor quitclaims and conveys the following described property ..."). In many states, however, any deed without an express statement of covenants of title is a quitclaim deed.

(3) Importance of Title Covenants

Title covenants or warranties serve two important functions in oil and gas conveyancing:

(1) if the covenants are breached, the grantee is entitled to recover damages suffered up to the amount of the consideration paid, plus interest and expenses incurred in defending the title. In a few states, including Louisiana, one who breaches covenants of warranty may be liable for all damages suffered, even in excess of the consideration received; and

(2) the presence of the covenants gives the grantee the protection of the doctrine of estoppel-by-deed, which may pass after-acquired title of the grantor.

For these reasons, most transactions creating or transferring oil and gas rights are completed with deeds containing covenants of warranty.

There are frequent exceptions, however. Persons active in the oil and gas industry often complete transactions on specially-drafted forms without warranties of title or on printed forms with the covenants struck out, particularly where the grantor's compensation is in the form of a retained interest. Quitclaim deeds are used often to clear clouds on title.

b. Oil and Gas Leases

Oil and gas leases are usually granted on printed forms, as are deeds of mineral and royalty interests. Many commercial printing houses offer a wide variety of lease forms. In addition, many oil companies, lease brokers and some large mineral-interest owners have printed their own lease forms. There are hundreds—or perhaps even thousands—of variations. Typical examples of oil and gas lease forms are included in the Appendix.

Oil and gas leases are different from ordinary leases of real property in at least three respects:

(1) the lessee acquires not only the right to use the premises but also the right to take substances—the oil and gas produced—from the land;

(2) the lessee's rights do not necessarily end after a term of years. In fact, they may be perpetual; they extend "as long as oil and gas is produced." An oil and gas lease creates a determinable interest, rather than a term of years;

(3) the lessee's right to use the land is not exclusive. The lessee's right is subject to the surface owner's uses that do not interfere with the lessee's efforts to acquire the substances covered by the lease.

For these reasons, the courts generally treat oil and gas leases like deeds of easement, or deeds creating a *profit a prendre,* or even deeds to the minerals in place, rather than like leases of real property.

Oil and gas leases generally contain covenants of title for the same reasons that they are included in mineral and royalty deeds—to give the grantee some protection against defects of title and the benefit of the doctrine of after-acquired title. Most printed forms contain only the covenant of warranty, however, obligating the lessor to protect the lessee against actual or constructive eviction by one with paramount title. Moreover, it is common for lessors to delete or disclaim all title covenants.

c. Other Instruments

Other instruments commonly used in creating and conveying oil and gas interests include assignments of interests, grants of right of way, mortgages, deeds of trust and numerous documents very much like documents used in real property conveyancing. As a general rule, the principles of law that control real property conveyances govern the adequacy and effect of oil and gas instruments.

2. WORDS OF GRANT

To convey an interest in oil and gas, a legal instrument must contain words of grant, just as with other interests in real property. There is no "magic" language; it is sufficient that the language show the grantor's intention that there be a present transfer of a present or future interest. A statement that "I give" or "I transfer" the interest probably will suffice. Obviously, a good drafter will not leave the matter open to question. On the premise that more is better, most deeds and leases contain detailed words of grant (e.g., "grant, bargain, sell, convey, transfer, assign, and deliver").

3. DESCRIPTION

The third formality for the creation or transfer of oil and gas interests is that there must be an adequate description of the property to which the interest attaches. In practice, this requirement divides into two standards: (a) legal validity, and (b) marketability.

a. Legal Validity

The standard of legal validity must be met for the instrument to be effective between the grantor and the grantee. The standard is not high. Courts apply the same rule they apply to real property interests in general and hold that a description in an oil and gas conveyance is legally adequate if it is sufficient to permit location of property with reasonable certainty. A description may be legally valid even if oral or other extrinsic evidence is necessary to locate the property; e.g., a grant of "1/32 perpetual non-participating royalty in the 40 acres upon which the house that Uncle Jack built for Aunt Jaime sets" might well be legally valid despite the unorthodox description.

b. Marketability

The marketability standard requires a description sufficiently certain to make the title freely assignable in commerce. The marketability standard is higher than the standard for legal validity. Though reference to the 40 acres where "the house that Uncle Jack built for Aunt Jaime sets" might be legally valid, it would not be a sufficient description upon which a New York, Denver, Houston, or Los Angeles banker would lend money. The marketability standard requires that the tract can be located solely by reference to the public records, without ambiguity, uncertainty, or reference to extrinsic facts.

c. Methods of Description

Most descriptions in oil and gas conveyances meet both the standard of legal validity and the standard of marketability. Generally, oil and gas conveyances use one of two description systems, or a combination of the two, as is done in ordinary real property transactions.

(1) Reference to Government Survey

The more frequently used description system is to locate the property by reference to a government survey, identifying it in the terms of one of the many land surveys conducted under governmental authority. The most common government survey description is the "standard" or rectangular system established by Congressional fiat in 1785. The "standard" system establishes six mile square "townships," located by reference to imaginary lines running north and south (principal meridians) and east and west (principal base lines). Each township is composed of 36 one-mile square "sections" of approximately 640 acres each.

Use of the "standard" system results in references to townships, sections, and quarter sections; e.g., "the SW/4 of the SE/4 of Section 13, Township 12 North, Range 5 West of the Indian Meridian, Canadian County, Oklahoma." Note, however, that the "standard" system is used only in approximately half the states, and not exclusively in many of

those. In Texas, for example, there have been surveys under four different governments—the Span-
ish, the Mexican, the Republic of Texas and the
State of Texas—none of which used the "standard"
system.

(2) Metes and Bounds

When property is not described by reference to
government survey, it is usually described by metes
and bounds. A metes-and-bounds description locates
property by reference to its exterior boundary lines.
Location is expressed in terms of natural or artifi-
cial "monuments" (such as creeks, rocks, and
stakes) and directions and distances. Metes-and-
bounds descriptions tend to be lengthy and poetic;
e.g., "beginning at the granite boulder on the north
side of the bridge over Oil Creek, thence Northeast-
erly 280° thirty rods to an iron stake, thence East
by Northeast to the white oak tree...."

One problem with metes-and-bounds descriptions
is that it may prove difficult to locate the monuments. The white oak tree and the granite boulder
referred to above may have looked distinctive to the
surveyor who drew the description, but time pulverizes even granite boulders, and oak trees multiply,
albeit slowly. Another problem is that the length of
metes-and-bounds descriptions increases the risk of
errors in copying from instrument to instrument. If
the error is in a direction, the description may not
"close" (i.e., the lines of the boundary may never
meet). If the error is in a distance, there will be a
gap in the boundary. The courts have developed

elaborate rules for rationalizing ambiguities or errors in description.

A special application of the metes-and-bounds description method is the recording of plat maps that incorporate metes-and-bounds descriptions in deeds by reference to lots and subdivisions. Another is the "bounded by" method sometimes used in oil and gas leases when it is inconvenient for the person taking the lease to obtain a full legal description. In the Appalachian states, oil and gas leases may describe the property leased by reference to the ownership of surrounding properties at the time the lease is granted; e.g., "Bounded on the North by the lands of Caroline Goldsmith, on the East by lands of Victoria Goldsmith and lands of Sarah Staley Lowe, on the South by the lands of Daniel Nathan, Alexandra Nathan, and Ellie Nathan, and on the West by State Route 161 and the lands of John Taft Lowe." Bounded-by descriptions may be confusing where ownership of surrounding properties has changed between the time of the grant of lease and the attempt to locate the property. But bounded-by descriptions are legally valid; it is possible to locate the property. The marketability of bounded-by descriptions may be questionable, however, and a survey or metes-and-bounds description is preferable.

4. PARTIES DESIGNATED

a. Identification of the Parties

There are two aspects of the requirement that a conveyance identify the grantor and grantee. First, an instrument must identify the parties grantor and grantee with reasonable certainty. The rationale of this rule is certainty and concern that *seisin*, the magic substance of property ownership, must always rest in someone. Compliance with this formality is usually a matter of making sure that all of the blanks of the deed form are completed.

b. Capacity of the Parties

The second and more troublesome aspect of the designation requirement is that those designated must have *capacity* to be a party. Not everyone has the legal right to make conveyances or to hold property rights. Minors, incompetents and drunkards, for example, all generally lack or have limited capacity to transfer interests in land. In oil and gas conveyancing, common capacity problems involve Native Americans (who may be beneficiaries of a trust relationship with the federal government), attorneys in fact, married couples, and concurrent and successive owners. Chapter 6 discusses some aspects of acquiring interests from persons with limited capacity.

5. EXECUTION

Execution, as that term is used with reference to conveyances, means completion of the instrument. Execution may involve as many as four separate elements: (a) signature, (b) attestation and acknowledgment, (c) delivery and acceptance, and (d) recording.

a. Signature

The Statute of Frauds requires that instruments transferring oil and gas interests, like all interests in land, be signed by the grantor. One's signature on a deed or lease attests to its validity. It is common to affix one's business signature rather than one's full given name. President James Earl Carter, Jr. signed his name as Jimmy Carter to documents of state. Even an "X" may be a valid signature if it is intended by the person signing it to be a signature, and if other special requirements are met.

Though there is no legal requirement that one sign one's given name, as a practical matter, it is important that a grantor's signature to a deed or a lease be the identical name shown on the instrument conveying rights to the grantor to avoid confusion over identity. Thus, if the record shows a deed granting the mineral rights in Blackacre to John Taft Lowe, a deed or lease from him at a later date should be signed by him as John Taft Lowe, and not as John Lowe or John T. Lowe, to avoid possible question of the chain of title.

Oil and gas instruments are usually in the form of *deed polls;* i.e., they are structured to be signed only by the grantor. When accepted by a grantee, deed polls are fully as binding upon the grantee as contracts signed by both parties. It does no harm, however, to have the grantee sign the instrument as well.

Most states do not require *consideration* to support creation or transfer of oil and gas interests. Oil and gas interests are classified as real property interests, and the common law did not require consideration to validate a property conveyance. Title passes if the instrument is properly executed and delivered. Most oil and gas conveyances contain recitals of consideration, however, to avoid creation of a resulting trust and to qualify the grantee as a bona fide purchaser for value under recording statutes.

In fact, the parties bargain for monetary consideration in most oil and gas transactions, and if the grantee does not actually pay the money promised there may be grounds for the grantor to rescind the deed or lease and recover title. Furthermore, a few states classify oil and gas leases as contracts, which must be supported by consideration. Louisiana goes even further and requires "serious" consideration.

b. Attestation and Acknowledgment

Attestation, or witnessing, means having persons who are not parties to an instrument testify that they saw the grantor sign the instrument (or, sometimes, that they recognize the signature) by affixing their signatures to the document as witnesses. *Acknowledgment* is the grantor's affirmation under oath that the signature is the grantor's own and, usually, that the grantor has the authority to sign and does so freely. Acknowledgments are usually given before a notary public, but in many states, recording clerks, judges, lawyers, or other officials are empowered to take acknowledgments as well.

Generally, neither attestation nor acknowledgment is necessary to make a conveyance valid. An instrument is valid as between the grantor and the grantee without attestation or acknowledgment, or with improper attestation or acknowledgment, if the parties have complied with all the other formalities. Joinder of the spouse or special acknowledgment may be required to validate a conveyance of property subject to marital rights, however. Moreover, in most states, proper attestation, or acknowledgment, or both are necessary to qualify a conveyance for recording.

Oil and gas instruments are often improperly attested or acknowledged. Probably the most common defect is that the grantor is not presented personally before the oath-giving officer to acknowledge the instrument, as most states require. Another common defect is witnessing by or acknowledgment before an employee or agent of the grantee, which sets up a challenge on the ground that the employee or agent had an interest in the transaction.

When a defective attestation or acknowledgment is challenged, usually by a subsequent purchaser who seeks to avoid having notice imputed by the recording statutes, the states split into three groups:

　　1. The strictest position is that the defectively attested or acknowledged instrument should not have

been allowed on the record and, therefore, will be ignored. The defect makes the recording ineffective to give notice even to those persons who may actually have seen it on the record. Recording gives no constructive, actual, or inquiry notice;

2.   The most liberal position, adopted in Colorado by statute, is that if the defectively attested or acknowledged instrument is recorded it serves as constructive notice to the whole world. Though the recorder should not accept it, the instrument's defects will be ignored if it is actually recorded;

3.   An intermediate position, and the majority rule, is that a defectively attested or acknowledged instrument does not give constructive notice (since it should not be on the record), but it will put those who see it on actual or inquiry notice of the grantee's claim to an interest.

c.   Delivery and Acceptance

The third element of execution is delivery and acceptance. *Delivery* is any act that shows clearly the grantor's intent that title be passed presently. Usually, delivery takes place when the grantor hands the deed to the grantee, but physical transfer of the instrument is neither required nor conclusive proof that delivery has taken place.

Delivery turns on the facts. Delivery may have occurred though the instrument is in the hands of a third party or even though the grantor still possesses it. Conversely, there may be no delivery even though the deed or lease has actually been given to the grantee. In each case the courts look for facts indicating the intent of the grantor and the grantee to pass title presently, without conditions precedent or a right of recall.

Acceptance is a showing by the grantee that the grantee wishes the transfer to be effective. With conveyances of oil and gas interests, as with real property transfers generally, acceptance is usually implied from the fact that the grantee takes the instrument; the grantee does not usually sign a deed or lease.

Disputes over delivery and acceptance are more common in oil and gas conveyancing than in other real property conveyancing because oil and gas interests are usually created and transferred without formal "closings," gatherings at which the deed or lease is signed, witnessed and acknowledged, and the agreed consideration paid. Often, oil and gas transactions are closed by mail or over the telephone. As a practical matter, the moral for grantees is "Get the deed or lease in hand." There is a strong presumption that an instrument in the possession of its grantee has been delivered and accepted.

d. Recording

The final step in conveying oil and gas rights is recording. In most states, recording is a practical requirement for validity rather than a legal requirement. As a general rule, an instrument is valid as between the grantor and the grantee even though it is not recorded. Recording merely protects the grantee against claims of subsequent purchasers or creditors.

Recording may be a legal requirement, however. In Kansas, recording or registration for taxation within a specified time is required to validate a mineral deed. In several states that have enacted marketable title acts or dormant minerals acts (see the discussion in Chapter 7), severed mineral interests can be preserved beyond the statutory limitations period only by special recording or by use.

B. BY INHERITANCE

Oil and gas interests may be acquired by inheritance, as a result of the provisions of a will or of the intestacy laws, as well as by conveyance. Where inheritance is the basis for the creation or transfer of such interests, the requirements that have to be met are those that apply to probate law and to estates generally.

C. BY JUDICIAL TRANSFER

Oil and gas rights also may be transferred by judicial action; e.g., when there is foreclosure of a mortgage or some other lien encumbering the property. Tax sales and administrators' or executors' sales are other examples. The order of a conservation agency compulsorily pooling property may also be a judicial transfer.

The requirements for valid creation or transfer of oil and gas interests by judicial action are strict, and a substantial source of litigation. Minor deviations from statutory procedures will be considered to be "mere irregularities" that will not invalidate the transfer, but more serious "jurisdictional defects" will. To avoid jurisdictional defects, the court that orders the transfer must have proper jurisdiction of the subject matter (including the amount), the property, and the parties to the litigation. The intricacies of jurisdiction of the courts is beyond the scope of these materials. As with transfer of interests by will or intestacy, the issues presented are not peculiar to oil and gas law, but are issues of real property law.

D. BY ADVERSE POSSESSION

One may also acquire title to oil and gas interests, like other real property interests, by using them like an owner. Despite the strong interest in permitting the public to rely upon record title, when one adversely possesses property by using it "like an owner" for a sufficient period of time, fairness and economic efficiency demand that the adverse possessor be recognized and legally protected as the owner.

Generally, what the courts require to establish adverse possession is possession of real property in an open and visible manner, continuously and exclusively for the limitation period, under a claim of ownership sufficient to put other parties on notice that the adverse possessor claims as an owner. Often, adverse possession will be under *color of title,* under a written instrument that the adverse possessor believes conveyed the property to him. Color of title is not necessary for adverse possession, however, except in a few states, including New Mexico. It is not necessary that the possessor personally hold the property for the full limitation period; where there is privity between possessors, their time in possession may be "tacked" together to meet the requisite period.

In modern times, states have codified the doctrine of adverse possession in statutes of limitations. Where the requisites of adverse possession are met for the statutory period, which ranges from five to twenty-five years, the record owner is barred by statute from suing to eject the adverse possessor or to quiet title. An adverse possessor will be entitled to a decree establishing a new and original title to the premises.

Though transfer of oil and gas interests by adverse possession is much less common than transfer by heirship or judicial sale, application of adverse possession to oil and gas interests creates special problems. These are solved by application of fundamental principles.

1. ARE BOTH THE SURFACE AND MINERALS ADVERSELY POSSESSED?

A common problem of adverse possession of mineral properties is the scope of the possession; does the adverse possession extend to both the surface and the minerals? This issue is answered by applying the principles of unity of possession, relation back, and paper transactions.

a. Unity of Possession

A fundamental principle of adverse possession is that the adverse possessor takes all that the record owner against whom he or she adversely possesses has. Therefore, if

O owns fee simple absolute, and

A adversely possesses *by farming* the surface for the statutory period,

A acquires title to both the surface and the minerals when the statutory period ends. If ownership of the minerals has been severed from the surface when the adverse possession begins, however, so that

O owns the surface interest only, and

X owns the mineral rights, and

A adversely possesses by farming the surface for the statutory period,

A acquires title only to the surface rights. Courts distinguish the situations on the basis of to whom A's adverse possession gives notice. Where O owns the fee simple absolute, A's use of the surface by farming puts O on notice that his rights are being challenged. If O does not respond, O loses everything he has. Where the mineral interest has been severed from the surface, however, A's possession of the surface gives no notice to X because A's surface use is not inconsistent with the rights X; if X sees A farming the surface of O's land, for all X knows, A's use may be with O's permission. Another way of rationalizing the result is by the public policy in favor of unity of title; where there is ambiguity, the courts rule in favor of less title fragmentation (and more title unity) because the public has an interest in efficient use of property, which is more likely where there are fewer owners of interests.

b. Relation Back

A second fundamental principle is that title earned by adverse possession relates back to the time of its beginning. Adverse possession is not interrupted by severance of minerals from the surface after adverse possession has begun. Therefore, if

O owns fee simple absolute, and

A begins adverse possession by farming the surface, and

O then severs the minerals by conveying them to X,

A gains title to the fee simple absolute when the statutory period runs. A's title relates back to the beginning of adverse possession. A way to understand the result is to see it as an application of the principle that one can give no better title than one has; O could only give X the mineral rights subject to the claims of A.

c. Paper Transactions

Why does the conveyance from O to X in the last example not interrupt A's adverse possession? Once A takes possession of the property adversely, A must be physically or constructively dispossessed to interrupt the adverse possession. Mere paper transactions are not enough. If X commenced drilling operations, however, that action would interrupt A's adverse possession because X's drilling would be inconsistent with A's claim to the minerals.

2.   WHAT MUST BE DONE TO ADVERSELY POSSESS SEVERED MINERALS?

Where mineral rights have been severed from the surface interest, mere use of the surface for the statutory period is not sufficient to establish title to the minerals by adverse possession. Except in Louisiana, however, one can acquire title to severed minerals by actually taking minerals for the statutory period.

The cases often say that title by adverse possession to severed minerals requires a continuous taking of the minerals for the statutory period. If one takes such statements literally, adverse possession of severed minerals will not begin until actual production is obtained from the land. If notice of the adverse claim is the key to adverse possession, however, actions less than actual production of the minerals should constitute adverse possession. If notice is the issue, adverse possession should begin when operations for drilling or mining are commenced upon the property. Likewise, the requirement that the adverse possession be continuous for the statutory period should be met by intermittent but obviously unconcluded operations. For example, suppose that A, an adverse possessor, commences drilling operations on January 1 and concludes drilling operations with a dry hole on April 1. A does not restore the access roads or drill pits and leaves pipe and equipment on the property until October 1, when drilling operations for a second well are commenced. A's adverse possession should be held to be continuous from January 1. Although A did not work on the land continuously, A's use of it was obvious for all to see and consistent with a claim to the mineral rights.

3. UNRESOLVED ISSUES

Virtually every state has many decisions on adverse possession. Surprisingly, there are several unresolved issues.

a. What It Takes to "Sever" Minerals

As noted above, whether or not the mineral interest has been severed from the surface interest at the time adverse possession begins determines what actions constitute adverse possession. Therefore, it is important to determine what constitutes a severance of the minerals.

There is no doubt that a grant of the minerals by a mineral deed severs the minerals from the surface. But what if the grant is not by a mineral deed but by an oil and gas lease? In states like Texas that hold that an oil and gas lease conveys an estate in the oil and gas to the lessee, it is clear that an oil and gas lease severs the minerals from the surface. In many states, however, an oil and gas lease gives the lessee something less than an estate in the oil and gas—a profit a prendre, a profit in gross, or a license. By the logic of the common law, creating such interests probably would not sever the minerals from the surface. Professors Howard Williams and Charles Meyers argued that an oil and gas lease should be treated as a severance of the minerals from the surface for purposes of adverse possession because the rights of entry and use given by an oil and gas lease are substantially identical to those of a mineral deed.

b.   How Much of the Mineral Is Acquired

A second unresolved issue of adverse possession of severed minerals is the amount of the mineral earned by adverse possession. For example, suppose

O owns the severed mineral rights under a 640 acre section, and,

A adversely possesses for the statutory period by producing oil and gas from the southeast 160 acres.

How much oil and gas does A earn? Does A become owner only of the oil and gas that will be drained by the well he has produced? Does A earn title to all of the oil and gas under the spacing unit, which may cover an area larger than that actually drained? Does A acquire title to all of the oil and gas under the entire 640 acre tract? Finally, what about oil and gas in deeper (or shallower) formations not being produced by the adverse possessor's well? Are they earned?

The cases give little guidance. In dealing with hard minerals, many courts have said that an adverse possessor earns title only to that amount of the minerals produced or loosened by the mining activities. Nonetheless, there is no reason for a record owner who learns of drilling operations on a portion of a tract by an adverse possessor to conclude that the adverse possessor's claims are limited to that portion. In the interest of unity of title, adverse possession of a part of a reasonably sized tract should give the adverse possessor title to the oil and gas to all depths under the whole spacing unit (if the adverse possessor holds without color of title) or under the area covered by the instrument (if the adverse possessor holds under color of title).

c. What Minerals Are Earned

A parallel problem is whether acquisition to title of oil and gas by adverse possession acquires for the adverse possessor rights to other minerals, such as coal. Some cases have held that adverse possession of hard minerals does not earn title to oil and gas. Again, in the interest of unity of title, the better result would be that adverse possession of one mineral earns title to all minerals belonging to the person against whom there has been adverse possession under the area worked or under the entire tract, depending upon whether the possession was under color of title.

CHAPTER 6

JOINT OWNERSHIP OF OIL AND GAS RIGHTS

In the United States, property rights are often owned jointly, by more than one person. Joint ownership of mineral rights is particularly common. In fact, fractionalized oil and gas interests are the rule rather than the exception, because owners often fail to designate mineral interests by will, so that they pass from generation to generation under intestacy laws. Therefore, it is relevant to consider the nature of the rights of joint owners. What kinds of relationships create joint ownership rights? Can one who owns a fraction of the mineral interest grant a lease or develop without permission of the other owners? Whose permission to develop must be obtained and how should permission be accomplished?

A. CONCURRENT OWNERS

At common law, and in most states today, there are three types of concurrent ownership:

Tenancy in Common—joint owners have separate but undivided interests in the property. Each owns a separate fraction, but it is not possible to identify which part belongs to any tenant. Mineral interests are frequently divided into tiny fractions in this manner.

Joint Tenancy—each joint owner owns the whole thing, subject to the right of survivorship of the other owners. The last owner alive takes all the interest. A joint tenancy interest may be "severed" by conveyance, which destroys the right of survivorship and converts it to a tenancy in common; e.g., if A, B and C are joint tenants and C conveys to D, D holds his or her interest as a tenant in common with the joint tenancy of A and B.

Tenancy by the Entirety—this is a form of concurrent ownership available only to husbands and wives. It is similar in effect to a joint tenancy in that each spouse's right is subject to survivorship, but different in concept in that the spouses are treated as one person; spouses have "unity of person," in addition to unities of time, title, interest, and possession. One spouse cannot sever a tenancy by the entirety by a conveyance, but a divorce will convert it to a tenancy in common or a joint tenancy.

The common element of all three ownerships is that all of the co-owners have the right to present possession of the property at the same time; their ownership is *concurrent*.

1. DEVELOPMENT BY CONCURRENT OWNERS

The most common issue with concurrent ownership is whether one or more of the owners have the right to develop minerals, or to lease for their development, without the consent of the other owners.

Suppose that Alexandra and Ellie are tenants in common of Blackacre in fee simple absolute. Alexandra owns a 90% undivided interest and Ellie owns a 10% undivided interest. Alexandra wishes to develop. Alexandra cannot locate Ellie, though she searches diligently (or, she finds Ellie, but Ellie refuses to cooperate in drilling). Alexandra proceeds anyway and completes a prolifically producing well. What rights has Ellie?

a. Minority Rule

In a minority of states, including West Virginia, there is precedent that it is waste for a cotenant (or a cotenant's lessee) to drill for oil and gas without the consent of the other owners. The rationale is the traditional view that any action that changes the nature or character of jointly owned land is waste, even if the action improves it. *Law v. Heck Oil Co.,* 145 S.E. 601 (W.Va.1928), is an example of this approach. In such states, Alexandra, the cotenant who wishes to drill, may be enjoined from development or held liable for damages as a trespasser, unless she can show that development was necessary to protect against drainage. Louisiana has also adopted the minority view in its Mineral Code, but with the modification that the majority rule applies when the cotenants who wish to drill own at least 80% of the mineral rights.

b. Majority Rule

The example is based on the landmark case of *Prairie Oil and Gas Co. v. Allen,* 2 F.2d 566 (8th Cir.Okl.1924). There the 90% tenant in common of the mineral interest in Oklahoma lands leased its interest to an oil company. After the oil company drilled successfully, Lizzie Allen, the owner of the surface and the remaining 10% mineral interest, sued the purchaser of production and the lessee. Ms. Allen contended that she was entitled to one-tenth of all production from the land, arguing that the oil company had no right to develop without her permission—that it was a trespasser to her interest.

The court rejected Lizzie Allen's argument that development without her permission was trespass. The court held that any tenant in common (or the tenant's lessee) has the right to remove minerals from the jointly-owned property because the only way to enjoy an interest in minerals is by developing them. Development is use of the interest, not destruction of it. On that basis, the court required an accounting to Lizzie Allen for her share of the production less her proportionate share of the costs of operating, after all drilling and completion costs had been recovered. It also noted that Lizzie Allen would have had no liability if the well had been a dry hole or had never produced enough to permit the operator to recover all costs.

The majority rule, adopted in Alabama, California, Florida, Georgia, Kansas, Kentucky, Missouri, Montana, North Dakota, Oklahoma, Pennsylvania and Texas, is that a tenant in common (or the tenant's lessee) has the right to develop minerals without the permission of other cotenants, or even over their objection. The developing owner must pay all costs, but has the right to recoup costs paid from production. Thereafter, the developing owner

must account to the non-consenting owners. Furthermore, the developing owner must not deny the
non-consenting owners' rights to develop independently or to lease for development, for that would
be an *ouster* of the other cotenants, making the
developing owner liable as a trespasser.

The majority rule also has implications for a
cotenant's operating rights. In *Anderson v. Dyco
Petroleum Corp.*, 782 P.2d 1367 (Okl.1989), the
Oklahoma Supreme Court held that non-contracted
owners of interests in a gas well did not have a
claim for common law conversion against the purchaser of production from contract parties because
working interest owners were cotenants, each of
whom has the right to develop and market.

2. A CRITICAL EVALUATION OF THE MAJORITY RULE

Several notes are in order about the majority rule
for development by cotenants. First, the rule of
Prairie Oil v. Allen has *not* been specifically adopted
in several jurisdictions that now produce substantial amounts of oil and gas. Most commentators
regard it as the better rule because it is closer
attuned to the trend of the law of waste and to the
effect of oil and gas development. One can make a
strong argument, however, that non-consenting cotenants should be able to insist that their share of
recoverable reserves be left in the ground, if not
that they should be able to bar development altogether; if one anticipates rising oil and gas prices,

early development is not necessarily in the owners' interest.

Second, note that *Prairie Oil v. Allen* involved a tenancy in common, not a joint tenancy or tenancy by the entirety. Its principle should apply equally to a joint tenancy because a joint tenant could convert the interest to a tenancy in common by conveyance. The principle may not apply to a tenancy by the entirety, however, because tenants by the entirety share "unity of the person"; i.e., the two are one legal entity and may not act separately. I discuss the rights of married persons below in this Chapter.

Third, business people do not often rely upon the majority rule. One reason is that there are frequent disagreements over what costs may be recouped by the developing owner. In the context of the example, suppose that the first well on the premises had been a dry hole and that production had been obtained only by drilling a second well. Should the costs of the dry hole be recoverable from the production of the second well? Most of the cases that have considered the issue base their decisions on whether the dry hole was of benefit to the non-consenting owner. However, the concept of "benefit" has proved to be elusive. One can make a strong argument that the non-consenting cotenant should pay his or her share of all costs that are not unreasonable or incurred in bad faith before sharing in production.

Another and perhaps more important reason that business people do not rely on the majority rule of the rights of concurrent owners is that it confers legal rights that may make little economic sense. Suppose that in our example Ellie has a 50% undivided interest (rather than 10%). If Alexandra relies upon the rule in *Prairie Oil & Gas Co. v. Allen,* Alexandra will bear 100% of the risk of loss of drilling a dry hole but will gain only 50% of the right to production if she is successful. Unless the prospect is superlative, Alexandra is likely to decide not to drill without Ellie's consent because the probable return on investment will not be worth the risk.

3.   OTHER METHODS OF OBTAINING THE RIGHT TO DEVELOP

Because of the economic realities, people in the oil and gas industry usually rely upon the rule of *Prairie Oil & Gas Co. v. Allen* only as a last resort or when very small interest owners refuse to participate in drilling. Instead, they use statutory or judicial devices to obtain the rights of lost or recalcitrant owners.

a.   Forced Pooling

The preferred way to obtain non-consenting interests for development is by forced or compulsory pooling. *Forced pooling* is the compulsory joinder of ownership rights in property within a proposed well spacing unit by exercise of the state's police power. As Chapter 2 discusses in conjunction with conservation laws, forced pooling is a legal device developed to permit government to establish minimum sized spacing units without destroying the correlative rights of small tract owners. All but one of the states with petroleum conservation laws have forced-pooling sections in their legislation. Approximately two-thirds of these permit the forced pooling of undivided fractional interests as well as separately-owned small tracts within the spacing unit.

How forced pooling works differs substantially from state to state. The basic concept is the same, however. The state exercises its police power to protect its citizens from over-drilling and correlative rights owners from drainage by forcing a non-consenting owner to accept administratively-determined fair terms. In some states (Oklahoma for one), forced pooling procedures are fast and relatively simple, so that forced pooling is the usual way of dealing with non-consenting owners. In other states (including Texas), the forced pooling procedures are so arduous or the scope of the legislation so limited that forced pooling is rarely used.

b. Judicial Partition

Judicial partition is the division by court order of undivided interests of equal dignity throughout the land. Partition was available only to possessory interests at common law. Therefore, the action ought not be available to divide concurrent interests in severed minerals in states that have embraced the non-ownership theory of oil and gas rights. Nevertheless, courts in most states have applied partition to mineral interests, regardless of ownership theory. Other nonpossessory interests, such as royalty interests or the mineral interest owner's possibility of reverter under a lease, are generally not entitled to partition.

Partition may be *in kind* (a division allocating specific portions to each owner) or *by sale* (conversion of the interests to cash and division of the money). In theory, partition in kind is favored because it disturbs land ownership less. Courts do not generally partition in kind property that produces oil or gas or that is likely to produce oil or gas, however, because a division of the land into tracts proportionate in size to the interests of the cotenants may not proportionately divide the minerals.

In a majority of states, partition is a matter of legal right. The complaining cotenant is entitled to partition either in kind or by sale, though the courts have the discretion to choose between partition in kind and partition by sale to balance equities. There is a minority view, however, adopted in Arkansas, Kansas, Mississippi, and Oklahoma, that the courts have the authority to deny partition altogether to prevent the remedy from being used for "fraud or oppression."

One of the attractions of partition from the view of the partitioning owner is that the partitioning owner is usually entitled to apportion costs and reasonable attorney's fees to the other owners, on the theory that partition benefits the property. A practical problem of partition is that it requires adversary proceedings in court that may drag on for years. As a result, the oil industry does not regard partition with favor.

c. Lost Mineral Interests

Forced pooling and judicial partition are remedies for the problem of non-consenting concurrent owners that may be applied either to recalcitrant mineral interest owners (those who can be located but will not agree to develop or lease) or to "lost" mineral interest owners (those who cannot be located). Lost mineral rights are a special problem because of the difficulty of obtaining jurisdiction over a lost mineral interest owner, and some states have taken special steps to deal with them, including service by publication.

In the last century and a half, many property owners in oil producing states have reserved fractional mineral rights from real estate conveyances, hoping that the rights would become valuable in the future. In many cases those interests did not become valuable, even for speculation, for generations. In the meantime, the severed rights had been further fractionalized by operation of residuary clauses of wills and intestacy laws. Severed fractional rights are now often owned by persons who are not aware that the rights exist. Tracing those persons and purchasing or leasing their rights has become a monumental problem for the oil and gas business— and a growth industry for lawyers and landmen.

In an attempt to unify titles, many states have enacted special legislation. A detailed consideration of the various statutes is beyond the scope of this

book, but the most important statutes can be classified as follows:

    1. *Prescription*—As is discussed in Chapter 3, in
Louisiana, mineral servitudes, mineral royalties, and
leases are extinguished by non-use for 10 years. Tennessee puts a statutory limit of 10 years on oil and gas
leases without development.

    2. *Marketable Record Title Acts*—Some states have
applied marketable record title acts to oil and gas rights
so that interests that conflict with a record chain of
title are extinguished. If the record does not contain a
specific reference to the interest within the statutory
period (usually 30 to 40 years), it is destroyed.

    3. *Dormant Mineral Acts*—Closely related both to
marketable record title acts and to prescription are
dormant mineral acts, statutes that permit mineral
interests not developed or "used" within a stated time,
usually 20 years, to be extinguished and returned to the
surface owners. Several state courts struck down such
laws, finding that they were in violation of the state or
U.S. Constitutions. In *Texaco, Inc. v. Short,* 454 U.S.
516 (1982), the Supreme Court approved the Indiana
Dormant Minerals Statute, opening the door to wide-
spread enactment. Since 1982, approximately a third of
the states have enacted dormant mineral acts. Some
dormant mineral statutes, like the one in *Texaco v.
Short*, are "self-executing"; they automatically terminate mineral interests not developed or "used" within a
stated time, unless they have been preserved by filing.
Others, like the Kansas statute at issue in *Scully v.
Overall*, 840 P.2d 1211 (Kan.App.1992), are designed to
identify lost mineral interests, which are extinguished
only if their owners do not reaffirm them by recording
after being placed on notice by the surface owners.

    4. *Taxation and Sale*—Some states subject severed
mineral interests to separate taxation. If the taxes are

not paid, the interests are sold at a sheriff's sale. A practical problem with such statutes is that officials charged with administration often neglect to assess taxes because of the expense and time involved. In Colorado, a statute permits the surface owner to require county officials to assess taxes on the severed mineral interests in the land.

5. *Receivers or Trustees to Lease*—Most major oil producing states have legislation permitting probate courts to appoint receivers or trustees to lease on behalf of lost mineral interest owners upon judicially-approved terms. Payments from such leases are held in escrow and eventually escheat to the state if not claimed. Oklahoma has gone a step further and provided for escheat of the underlying mineral interest at the same time as the proceeds.

B. MARITAL RIGHTS

Both common law and state statutes provide substantial legal protection for spouses against disinheritance. The rights created are a special application of concurrent rights. They also present special problems in oil and gas development.

There are three kinds of general marital rights that frequently have an impact on the creation or exercise of oil and gas rights.

1. *Dower*—At common law, *dower* was the interest a surviving wife received in the inheritable lands owned by her husband during marriage. She received a life estate in one third of such lands. The corresponding interest of a surviving husband was *curtesy*, a right given to a surviving husband who had proved his manhood by fathering a male heir born alive, to a life estate in all the property owned by his wife during marriage.

In many states, the distinction between the two interests has been abolished by statute so that surviving spouses are entitled to equal interests in property acquired during marriage (usually a ⅓ life estate), upon the death of the partner. Both at common law and in modern times, however, the record may not show a dower or curtesy interest.

2. *Homestead*—Many states have enacted legislation intended to protect property used as the family home against attachment and sale by creditors. Homestead statutes function in part by barring creation and transfer of rights to property unless both spouses join. In some states, homestead must be noted on the deed and actual occupancy of the land claimed as the homestead is not required. In other states, homestead is a question of fact, and a formal legal claim is not required. Whatever is necessary to establish homestead, clear title to oil and gas interests may not be effectively created in homesteaded property without joinder of both spouses, even where the record shows title in one spouse.

3. *Community Property*—In nine states, including Texas, Louisiana, California and New Mexico, community property statutes create a kind of marital partnership in property acquired during marriage. In community property states, each spouse is presumed to own one-half of all property acquired by either spouse during marriage. Though exceptions are made for property acquired by one spouse by inheritance or with assets owned before marriage, the presumption is strong that property acquired during marriage is subject to the other spouse's right. As with dower and homestead rights, community property rights may not be noted on the record; i.e., the property may appear to be wholly-owned by one spouse.

Both spouses usually execute documents creating oil and gas interests, even where the record shows ownership only by one spouse. A better practice is for the spouse who claims no interest, or only a dower or homestead interest, to sign the instrument specially; i.e., the lease or deed should show only the record owner as grantor and the spouse should sign solely to release any rights of dower, homestead, or other marital interest in the premises. Otherwise, the joining spouse may argue for a share of payments provided for under the instrument in the event of a divorce.

C. DEBTORS/CREDITORS

Although in many states secured creditors (e.g., mortgagees or deed-of-trust beneficiaries) hold legal title to the property subject to their claims, there is no doubt but that the right to create and to transfer oil and gas rights belongs to the debtor. Whatever the legal fiction as to the state of title, a security interest is limited to protection of the creditor's right to collect its money, so the debtor (the mortgagor) should have the right to convey oil and gas rights.

Both grantors and grantees of oil and gas rights need to look closely at the terms of security instruments, however. The terms of the mortgage, deed of trust, or other document creating the security interest may make the creditor's acquiescence essential. Many mortgages and deeds of trust contain "due-on-sale clauses"; e.g., "if the ownership of any portion of the premises shall be changed ... then, at the mortgagee's discretion, the entire indebtedness secured hereby shall become immediately due and payable." Others contain assignments of proceeds; e.g., "there are specifically assigned to the mortgagee all rents, revenues, damages, and payments . . . on account of any and all oil, gas, mining, and mineral leases, rights or privileges of any kind now existing or that may hereafter come into existence." Such provisions may not be enforceable in some states, but they are certain sources of dispute between oil and gas interest owners and holders of security interests. Moreover, unless the secured party consents to the grant of a lease or other interest, foreclosure of a prior secured interest will extinguish the oil and gas interest conveyed. As a matter of practice, grantors and grantees of oil and gas interests commonly seek waivers of priority or subordination agreements from secured interest owners.

The vendee's position under a land contract or contract for deed is different from that of a mortgagor only as to the procedure followed to convey. The traditional remedy of the land contract vendor upon default has been to repossess the land and to declare the vendee's equitable title to have been extinguished. Since it is the vendor who will reacquire the full title in the event of default, an oil and gas lessee typically seeks a ratification with a present grant of after-acquired rights instead of a waiver or a subordination of the vendor's rights.

D. FIDUCIARIES/BENEFICIARIES

Another special situation of joint ownership occurs when a fiduciary holds title or exercises rights of management for a beneficiary. Fiduciaries did not have the right at common law to lease for oil and gas development or to create other oil and gas interests because of the traditional view of waste that barred any change in the state of the property. Many states have changed that rule for oil and gas leasing, enacting statutes that authorize a fiduciary to lease unless the trust instrument precludes it. Most trust instruments specifically confer upon the trustee the right to lease and to create other oil and gas rights. Therefore, as a general rule, fiduciaries are able to create and transfer oil and gas rights, even though these rights may extend beyond the term of the fiduciary relationship.

The powers of a fiduciary are often subject to statutory conditions and limitations that vary from state to state. For example, although a personal representative has a statutory power to lease on behalf of the estate in Texas, the same statute limits the lease primary term to five years. When the fiduciary relationship is created by a trust instrument, similar variations are possible because the terms of the trust prevail over more liberal statutory provisions.

As a result, leases and other interests granted by fiduciaries are frequently the source of title problems. One must give meticulous attention (1) to the terms of the instrument establishing the fiduciary relationship and (2) to the requirements of state law.

E. EXECUTIVE/NON–EXECUTIVE OWNERS

The executive right is the power to lease minerals. Frequently, the executive right is severed from the other incidents of mineral ownership. For example, O might convey to A, reserving to himself half the minerals and the exclusive right to lease all of the minerals. By so doing, O could maintain better control over development. O would have half the mineral interest and the executive right to A's half non-executive mineral interest. To obtain a lease covering A's half mineral interest, a prospective lessee would have to deal with O, not A.

The executive right is also present when there is a royalty burdening the property. If O conveys a 1/16 nonparticipating royalty to A, reserving to himself all the minerals, O has the executive right by virtue of his mineral ownership and A has a non-executive right, since his royalty interest has no right to lease.

The executive right is just one of the incidents of mineral ownership. Generally, the executive right does not entitle its holder to the portion of lease benefits accruing to non-executive mineral interests. In Louisiana, the executive right owner is entitled to bonus and delay rentals, but in other states non-executive mineral interest owners retain the right to all lease payments accruing to their interests. It is unclear whether the executive right includes the power to conduct operations on the land as well as lease it. There is a division whether the executive has the power to pool the non-executive rights. In Texas, it has been held that the executive has no such power, but Louisiana has permitted the executive to pool the non-executive interest.

A frequent source of dispute is the duty owed by the executive to the non-executive. What obligation does O have to A in the examples above to exercise the power to lease? Can O decline to lease on any terms? Article 109 of the Louisiana Mineral Code says O can, but *Federal Land Bank of Houston v. United States*, 168 F.Supp. 788 (Ct. Cl. 1958), held squarely to the contrary.

Another issue of executive rights is what obligation O owes A in the examples above to negotiate a "good" lease. Some cases indicate that there is no duty other than to act in good faith, which is defined as an absence of bad faith, because O's self interest will protect A. Most courts that have addressed the issue have found an implied duty of utmost good faith and fair dealing. The utmost good faith and fair dealing standard requires that the executive act with reasonable regard for the interests of the non-executive and be willing to execute a lease for the non-executive on the same terms and conditions as a reasonably prudent landowner would have done had there been no non-executive interest. A few courts have imposed a fiduciary obligation, which requires the executive to subordinate his interests to those of the non-executive rights owner. In *Manges v. Guerra*, 673 S.W.2d 180 (Tex.1984), the Texas Supreme Court mixed the concepts, finding a fiduciary duty of utmost good faith that requires the executive to acquire for the non-executive every benefit that the executive rights owner exacts for himself, and imposing exemplary damages upon the executive for his failure to meet the standard. Subsequently, in *Mims v. Beall*, 810 S.W.2d 876 (Tex.App.1991), a Texas Court of Appeals interpreted *Manges* to bridge the utmost good faith and fiduciary standards. The duty owed, reasoned the *Mims* court, is utmost good faith, which requires that the executive acquire for the non-executive every benefit that he exacts for himself. Since the duty is fiduciary in nature, however, a court may award punitive damages for breach.

F. LIFE TENANTS/REMAINDERMEN

The most common successive interests, when ownership is divided between present and future rights, are those of life tenants and remaindermen. Typical problems in dealing with life tenancies and remainder interests are (1) the power to grant, (2) division of proceeds, and (3) the open-mine doctrine.

1. POWER TO GRANT

a. In Common Law States

At common law, neither a life tenant nor a remainderman can develop oil and gas, grant a valid oil and gas lease, or create any other oil and gas interest without permission of the other, because neither possesses the full rights to the property. A life tenant has the right of present use, but must conserve the estate for the remainderman. A life tenant cannot grant an oil and gas lease, because taking minerals would diminish the estate that the life tenant must conserve, and because the term of the lease (typically "so long as oil and gas are produced") might exceed the life estate. The remainderman on the other hand, eventually will have full rights to the property, but the remainderman lacks the right to present use that any grantee of an interest in oil and gas will require.

Welborn v. Tidewater Associated Oil Co., 217 F.2d 509 (10th Cir.Okl.1954), illustrates the principle. One who held a life estate in a certain parcel also served as legal guardian to a minor remainderman. In 1943, acting in her capacity as guardian, Smith issued a lease to Welborn of the remainder interest. In 1952, while the Welborn lease was still effective according to its stated terms, both the remainderman (by now an adult) and the life tenant granted an oil and gas lease that was subsequently assigned to Tidewater. When Welborn sued Tidewater for slander of title, the court held that Welborn had no right to go on the property to explore for, develop, or produce oil and gas, so Welborn had no title that could be slandered by a lease executed jointly by the life tenant and remainderman.

If a life tenancy is created by an instrument, rather than by operation of law, the relationship of the life tenant and remainderman may be changed from the common law standard either specifically or by inference. For example, if a life tenant is specifically given the right to lease or otherwise dispose of the property, the weight of authority is that the life tenant has the right to grant an oil and gas lease even though it may extend beyond his or her lifetime. The right to lease may be inferred from a grant of a life tenancy in the minerals; if the grantor intended to give the life tenant use of the minerals, that intent requires that the life tenant possess the right to develop or lease for development. On the other hand, if the instrument merely creates a life estate "without impeachment for waste," the life tenant has no duty to conserve the minerals against depletion under an oil and gas lease, but there is an unanswered question as to whether the life tenant has the right to grant lease rights beyond his or her lifetime.

b. In Louisiana

In Louisiana, the analogous interests to life tenant and remainderman are the *usufruct* and *naked owner*. The usufruct has no right to take minerals, to lease, or to share the benefits of leasing, however, as a general rule. The usufruct is entitled only to the benefit of the use of the surface unless the instrument creating it provides otherwise. The naked owner has all rights to oil and gas.

c. Common Leasing Practice

Generally, grants of oil and gas rights from life tenants and remaindermen are obtained over the signatures of both. An oil and gas lease may be obtained (1) by having the life tenant and remainderman sign the same lease, (2) by having the life tenant and remainderman sign separate leases, or (3) by having the life tenant grant a lease which is then ratified by the remainderman. The third practice is preferred by oil companies for two reasons. First, having the life tenant sign a lease that is then ratified by the remainderman avoids questions as to how to divide payments under the lease. The life tenant is designated as the lessor to whom payments are to be made, and the remainderman ratifies the lease terms. Second, a remainderman presented with a ratification is less likely to demand payment of a bonus or a share of the lease proceeds than if he or she is asked to execute a lease.

Each of the three approaches may lead to problems. If the life tenant and the remainderman execute the same lease, an ambiguity as to how the bonus, delay rentals, and royalties provided for in the lease are to be paid may result, unless the lease spells out the division. As Chapter 8 discusses, ambiguities over how delay rentals are to be divided may result in termination of the lease. Where the life tenant and the remainderman execute separate leases, the lessee may be required to make double lease payments unless the leases are carefully drafted. Some courts have held that the lessee must pay whatever bonus, delay rentals and royalty each lease provides for the lessor it names. The third alternative, obtaining a lease from the life tenant and a ratification from the remainderman, may lead to the transaction being set aside for fraud, misrepresentation, or overreaching, if its nature is not disclosed to the remainderman. Neither the life tenant nor the remainderman has the right to develop oil and gas without the other. Consequently, the ratification form presented to the remainderman will contain words presently granting the remainderman's future interest to the lessee under the terms of the lease being ratified, as well as ratifying the life tenant's lease. A ratification form containing words of grant as well as words of ratification is more than a mere ratification; it is a lease, and the lessee should disclose that fact.

2. DIVISION OF PROCEEDS

Where a life tenant and remainderman grant an oil and gas lease without agreeing specifically upon division of proceeds under the lease, how should the proceeds of the lease—the bonus, delay rentals, royalty and shut-in royalties—be paid?

The courts have generally allocated funds between the life tenant and the remainderman on the basis of classification of the funds as income or corpus. Funds classified as income are paid to the life tenant. If classified as corpus, a return of the "body" of the trust, the funds are invested to yield income (which is paid to the life tenant) and held as principal to be turned over to the remainderman when the life tenant dies.

When applied to oil and gas lease proceeds, application of the general rule rarely satisfies either the life tenant or the remainderman. Delay rentals (which have traditionally been a nominal dollar per acre per year) are uniformly classified as income and paid to the life tenant. Bonus payments, paid to induce the lease grant, and royalty payments are usually allocated to principal and invested. The interest from investments is paid to the life tenant, but the remainderman gets nothing until the life tenant dies. In Arkansas and Oklahoma, bonus is allocated to the life tenant. Generally, however, the life tenant is paid only delay rentals and interest on bonus and royalties, and the remainderman receives nothing until the life tenant's death. Often, the life tenant and remainderman will agree in advance upon allocation of lease proceeds. If they agree, all of the proceeds can be distributed.

3. THE OPEN–MINE DOCTRINE

The open-mine doctrine, borrowed from the law of hard minerals, changes the general rules for division of oil and gas lease proceeds. Where there is an "open mine" on the property when the life tenancy is created, the life tenant is entitled to all lease payments, including any bonus and royalties (as well as the right to work the mine in absence of a lease). One rationale for the open-mine doctrine is the presumed intent of the life tenancy's creator that the life tenant should have the use of the property as it was when the life tenancy was created.

Generally, a mine is held to be "open" when an oil and gas lease exists when the life tenancy is created; the grant of a lease "opens" the mine.

Contrary to the rule for hard minerals, when there is a producing well on the lease at the creation of the life tenancy, the life tenant is also entitled to the proceeds from additional wells drilled. Texas and Oklahoma, at least, limit the open-mine doctrine to the term of the lease in existence when the life tenancy is created. The life tenant may not grant additional oil and gas leases on the property or extend existing leases.

The Louisiana Mineral Code adopts a version of the open-mine doctrine as an exception to the general rule that the naked owner is entitled to the benefits of leasing. If a well capable of producing exists on the land or on land pooled with it when the usufruct is created, then the usufruct is entitled to royalties on actual or constructive production. Further, the usufruct has the right to lease the interest subject to the usufruct and to retain any bonus and rentals.

G. TERM INTERESTS

Theoretically, the position of a holder of an estate for years is the same as a life tenant. The estate-for-years owner lacks the power to grant an oil and gas lease because development of petroleum would be waste and because the lease may be extended beyond his or her estate for years by production. The estate-for-years owner should be benefitted by the open-mine doctrine. In practice, however, grants of estates for years are rarely intended to include the minerals as well as the surface.

But one frequently sees defeasible-term interests in oil and gas. For example, O may convey to A mineral rights "for 10 years and so long thereafter as oil or gas are produced...." Such language gives A rights that will terminate at the end of the 10 years without production, but that will be extended by production as long as production lasts.

Defeasible-term interests present the same interpretative difficulties as the term clause of an oil and gas lease. Should "production" in a defeasible-term deed mean the same thing as "production" in the term clause of an oil and gas lease? In Texas, courts have held that it should because the likelihood is that the parties intended that result by their choice of language. Oklahoma has rejected the notion, adopting Professor Eugene Kuntz' analysis that leases contemplate development by the lessee while defeasible-term interests are held for speculation. Accordingly, in *Fransen v. Eckhardt,* 711 P.2d 926 (Okl.1985), the Oklahoma Supreme Court held that a defeasible term mineral interest for thirty years and so much longer as oil or gas were "produced from said land in paying quantities" terminated where there was a well on the premises capable of production but not actually producing at the end of the term; Oklahoma's capability-of-production rule would have preserved a lease with similar language, as Chapter 8 discusses. Louisiana's Mineral Code also applies a different standard to interruption of prescription for mineral servitudes than for oil and gas leases. In contrast to Oklahoma, it sets a lower standard for servitudes

than for leases. Article 38 makes good faith operations sufficient to interrupt prescription of mineral
servitudes, while actual production is required for
leases.

A related issue is whether lease provisions for
constructive production, such as a shut-in royalty
clause, constitute "production" under a defeasible-
term deed? *Archer County v. Webb*, 338 S.W.2d 435
(Tex.1960), reasons that the constructive-produc-
tion provision must be in the deed; it cannot be
"bootstrapped" from a later oil and gas lease.

Defeasible-term interests present other problems
analogous to lease interpretation disputes. Does a
reference to "production" require "production in
paying quantities," as it generally does in oil and
gas leases? Should whether a cessation of production is temporary or permanent be judged by the
same factors applied to leases? Again, authority is
divided.

Moreover, the issues are close questions. The
reasons underlying the development of the interpretative rules for leases do not apply to defeasible
term mineral interests. Production must be "in
paying quantities" to extend an oil and gas lease,
because the parties enter into the lease with an
expectation of profit from development and the
lessee has it within its control to make production
profitable. In contrast, defeasible-term mineral interests are usually held for speculation, and their
owners often lack either the right or the expertise
to develop themselves. This reasoning may lead to

contrary results, however. One may conclude, as did the Oklahoma court in *Fransen v. Eckhardt*, that because of the element of speculation, a more strict definition should be adopted for defeasible-term interests than for leases. In the alternative, one may conclude that defeasible-term interests should be subject to a more liberal standard, as in Louisiana, because their owners are often unable to protect themselves. One may also conclude that the terms of oil and gas leases and defeasible-term interests should be given the same meaning because that probably was what the parties intended and because such an interpretation will be more certain. Finally, one may distinguish between defeasible-term mineral interests and defeasible-term royalty interests. Except in a few states, there is little case law on these and similar issues.

CHAPTER 7

INTERPRETIVE PROBLEMS IN OIL AND GAS CONVEYANCING

Oil and gas conveyances often present interpretive problems. Those problems are usually dealt with by well-established rules of judicial construction that yield little certainty or, where they are certain, may seem unfair in result. In this Chapter, we will examine common conveyancing problems with the purpose of identifying them and learning to avoid them.

A. STEPS IN JUDICIAL INTERPRETATION

The first duty of a court trying to interpret a conveyance is to give effect to the intent of the grantor and grantee. Though certainty of title is desirable, and a close second in priority, the controlling policy is to recognize owners' rights by giving effect to the parties' intent. To ascertain the parties' intent, courts have developed a three-step process for interpreting conveyances of real property interests, including oil and gas rights:

(1) determine the intention of the parties from all the terms of the instrument;

114

(2) if the intention of the parties is doubtful, use construction aids and rules of construction to clarify their objective intent;

(3) if the instrument is still ambiguous, consider parol or other extrinsic evidence.

1. INTERPRETATION OF THE INSTRUMENT AS A WHOLE

A court's first step in interpreting an instrument is to look to all of its terms. Courts seek the parties' intent, but because of the importance the law places on certainty in real-property ownership, courts seek intention objectively, by examining the terms of the instrument rather than by asking the parties what they intended. Courts review the instrument in question as a whole and attempt to reconcile or *harmonize* all of its terms. This first step is frequently referred to as the *four corners rule,* because a court looks to the four corners of the instrument to ascertain the parties' intent. Application of the four-corners rule often leads to literal interpretations in which the result turns on the drafter's choice of a word or a phrase or even the placement of a comma.

2. USE OF CONSTRUCTION AIDS AND RULES OF CONSTRUCTION

When a court remains in doubt about the intent of the parties to an instrument after examining its four corners, it may apply a variety of discretionary construction aids and rules of construction. For example, the instrument may be construed against the interests of the party who prepared it, who was in a position to have made its intent clear. Typed or handwritten provisions will prevail over printed provisions, because they are more likely to express the intent of the parties. General terms following specific terms will be interpreted by the rule of *ejusdem generis* to refer to terms of the same kind or class as the specific terms.

Construction aids and circumstantial tests are not certain to lead courts to the parties' intent. At best, they provide objective inferences of what the parties' intent might reasonably have been. Many construction aids further policy goals unrelated to intent. For example, the rule that an instrument will be construed against the party who drafted it promotes certainty in title and care in drafting, rather than providing an insight into what the parties probably intended.

3. CONSIDERATION OF EXTRINSIC EVIDENCE

Courts frequently find it impossible to locate a clear inference of the parties' intent from the terms of an instrument, even with the help of construction aids. For example, as is discussed in conjunction with the meaning of "minerals" below, a mineral deed conveying "oil, gas and other minerals" gives little guidance as to what other substances the parties may have intended to include within the phrase "other minerals." Therefore, as a last resort, courts examine the attendant circumstances of the conveyance. They may consider parol (oral) evidence, as well as the performance of the parties before the dispute, and extrinsic evidence in the form of letters, memoranda, or records bearing upon the negotiations that led to the ambiguous conveyance.

4. APPLICATION OF THE INTERPRETIVE STEPS

Knowing the steps courts follow in interpreting conveyances helps in understanding the process of judicial decision making. It is of little assistance, however, in predicting the result of particular disputes. Since the intent of the parties to the conveyance is the interpretative goal, determination of what the instrument fairly says, which construction aids to use, and what extrinsic evidence is sufficient to establish intent rests within the discretion of the courts. As a result, litigation is the only certain way to resolve many interpretive problems of oil and gas conveyancing.

B. WHAT IS THE MEANING OF "MINERALS"

The problem of what substances are included in a grant or reservation of "minerals" is a good example of the difficulties of applying the principles of judicial interpretation. The meaning of a general reference to "minerals" in a grant or reservation is of great economic significance. Commercial uses have been developed for many substances that had little or no commercial value a generation ago. In addition, reserves of many important natural resources are growing short, so that marginal deposits previously not considered worth developing may have substantial value. As a result, there is frequent litigation over ownership of substances that may have been granted or reserved as "minerals." Except in Pennsylvania and a few other states, the courts have held that oil and gas are "minerals."

Problems similar to those encountered in construing "minerals" may arise with respect to specifically-named substances. For example, what is "gas"? Helium produced in conjunction with natural gas has been held to be "gas," even though it is not combustible. Especially troublesome is whether a grant or reservation of "coal" carries with it ownership of coalbed methane gas. The United States Supreme Court held in *Amoco Production Company v. Southern Ute Indian Tribe*, 526 U.S. 865 (1999), that the meaning of "coal" and "coalbed methane" should be determined by the "plain meaning" of those terms in 1909 and 1910. The Court also applied a "social purpose" test, looking to the circumstances that applied at the time of the reservation, notably the view of coalbed methane as a dangerous waste.

The dispute over the meaning of "minerals" is common with "hard" minerals. Uranium is a good example. Suppose that the record of title to Blackacre shows that O, as owner in fee simple absolute, conveyed the land in 1950 to A, reserving the "oil, gas and other minerals." There have been subsequent transfers of both the surface interest and the severed mineral interest so that ownership is now vested in P, who owns the "oil, gas and other minerals" and D, who owns the remainder of the interest in the land. If a mining company wishes to obtain the right to strip mine uranium from the premises, should it take a lease from P or D? Is uranium a "mineral" or does it belong to the surface owner?

1. THE TRADITIONAL APPROACH OF THE COURTS

Our legal system has not dealt effectively with disputes like that between P and D. Courts have traditionally tried to determine what substances O and A, the original grantor and grantee, intended should be minerals. Out of reverence for the importance of certainty to the land title system, judges have tried to ascertain O and A's intent by examining objective factors rather than by asking them what they intended.

Usually, the courts' analysis begins with a review of the four corners of the document, seeking the intent of the parties in using the word "minerals" by considering all of the deed's terms. This process is often futile. Mineral grants and reservations usually do not contain enough verbiage to raise clear inferences.

The next step of the process is to apply one or more of a variety of construction aids and circumstantial tests to determine O and A's intent. As discussed in Part A, these "rules of construction," are not rules of law that judges must follow. They are "rules of thumb" that provide objective clues to what the parties might have intended or that further public policies. In addition to construction against the grantor, the following rules of construction have been applied to clarify "minerals":

ejusdem generis—general words that follow specific words are limited to things of the same kind or class as those specifically stated, so that a reservation of "oil, gas, and other minerals" reserves other minerals "like" oil and gas;

community-knowledge test—a substance is considered to be a "mineral" if it was regarded as such by the community in which the instrument was given at the time of the conveyance;

exceptional-characteristics test—a substance is a "mineral" if it possessed exceptional characteristics that gave it special value at the time of the conveyance;

rule of practical construction—the actions of the parties contemporaneous with or subsequent to the conveyance are considered to establish the intention of the parties. If the negotiations concerned only oil and gas rights, only substances produced in conjunction with oil and gas are likely to be "minerals";

surface-destruction test—when production of a substance requires destruction of the surface, the substance is not a "mineral" because the original parties would not have intended that the mineral interest owner be given the right to destroy the beneficial use of the property by the surface owner.

Rules of construction are not very helpful. First, rules of construction merely suggest what the parties may have intended, and the inference may not be very strong. For example, though the community-knowledge test would include oil and gas in a reservation of "the mineral interests in said land" when oil and gas were known to exist in the area, "the nagging question remains ... if its retention were a part of the consideration for the deed, why did not the grantor write plainly 'minerals including oil and gas'?" Edward Horner, Lignite—Surface or Mineral, 31 *Ark.L.Rev.* 75, 97 (1975).

Second, the sheer number of rules of construction and the lack of agreement as to which should be applied, and in what circumstances, virtually guarantees confusion. Some states have rejected some of these tests while accepting others, but with few exceptions, there are no rules as to when to use any rule of construction. Frequently, the courts use more than one test in the same case.

Finally, the interpretive process often produces results that cannot be demonstrated to be fair. Whether a particular substance should be considered a "mineral" or should belong to the surface owner is not an issue that produces much emotion in the abstract. Even when the question is presented in a specific context, the indicia usually are so contradictory and overlapping that it is rare that one who reads the cases will conclude that a wrong has been made right, whatever test is used.

The flaw in the process, as Professor Eugene Kuntz noted more than sixty years ago, is that the courts seek to ascertain intention in situations in which the parties probably had none. Had the parties been aware that the disputed substances were present or that they would have substantial value in the future, the drafter would have named them or excluded them specifically. In sum, the construction process typically applied by courts results in a legal fiction, rather than a finding of true intent. The search for intent in each case makes the meaning of "minerals" uncertain in all cases. And title disputes depreciate the value of both interests.

As the years have passed and the number of cases raising the issue of what substances are "minerals" has multiplied, a trend has developed toward developing a definition of "minerals" as a rule of law. Texas has been the leader in this attempt. Its experience is instructive.

2.   THE TEXAS EXPERIENCE

Until 1971, the Texas courts took the traditional approach to determining what substances are minerals, looking for the specific intent of the parties by objective tests. "Other minerals" was given its "ordinary and natural meaning," unless the intent of the parties to the contrary was clear. Where they found construction aids necessary, Texas courts rejected the *ejusdem generis* rule, as well as a scientific and technical definition of the substance. Texas used the exceptional-characteristics test, which classifies as minerals those substances that possess exceptional or peculiar characteristics that give them special value. In addition, whether the recovery of a substance would destroy the surface was considered as a "factor which is used with others."

a. The Surface Destruction Test

In 1971, in *Acker v. Guinn,* 464 S.W.2d 348 (Tex.1971), the Texas Supreme Court abandoned the attempt to ascertain the specific intent of the parties, commenting that "[v]arious approaches and rules of construction have been used to determine this intention, and the holdings are not uniform." In holding that the iron ore at issue belonged to the surface owner *as a matter of law,* the court reasoned that:

> "It is not ordinarily contemplated [by the parties to a deed] ... that the utility of the surface for agricultural or grazing purposes will be destroyed or substantially impaired. Unless the contrary intention is affirmatively and fairly expressed, therefore, a grant or reservation of 'minerals' or 'mineral rights' should not be construed to include a substance that must be removed by methods that will, in effect, consume or deplete the surface estate."

This test came to be called the *surface-destruction test.* It transformed what had been a discretionary rule of construction into a rule of law for determining ownership.

Between 1971 and 1983, the Texas courts struggled to make the surface-destruction test workable as a rule of law, but there was substantial confusion about how the test was to be applied. Some questions were answered by two opinions in *Reed v. Wylie*, 554 S.W.2d 169 (Tex.1977) and 597 S.W.2d 743 (Tex.1980), which evolved the surface destruction test to the following:

> "A substance is not a "mineral" within the meaning of a grant or reservation of "minerals," if substantial quantities of that substance lie at or near the surface in the reasonably immediate vicinity so that one of the reasonable methods of its removal at or after the conveyance would be by strip or open pit mining. If a substance is not a "mineral," the surface owner retains ownership of it at whatever depth below the surface it may be found."

The Texas courts never answered all the legal questions, however; for example, how near is "near the surface," and how close is the "reasonably immediate vicinity"? Furthermore, ownership depended upon facts about deposits of the substances at issue that had to be determined on a case-by-case basis. Ownership of a substance could not be determined by a review of the title records, which led to a surge of litigation.

b. The Ordinary and Natural Meaning Test

In *Moser v. United States Steel Corp.*, 676 S.W.2d 99 (Tex.1984), the Texas Supreme Court gave up trying to make the surface-destruction test work and adopted another rule designed to promote title certainty. Conceding the shortcomings of the surface-destruction test, the court held that uranium was a mineral as a matter of law, reasoning that "a severance of minerals ... includes all substances within the ordinary and natural meaning of that word, whether [or not] their presence or value is known...." The court held that a mineral owner has the right to take minerals even if removal causes destruction of the surface. It required compensation from the mineral owner to the surface owner for surface destruction, however, unless the substance was specifically defined as a mineral in the grant or reservation.

The court stated two exceptions to the new rule to protect those who had relied upon the surface destruction test. First, substances that the Texas courts had previously held to be non-minerals as a matter of law would continue to belong to surface owners. The court specifically identified building stone and limestone, caliche and surface shale, water, sand and gravel, near-surface lignite and coal, and near-surface iron ore. Second, the court announced that it would apply the new rule prospectively only, to deeds executed after June 8, 1983.

The "ordinary and natural meaning" test of *Moser* is not likely to achieve the laudable goal of title certainty. First, the test is uncertain. *Moser* is silent as to how and when the courts will determine what is the ordinary and natural meaning of "minerals." It appears that the ordinary and natural meaning test is nothing but a variation of the "community knowledge" rule of construction discussed above. Second, *Moser*'s scope is not clear. The Texas Supreme Court specifically limited the ordinary-and-natural-meaning test to those substances it had not previously held to belong to the surface as a matter of law, but it did not provide an exhaustive list of the surface-owned substances. In addition, the opinion is unclear as to whether it applies to leases as well as to deeds and to royalty interests as well as mineral interests. Third, the *Moser* case did not require the Texas Supreme Court to determine precisely when compensation is due to the surface owner or how it is to be calculated. Finally, the surface-destruction test remains the law for the interpretation of the hundreds of thousands, perhaps millions, of mineral grants and reservations prior to June 8, 1983.

3. A PROPOSED SOLUTION

The Texas cases illustrate the difficulty of trying to formulate a rule of law that allocates ownership of substances between the surface owner and the mineral owner. Elevating one or another of the rules of construction to a rule of law opens the proverbial can of worms because rules of construction are inherently imprecise, and elevating their status does not make them any more certain.

A better approach would be to separate the issues of ownership and enjoyment by a broad general definition of "minerals." Professor Eugene Kuntz said it best:

"[T]he courts are seeking to give effect to an *intention* to include or exclude a *specific substance*, when, as a matter of fact, the parties had nothing specific in mind on the matter at all. . . . The intention sought should be the *general intent* rather than any supposed but unexpressed specific intent, and, further, that general intent should be arrived at, not by defining and redefining the terms used, but by considering the *purposes* of the grant or reservation in terms of the manner of enjoyment intended in the ensuing interests.

When a general grant or reservation is made of all minerals without qualifying language, it should be reasonably assumed that the parties intended to sever the entire mineral estate from the surface estate, leaving the owner of each with definite incidents of ownership enjoyable in distinctly different manners. The manner of enjoyment of the mineral estate is through extraction of valuable substances, and the enjoyment of the surface is through retention of such substances as are necessary for the use of the surface. . . .

Applying this intention, the severance should be construed to sever from the surface *all substances presently valuable in themselves, apart from the soil, whether their presence is known or not, and all substances which become valuable* through development of the arts and sciences." Kuntz, The Law Relating to Oil and Gas in Wyoming, 3 *Wyo.L.Rev.* 107, 112–13 (1947), reprinted 34 *Okla.L.Rev.* 28, 33–34 (1981) (Emphasis in original).

Professor Kuntz' analysis has been termed the "manner-of-enjoyment" theory. It has been cited favorably by various courts, including the Texas Supreme Court in *Acker v. Guinn,* the *Reed v. Wylie* cases, and *Moser,* but never applied in pure form to solve the interpretive problem of a general grant or reservation of "minerals."

Probably the major reason that the manner-of-enjoyment theory has not been embraced by the courts is the assumption that its adoption would give the mineral owner the right to destroy the surface (albeit with compensation) if that were necessary to get the minerals. That result is not logical-

ly required. The mineral owner's ownership of all
substances that have or may acquire value apart
from the soil can be recognized while the mineral
owner's right to use of the surface is limited to
techniques that are not surface destructive. That
was done by an Arizona appellate court in *Spurlock
v. Santa Fe Pacific Railroad Co.*, 694 P.2d 299
(Ariz.App.1984), in which the court held that all
commercially-valuable substances belonged to the
severed mineral owner, but that the mineral owner
had an obligation not to destroy the surface owner's
potential use when the mineral owner took substances that were not known to be commercially
valuable at the time of the deed. Under such an
approach, the mineral owner would be forced to
negotiate an accommodation with the surface owner
or to await (or develop) methods of extraction that
would not destroy the surface.

Any approach to defining "minerals" that would
shift the focus from the illusory specific intention of
the parties to the reasonableness of operations on
the surface would be a substantial step forward
from where we are now.

C. THE MINERAL/ROYALTY DISTINCTION

1. THE SIGNIFICANCE OF THE DISTINCTION

Whether an interest is a mineral interest or a
royalty interest is an important distinction, as
Chapter 3 discusses. A mineral interest possesses

the right to develop or to lease, and to keep the proceeds of leasing. A royalty interest lacks those rights, but has a right to a share of production or production revenues or value free of the costs of production. Which is preferable depends upon the circumstances, as the Montana Supreme Court pointed out in *McSweyn v. Musselshell County, Montana*, 632 P.2d 1095 (Mont.1981). Even if there is never production from the land, the mineral interest may have substantial value because its owner has the right to lease and to receive bonus and delay rentals. On the other hand, if there is production, a royalty interest is usually preferable to an equally-sized mineral interest because it is cost free.

2. COMMON INTERPRETIVE PROBLEMS

Disputes over whether an interest is a mineral interest or a royalty may arise either from the language of the conveyance or from the general situation. To illustrate both, suppose that at a time when O owned the fee simple absolute and there were no oil and gas leases outstanding, the record showed a conveyance from O to A of "1/2 of the royalty in the oil, gas, or other minerals in and under the said above-described lands." Must an oil and gas lease be granted by A in order for a lessee to acquire full lease rights?

There is no clear-cut answer. At first glance, the language in the example may appear to create a royalty interest, because it refers specifically to "royalty." On the other hand, the remainder of the description "in the oil, gas or other minerals in and under," is more consistent with an attempt to describe minerals in place than an interest in production if and when it occurs. Furthermore, a 50% royalty interest, one that would give its holder the right to 50% of all production cost free, is an unusually-high burden. An inference may arise from the size of the fraction that the parties intended to give a mineral interest. Another possibility is that the reference to 50% of the royalty is to 50% of any royalty that may be provided for in a future oil and gas lease. There was no lease on the property when the conveyance was made, however, and the language does not refer to future leases.

The major reason that the mineral/royalty distinction is so hard to deal with is that the courts turn themselves inside out trying to ascertain the intent of the parties. The result, as with the problem of what is a "mineral," is incomprehensibility and inconsistency in the decisions.

French v. Chevron USA, Inc., 896 S.W.2d 795 (Tex.1995), is a good example. There the Texas Supreme Court construed a conveyance entitled "Mineral Deed" that stated that it granted a 1/656.17 "interest in and to all of the oil, gas and other minerals, in, under and that may be produced," but which also provided that "it is understood and agreed that this conveyance is a royalty interest only" and that the grantee obtained from the conveyance no interest in delay or other rentals, revenues from leasing, or the right to control leasing or development of the lands; those interests were reserved in the grantor. After reciting the attributes of a mineral interest and noting that those attributes could be severed from the mineral estate but are impliedly transferred with the mineral estate unless specifically reserved, the court *harmonized* the terms of the instrument by concluding that the conveyance transferred a mineral interest, but reserved all rights other than the right to receive a share of lease royalty in the grantor. "The meaning of this grant is to convey an interest in the nature of a royalty—a mineral interest stripped of appurtenant rights other than the right to receive royalties." Thus, the effect of the deed was to convey the royalty that would accrue to a 1/656.17 percent mineral interest.

a. Guidelines to Interpretation

Because the precedents from state to state, and even within certain states, are so diverse, it is difficult to generalize about what language will create a mineral interest or a royalty interest.

No one factor in an instrument is determinative to establish the intention of the parties to create a particular interest, but a specific statement of intention in the granting clause or in a clause immediately following the granting clause will probably be given more weight than any other factor, including the words of grant. *Atlantic Refining v. Beach*, 436 P.2d 107 (N.M.1968), is a good illustration. There, a document headed "Mineral Deed" mixed mineral interest and royalty references. In the

granting clause, the instrument conveyed an undivided 1/16 mineral interest, but a clause following
stated an intention to retain all rights to delay
rentals and to convey "one half of the royalty." The
Supreme Court of New Mexico affirmed the trial
court and held that the deed reserved a royalty
interest of 1/2 of the usual 1/8 royalty, giving effect
to the intention language of the deed rather than to
the literal terms of the granting clause. The court
considered the title of the instrument, the language
of the grant, and the reference to easements of
access and egress for development, as well as the
statement of intention. No one factor was determinative, but the intention statement was of prime
importance.

Courts are likely to hold that use of terms such
as "minerals," "mineral interest," or "oil and gas
rights" create mineral interests, unless other provisions of the instrument conflict with that conclusion. Likewise, use of the term "royalty" is generally considered to indicate an intent to create a
royalty interest. In the vernacular, "royalty" is
often used synonymously with "mineral interest,"
however. In Oklahoma, when there is no lease in
existence at the time of the conveyance and the
royalty is not stated as a specific percentage of
production (e.g., "1/2 of 1/8 royalty"), cases hold
that a reference to royalty denotes a mineral interest. Reference to royalty also created a mineral
interest in *Corlett v. Cox*, 333 P.2d 619 (Colo.1958),
which has since been legislatively overturned. The
Colorado Supreme Court relied on a now-defunct

common law rule that a grant of the rents or profits of land is a grant of the land itself. It held that a reservation of "6¼% of all gas, oil and minerals that may be produced on any or all of the above mentioned land, or in other words ... 1/2 of the usual 1/8 royalty" created a mineral interest.

Many drafters attempt to define the incidents of the interest rather than to give it the title of "mineral interest" or "royalty interest." This is usually an effective method of description, unless they mix conflicting descriptions. Deed references describing oil and gas in the ground (e.g., "1/32 of the oil and gas in and under" or "in and under and that may be produced from") are likely to be interpreted as mineral interests, even in states that follow the non-ownership theory where they cannot be given literal effect. Deed references that seem to convey an interest in oil and gas after they are produced are likely to be treated as creating royalty interests. Thus, in *Barker v. Levy*, 507 S.W.2d 613 (Tex.Civ. App.1974), a Texas appellate court held that a reservation of 1/160 of the "minerals that may be produced and saved" created a royalty interest. In several states, however, "produced and saved" language creates a royalty only if the language also indicates that the right to production is cost free. At least one prominent commentator, Professor Richard Maxwell, suggests that the real distinction between a mineral interest and a royalty is that a royalty is free of costs of production while a mineral interest is subject to expenses. A reference to sharing the costs indicates a mineral interest. A statement that the interest is cost free suggests a royalty.

In summary, a deed grant or reservation is likely to be considered a mineral interest if it has the following incidents:

   i.   the deed calls it a mineral interest;

   ii. the grant or reservation is of oil and gas "in and under and that may be produced from" or "in and under said land" or other language that describes oil and gas in place;

   iii. the interest is cost bearing and profit sharing;

   iv. the interest has the right to lease and share in lease benefits; i.e., bonus, royalties, delay rentals, and shut-in royalties.

On the other hand, a grant or reservation is likely to be construed as a royalty interest if:

   i.   the deed or reservation calls it a royalty;

   ii. the grant or reservation is of oil and gas "produced and saved" or "produced, saved, and marketed," or other language that describes oil and gas after it has been produced;

   iii. the interest is not cost bearing and profit sharing, but a percentage of gross production;

   iv. the interest has no right to lease or share in lease benefits.

When only some of the distinguishing incidents are present, or when the incidents of mineral interests and royalty interests are mixed, the mineral/royalty problem arises.

b. Avoiding Ambiguity

One cannot avoid the problem of the mineral/royalty distinction by using commercially-printed form deeds. Often, royalty deed forms (but not the one included in the Appendix) contain language granting easements for "the right of ingress and egress at all times *for the purpose of mining, drilling and exploring* said lands for oil and gas and other minerals and removing the same." Many title attorneys believe that such language is more appropriate for a mineral deed (because a royalty interest has no right to operate) and declare such a royalty deed form ambiguous.

The best way to avoid ambiguity is to draft by reference to the incidents of the interest created, rather than by using "magic" language. "Mineral interest" and "royalty interest" are shorthand terms devised by the courts to describe the most common bundles of rights that parties to a severance wish to create. Other groupings are possible. By referring specifically to the individual rights that make up the interest, the drafter can make clear whether there is intended a mineral interest, a royalty interest, or some hybrid of the two. The royalty deed form in the Appendix is a good attempt at drafting by reference to characteristics. The summaries at the end of subsection *a*, above, may be used as rudimentary checklists.

D. FRACTIONAL INTEREST PROBLEMS

Oil and gas interests are more frequently divided into fractional parts than any other kind of real property. As a result, lawyers and landmen, many of whom went to law school or into land management to avoid the mathematics required for the sciences, find themselves working with fractional interests that typically extend to seven decimal places. Often they do not handle the creation of fractional interests well. Disputes about how much is conveyed are common. In this section we will review common problems that arise in conveying fractional interests.

1. DOUBLE FRACTIONS

When one who owns less than all of the mineral interest or royalty interest conveys or reserves a fraction, there may be ambiguity whether the grant or reservation is intended to be a fraction of the whole or a part of the fraction owned by the grantor. This is called the *double-fraction* problem.

Suppose, for example, that

Alexandra owns the surface and an undivided ½ mineral interest in Blackacre, which is subject to an oil and gas lease; and

Alexandra conveys to Ellie without warranty "Blackacre, reserving an undivided ¼ of any lease royalty on the minerals in, under and that may be produced from the above-described land";

What royalty fraction does Alexandra retain?

It is unclear from this language whether Alexandra retains 1/4 of the whole lease royalty or 1/4 of the royalty to which Ellie will be entitled by virtue of her ownership of 1/2 the minerals. Alexandra cannot reserve more than she had to give Ellie, which suggests that she intended to reserve 1/4 of the royalty paid on the 1/2 of the minerals she conveyed to Ellie. It is possible, however, that Alexandra intended to reserve a royalty from the half interest that she conveyed which would be measured by the full lease royalty. There is a *double-fraction problem*.

Courts seek to solve the double-fraction problem by the steps of judicial interpretation considered in part A of this chapter. They interpret the language of deed grants or reservations strictly, applying two rules of construction that are particularly important.

a. The In–Sequence Rule

The interests created by an oil and gas conveyance are interpreted in sequence; a court will usually interpret the language describing what Ellie is granted before it examines the language of Alexandra's reservation. The *in-sequence* rule is a rule of construction for property law generally.

A special application of the in-sequence rule is what is called the *100% rule*. The 100% rule may be stated as follows:

> A deed that does not specifically limit the quantity conveyed, will be interpreted to describe 100% of the property described, both surface and minerals.

The 100% rule also applies to real property conveyances generally.

Both rules are important tools of the courts in achieving unity of titles. They may result in a

narrow construction of deeds that seems neither
certain nor fair, however. For example, in *Spell v.
Hanes*, 139 S.W.2d 229 (Tex.Civ.App.1940), the
grantors, who owned an undivided 5/8 interest in
the minerals, conveyed "an undivided 1/4 interest
in and to all of the . . . minerals," and described the
land. Following the grant, the phrase was added
"Above grant is to apply to our undivided interest
in and to the above described lands." That language
suggests to this writer an intention to grant 1/4 of
the grantors' 5/8 interest. Despite the intention
language, the Texas appellate court held that the
deed conveyed 1/4 of all the minerals. The court
gave effect to the granting clause, saying that the
intention language merely indicated what interest
the grant should be charged against.

b. The Literal–Interpretation Rule

The second rule of construction applied to the
double-fraction problem, as well as to other deed
ambiguities, is the *literal-interpretation rule*. Words
of conveyances are given their literal meaning; the
drafter of a formal instrument of conveyance is
deemed to mean exactly what he or she says. The
rule is simple to state, but difficult to apply, at least
if one clouds one's mind with thoughts of what the
parties probably intended. *Black v. Shell Oil Co.*,
397 S.W.2d 877 (Tex.Civ.App.1965), is an example.
The grantors, who owned an undivided 1/2 mineral
interest, conveyed "an undivided one-half (1/2) interest" in minerals, "It being the intention of
grantors herein to convey one half of the minerals

out of the interest owned by them." (Emphasis added). The grantor's successors contended that the deed conveyed 1/2 of the 1/2 the grantors had. The court held that the deed was not ambiguous, that "out of" designated the interest from which the 1/2 mineral interest was to be taken; "out of" means "from." The court noted that reference to "of" instead of "out of" would have achieved the result urged by the grantors' successors.

Averyt v. Grande, Inc., 717 S.W.2d 891 (Tex. 1986), the case upon which the facts of the double-fraction problem example above are based, is another application of the literal interpretation rule. There the Texas Supreme Court made a distinction between a deed reference to *land described* and a deed reference to *land conveyed.* The court reasoned that if a deed reserves a fraction of the minerals under the land *conveyed,* it reserves a fraction of the mineral interest owned by the grantor at the time of the conveyance. Where a deed reserves a fraction of the minerals under the land *described,* however, it reserves a fraction of the minerals under the entire tract, regardless of the size of the interest actually conveyed. Applying that reasoning to facts similar to the example, the court concluded that Alexandra reserved 1/4 of the entire lease royalty because the royalty reservation referred to the "above-described land"—all of Blackacre rather than just the interest Alexandra owned when she conveyed to Ellie.

Results like those in *Black v. Shell Oil Co.* and *Averyt v. Grande* are literally correct, but they may leave you with an uncomfortable feeling that the intention of the grantor was not achieved. As Professor Patrick Martin has noted, however, the courts are trying to give effect to the intention that the deed expresses rather than to whatever subjective intention the parties may have had. Unfair though the approach may appear, in the long run the literal-interpretation rule lessens uncertainty and litigation by encouraging careful drafting.

c. Avoiding Ambiguity

Good drafting will avoid the double-fraction problem. Whenever one who owns a fraction conveys or reserves a fraction, the grant or reservation should specify how it is to be measured. In our example, there would have been no ambiguity had Alexandra reserved "1/4 of 100% of any lease royalty." Likewise, there would have been no ambiguity if Alexandra had reserved "1/4 of any lease royalty payable to the fraction of the mineral interest that I hereby convey."

2. OVERCONVEYANCE

A second frequently-encountered problem in conveyances of fractional oil and gas interests is overconveyance; transactions in which the total of the fractions reserved and conveyed is greater than 100%. It may be helpful to think of this ambiguity as *the sum of the parts is greater than the whole* problem, although it is usually referred to as the *Duhig problem*.

An illustration may help. Suppose that

Daniel conveys "Blackacre" to Alexandra, reserving an undivided ¼ mineral interest; and

Alexandra conveys "Blackacre" to Ellie by warranty deed, "reserving to Alexandra an undivided ¼ of the mineral interest."

What does Alexandra retain?

The issue is whether Ellie takes the surface and 1/2 of the mineral interest, or the surface and 3/4 of the mineral interest, or (perhaps) the surface and 9/16 of the mineral interest. Clearly Alexandra takes subject to Daniel's retained 1/4 mineral interest if Daniel's deed to Alexandra was recorded. Clearly, as well, Alexandra's *intent* was to retain 1/4 mineral interest for herself; Alexandra's reservation says so. The literal result of the grant of "Blackacre" by warranty deed when the 100% rule is applied, however, is to *guarantee* that 100% of Blackacre is transferred, except for any interest specifically reserved. If that reasoning is applied here and effect given to Alexandra's intent as well, there will be an overconveyance (Ellie's 3/4 + Daniel's 1/4 + Alexandra's 1/4 = 125%); the sum of the parts will be greater than the whole.

a. The *Duhig* Rule

Courts generally deal with the problem of overconveyance by warranty deed by deducting the overconveyance from the grantor's interest, to the extent that is possible, by application of what is called the *Duhig* rule, after the Texas case of *Duhig v. Peavy–Moore Lumber Co., Inc.*, 144 S.W.2d 878

(Tex.1940). The *Duhig* rule may be summarized as follows:

> Where a grantor does not own enough interest to give full effect both to the granted interest and to a reserved interest, courts will give priority to the granted interest (rather than to the reserved interest) until the granted interest is fully satisfied.

Thus, in our illustration (based on a Wyoming case, *Body v. McDonald*, 334 P.2d 513 (Wyo.1959)), Alexandra retains nothing despite her clear intent. The *Duhig* rule has been adopted specifically or in effect in Texas, Colorado, Oklahoma, New Mexico, Wyoming, Louisiana, Mississippi, Alabama and Arkansas.

As adopted by the Texas Supreme Court, the *Duhig* rule is an analogy to estoppel by deed, the doctrine that one who grants a warranty deed and does not have title at the time of the warranty but later acquires it, passes the title through without further action. Alexandra's conveyance to Ellie is held to be conveyance of the whole by ordinary conveyancing principles. Alexandra's reservation of 1/4 is deemed to be 1/4 of the whole by those same principles. Since giving effect to Alexandra's reservation breaches Alexandra's warranty to Ellie, Alexandra is held estopped to assert the reservation to the extent of the overconveyance. Another view of the principle is that the conveyance with covenants of warranty to Ellie shows Alexandra's intent to convey the surface and 3/4 of the mineral interest, since that is what it literally says. Therefore, Alexandra's reservation of 1/4 refers to the prior outstanding interest. By either view, the overconveyance is charged against Alexandra.

The *Duhig* rule is significant in oil and gas conveyancing because of the element of certainty that it brings to titles. Without such a rule, the ambiguity inherent in our illustration could be solved only by litigation. Where the rule is applied, a title searcher can rely upon the record state of title.

b. Departures From the Rule

How rigidly the *Duhig* rule should be applied is an unresolved issue. What if the grantee has actual or constructive notice of the unmentioned outstanding interest, for example? Should fairness bar application of the rule? Generally, the rule has been applied as a matter of law. *Gilbertson v. Charlson*, 301 N.W.2d 144 (N.D.1981), rejected the *Duhig* rule where the grantee had actual notice of one outstanding interest and constructive notice of another. The North Dakota Supreme Court decided the case on ordinary principles of equitable estoppel, which is based on the actions or statements of the parties rather than the formal representations of the deed. Since the grantee knew or ought to have known of the outstanding interests, she was not misled by the improper warranty. Were similar reasoning applied in our illustration, Ellie would take 1/2 mineral interest and Alexandra's reservation of 1/4 mineral interest would be given full effect if Ellie knew of Daniel's outstanding interest when the conveyance was made. Subsequently, however, in *Sibert v. Kubas*, 357 N.W.2d 495 (N.D.1984), the

North Dakota Supreme Court limited *Gilbertson v. Charlson* to its facts. And in *Acoma Oil Corp. v. Wilson*, 471 N.W.2d 476 (N.D.1991), the court applied the rule to an over-conveyance caused by an outstanding royalty interest despite the fact that the grantee had knowledge of the existence of the outstanding interest.

In another case, *Hartman v. Potter*, 596 P.2d 653 (Utah 1979), the court simply ignored the *Duhig* rule. There the grantor owned 3/4 mineral interest, conveyed by warranty deed and reserved 1/2 mineral interest. The Utah Supreme Court found that, since the grantee knew of the previously outstanding interest and since the grantor could not grant what the grantor did not own, the grantor reserved 1/2 of the 3/4, or 3/8 mineral interest. Similar reasoning applied to our example would result in awarding Ellie 9/16 mineral interest and Alexandra 3/16 mineral interest.

Professor Willis Ellis criticized decisions that fail to apply the *Duhig* rule as abandoning objective interpretation standards for the dubious equity that consideration of subjective factors may bring. Fair though decisions like *Gilbertson v. Charlson* and *Hartman v. Potter* may be if the grantor has actual knowledge of the previously reserved interest, they undercut the function of warranty deeds in the record title system. The ability of title searchers to rely on the record is key to the operation of the land title system. If title searchers must investigate the knowledge of the grantee, title searches become slower, more expensive, and less certain. In addition, the *Gilbertson v. Charlson* and *Hartman v. Potter* decisions are inconsistent with the presence of warranties in the deeds. A covenant of title is essentially meaningless if it guarantees only the interest the grantor actually owns.

In states that have recognized the *Duhig* rule, the equitable remedy of deed reformation is available to correct unfairness that results when the rule prevents the intention of the grantor and grantee from being given effect. Even recognizing that reformation will not bring equity in every case (because, for example, it may not be available where the grantee has conveyed to a third party), application of the *Duhig* rule seems preferable to the alternative.

c. Application to Leases as Well as Deeds

An unresolved issue in many states is whether the *Duhig* rule applies to leases as well as deeds. In *McMahon v. Christmann*, 303 S.W.2d 341 (Tex. 1957), the court refused to do so. In a typical leasing transaction, a lessor who owned a 1/6 mineral interest granted a lease that contained a warranty not limited to the lessor's fractional interest and a lesser interest clause that permitted the lessee to reduce lease payments proportionately if the lessor owned less than 100% of the mineral interest. The lease provided for a 1/8 landowners' royalty and an overriding royalty of 1/32 of oil and gas produced "without reduction." The lessee contended that the lessor was barred by the *Duhig* rule from enforcing the overriding royalty "without reduction," since the lessor had warranted full title but had possessed only 1/6.

With reasoning that other courts probably will find compelling, the Texas Supreme Court refused to extend the *Duhig* rule to oil and gas leases. The court said that oil and gas leases are a special conveyance. A lessor customarily grants a lease of the whole mineral interest although the lessor owns only a fraction, leaving the lessee to reduce payments proportionately by application of the lesser-interest clause; i.e., the parties to such transactions do not intend that estoppel apply. Furthermore, the court noted, oil and gas leases are commonly prepared by lessees, not by lessors, so there is no reason to interpret an ambiguity against the lessor.

d.   Limitation to Warranty Deeds

It is unclear whether the *Duhig* rule will be limited to conveyances by general warranty deeds. It is generally accepted that quitclaim deeds are not subject to the rule. In *Opaline King Hill v. Gilliam*, 682 S.W.2d 737 (Ark.1985), the Arkansas Supreme Court reasoned that it would be illogical to find an overconveyance where a grantor had not claimed that the grantor owned anything. *Miller v. Kloeckner*, 600 N.W.2d 881 (N.D.1999) applied the doctrine to a special warranty deed. A harder question is whether the *Duhig* rule should apply to deeds that are neither general nor special warranty deeds. As noted above, the *Duhig* rule is viewed either as an analogy to estoppel by deed or as a device to give effect to the grantor's stated intent. By either view, should the rule not then apply whenever a grantor says in a deed that the grantor owns property and that he or she conveys that property? Following such reasoning, a Texas court held in *Blanton v. Bruce*, 688 S.W.2d 908 (Tex.App.1985), that the *Duhig* rule applies whenever a deed purports to convey a definite interest in property.

e. Avoiding the Overconveyance Problem

Overconveyance (and the *Duhig* rule) can be avoided by careful drafting. At least three alternatives are available to the drafter:

(1) the reservation can specifically refer to all previously reserved or conveyed interests. For example, there would be no overconveyance in our illustration if the conveyance to Ellie provided that it reserved to Alexandra ¼ of the mineral interest "in addition to the ¼ mineral interest previously reserved to Daniel" or "excepting all previously reserved interests";

(2) the reservation may be coupled with an intention clause that makes clear what the interests of the parties are to be; e.g., "reserving to Alexandra an undivided ¼ mineral interest, it being the intention of the parties that Ellie shall have an undivided ½ mineral interest and that Alexandra shall retain an undivided ¼ mineral interest, in addition to the ¼ mineral interest previously reserved to Daniel";

(3) the grant can be worded to avoid ambiguity; e.g., "Alexandra grants Ellie all the surface rights and ½ of all the minerals in and under and that may be produced from" Blackacre. If the grant is properly worded, there is no need for language reserving an interest.

Of course, more than one of these alternatives may be used in combination.

3. MINERAL ACRES/ROYALTY ACRES

a. **Mineral Acres**

A *mineral acre* is the full mineral interest under one acre of land. Often grants or reservations are made in terms of mineral acres to avoid the double-fraction problem. Conveyancing in terms of mineral acres is a useful tool when the intention of the parties is to establish a minimum limitation on the grant or reservation; i.e., the grant of "an undivided 25 mineral acres in Blackacre" is definite and certain.

There are potential problems, however, in conveyancing by reference to "mineral acres." One is that a grant of mineral acres is not necessarily the equivalent of a fractional-interest conveyance. For example, if the parties think that Blackacre contains a total of 100 acres, the parties may intend that a grant of "25 mineral acres in and under Blackacre" be the equivalent of an undivided 1/4 mineral interest. If Blackacre is either more or less than 100 acres, however, 25 mineral acres will be, respectively, less or more than an undivided 1/4 mineral interest.

In addition, if one mixes references to mineral acres and undivided fractional interests in a grant or reservation of an interest in property that subsequently turns out to be either larger or smaller than the parties originally anticipated, the stage is set for litigation; e.g., suppose that Alexandra, who believes that Blackacre totals 100 acres, conveys "reserving 25 mineral acres, being an undivided 1/4 mineral interest" and a subsequent survey shows that there are 105 acres in Blackacre? Here reference to mineral acres is in conflict with the reference to the fractional mineral interests; 1/4 mineral interest in 105 acres is the equivalent of 26.25 mineral acres. There is an inherent ambiguity that must be resolved.

b. Royalty Acres

Occasionally, one sees references to "royalty acres." Professors Howard Williams and Charles Meyers defined "royalty acre" as the full lease royalty (whatever percentage may be specified in present or future leases) under one acre of land. In *Dudley v. Fridge*, 443 So.2d 1207 (Ala.1983), however, the Alabama Supreme Court held that a royalty acre was the full 1/8 royalty on an acre of land, which used to be the "standard" royalty percentage. A few cases define a royalty acre as the full production from one acre. Prudence suggests that one avoid the term, unless it is defined carefully.

E. CONVEYANCES OF LEASED PROPERTY

Conveyances of property subject to oil and gas leases have led to disputes. Three common problems are (1) the "subject to" problem; (2) apportionment of royalties; and (3) top leasing.

1. THE "SUBJECT–TO" PROBLEM

a. Purpose of the "Subject to" Clause

The "subject-to" clause in a mineral deed states that the deed is subject to existing oil and gas leases. It has two purposes. First, the subject-to clause protects the grantor against claims for breach of warranty because of an outstanding lease and avoids the *Duhig* problem discussed earlier in this chapter. Second, the clause is intended to make clear that the grantee is to receive an interest in unaccrued rentals and royalties under the lease.

The second goal probably need not be of concern today, for it is now clear that conveyance of land subject to a recorded oil and gas lease both binds the grantee to the terms of the lease and entitles the grantee to any unaccrued benefits. An early Texas case held that unaccrued lease benefits passed to the grantee only if there was a specific assignment, however. As a result, the subject-to clause was placed in mineral deed forms immediately following the granting clause, rather than as an exception to the warranty, to make clear the grantee's right to unaccrued benefits. The mineral deed in the Appendix contains a subject-to clause in the paragraph following the granting clause.

b. The Two–Grants Problem

The "subject-to" clause is a source of ambiguity when the interests referred to in the clause are inconsistent with those of the granting clause. When that occurs, an ambiguity arises whether the "subject-to" provision states an exception to the warranty or describes a second grant, in addition to the one described in the granting clause. A classic case in point is *Hoffman v. Magnolia Petroleum Co.*, 273 S.W. 828 (Tex.Com.App.1925), which applied what is called the *two grants* theory. There the lessors, who owned one half the mineral interest in 320 acres subject to an oil and gas lease, conveyed to the plaintiff their mineral interest in 90 of the 320 acres. The granting clause was followed by a subject-to clause that referred to the lease and provided specifically that "It is understood and agreed that this sale is subject to said lease, but covers and includes one-half of all the oil royalty and gas rental or royalty due to be paid *under the terms of said lease.*" (Emphasis added). The plaintiff successfully argued that his right to payments under the lease was not limited to those that accrued to the 90 acres; that the deed contained two grants, one of a reversionary right to the mineral interest in the 90 acres and another of one-half the benefits under the existing lease from the whole 320 acres.

In *Paddock v. Vasquez*, 265 P.2d 121 (Cal.App. 1953), a California appellate court applied the two-grants theory to inconsistent fractions to affect the size of the interest conveyed. A grant of a three percent mineral interest in property subject to an oil and gas lease providing for a 1/8 royalty was followed by a subject-to clause that stated that the grantee was to receive 6/25 of all payments that might accrue under existing or future leases.

Though the parties probably had erroneously completed the deed on the mistaken premise that the grantee should receive a share of the royalties under the existing lease equal to three percent of production without deduction for costs (6/25 × 1/8 = 3%), the court awarded the grantee 6/25 of the royalty under any future lease in addition to a three percent mineral interest. In the context of *Paddock v. Vasquez*, the two-grants doctrine is particularly appalling because the court's interpretation of the second grant substantially eclipses the grant of the mineral interest.

The courts do not consistently apply the two-grants theory; as Professor Ernest Smith has commented, there is no clear indication in many cases that the court is even aware of it. In *Heyen v. Hartnett*, 679 P.2d 1152 (Kan.1984), the Kansas Supreme Court ignored the two-grants rule. There a grantor had quitclaimed "an undivided 1/16 interest in and to all oil and gas and other minerals," but in the subject-to clause provided that if the land was covered by a valid lease, the grantee "shall have an undivided 1/2 interest in the Royalties, Rentals, and Proceeds therefrom." The court found that the deed was ambiguous and concluded that it was intended to convey an undivided 1/2 interest in the minerals, reasoning that the drafter had mistakenly assumed that a 1/2 interest in property subject to a lease that provided for a 1/8 royalty was 1/16 of the minerals.

Even in Texas, where the two-grants theory began, it has been unevenly applied. In *Alford v.*

Krum, 671 S.W.2d 870 (Tex.1984), the lease contained three relevant provisions. In the granting clause, Alford granted to Krum "one-half of the one-eighth interest" in minerals. The subject-to clause provided that the grant was subject to a lease, but covered and included 1/16 of the lease royalty payable. A provision followed that if the lease in effect should terminate, Alford and Krum would each own "a one-half interest in all oil, gas, and minerals in and upon said land together with a one-half interest in future rents." Without discussing the two-grants theory, the Texas Supreme Court held that the granting clause should control because it expressed the "controlling language" of the intent of the parties; the later provisions were "repugnant to the grant." More recently, however, in *Luckel v. White*, 819 S.W.2d 459 (Tex.1991), the Texas Supreme Court "harmonized" all of the deed clauses, implicitly recognizing the two-grants rule. *Luckel* seemed on all fours with *Alford*; a royalty deed covering property subject to a lease granted a 1/32 royalty interest and a "future lease" clause stated that the grantee would be entitled to 1/4 of any and all royalties reserved under future leases. The lower courts had applied *Alford*'s repugnant-to-the-grant rule to hold that the *Luckel* deed conveyed a fixed 1/32 royalty. The Texas Supreme Court held, however, that *Luckel*'s future lease clause was clear and unambiguous, the deed presently conveyed the possibility of reverter, and the grantee owned 1/4 of the royalty reserved in all future leases. The court overruled *Alford v. Krum*,

stating that the courts must "harmonize" all of a
deed's provisions. But in *Concord Oil Company v.
Pennzoil Exploration and Production Co.*, 966
S.W.2d 451 (Tex.1998), a mineral deed granted "an
undivided one-ninety sixth (1/96) interest in and to
all oil, gas and other minerals in and under, and
that may be produced from" property being conveyed. The deed also stated that "this conveyance is
made subject to the terms of any valid subsisting
oil, gas and /or mineral lease or mineral lease or
leases on above described land or any part thereof,
but covers and includes one-twelfth (1/12) of all
rentals and royalty of every kind and character that
may be payable...." By examining and "harmoniz-
ing" the entire deed to determine the intent of the
parties, five members of the court in two opinions
held that the deed in question represented a single
conveyance of a one-twelfth (1/12) mineral interest
instead of two separate grants, with the one-twelfth
grant being limited to the lease existing at the time
of the conveyance. The majority opinions relied
heavily on the premise that the deed language contemplated that only a single estate would be conveyed. Four dissenting members of the court "harmonized" the four corners of the deed to conclude
that the deed contained "two grants," one of a
mineral interest and another of rents and royalties.

c. Avoiding "Subject to" Ambiguities

The key to avoiding the two-grants problem and
other ambiguities of the subject-to clause is to recognize the limited purpose of the subject-to clause

in modern conveyancing. Historically, the clause was intended to except outstanding leases from the scope of the grantor's warranty and to make it clear that the grantee was to receive a share of lease benefits proportionate to the interest in minerals conveyed by the deed. Ambiguities arise when drafters make the mistake of using the subject-to clause to reserve an interest in the grantor, or when they become confused about the size of the fractional interests involved.

In time, the subject-to clause may wither away, to be replaced by a simple exception to the warranty. A separate assignment of lease benefits to the grantee should not be necessary. For now, the subject-to clause should *never* be used as a reservation. If the grantor wishes to reserve or convey an interest in an outstanding lease different from the mineral interest reserved or conveyed, that interest should be specifically and carefully drafted in a separate reservation clause.

Drafters can minimize confusion over the size of fractional interests by remembering that fractions referred to in the granting clause and the subject-to clause should be consistent. When the subject-to clause has blanks that must be completed by the grantor, as do many older mineral deed forms, the numbers inserted in the two clauses should be the same.

Many mineral deed forms, like the one in the Appendix, contain what has come to be called a "Hoffman clause":

"This sale is made subject to any rights now existing
under any valid and subsisting oil and gas lease of
record heretofore executed; it being understood and
agreed that said Grantee shall have, receive, and enjoy
the herein granted interest in and to all bonuses, rents,
royalties and other benefits which may accrue under
the terms of said lease *insofar as it covers the above
described land....*" (Emphasis added).

This language clearly avoids the two-grants problem
because it specifically states that the grantee will
receive lease benefits only "insofar as it covers the
above described land." The language also minimizes
the risk of confusion over fractions by eliminating
the need for the parties to complete blanks in the
subject-to clause.

2. APPORTIONMENT OF ROYALTIES

As has been discussed, a grantor who transfers
property subject to an existing oil and gas lease
generally transfers unaccrued lease payments. The
courts reach this result on the basis either that the
lease royalty is reserved from the lease and conveyed with the land, or that the lessee's promise to
pay is a covenant that runs with the land. But what
if the transfer is of a subdivided part of the leased
land? How should lease benefits be apportioned?
There is a split of authority as to apportionment of
royalties that creates another special problem of oil
and gas conveyancing.

An illustration may help. Suppose that O, the
owner of fee simple absolute in both the surface and
minerals of a 640 acre section leases the property to

A Company. O then sells the east 320 acres to X, subject to the oil and gas lease. If at the end of the first year A Company wishes to pay delay rentals, in what proportion should the payment be made to O and X? If A Company drills a well and obtains production, how should royalties be paid? The following diagram illustrates the problem:

LEASE

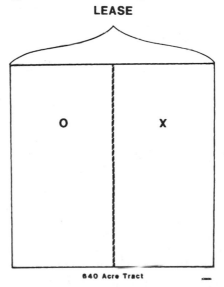

840 Acre Tract

There is no dispute over how payments of delay rentals should be made where there has been a subdivision of a leased property. Unless the grantor has retained the right to receive delay rentals explicitly (and assuming lease provisions requiring notice to the lessee of changes in ownership, such as those in paragraph 8 of the Texas lease in the Appendix have been met), payments of delay rentals must be apportioned between the owners of the land; i.e., O and X will each get half. This is an application of the usual rule that rents from real property are apportioned.

a. The Non–Apportionment Rule

A different rule is usually applied to royalties on oil and gas production. In most states, lease royalties are not apportioned among the owners of subdivided property. Instead, the owner of the tract where the well that produces the oil and gas is located is entitled to all royalties due under the lease.

The majority non-apportionment rule is an application of the rule of capture. The leading case is from Texas, *Japhet v. McRae*, 276 S.W. 669 (Tex. Com.App.1925). The reasoning of the courts is that royalties are different from rents. Royalties are not payments that issue equally from each and every part of the land. A royalty interest is a right to production if and when it occurs. The rule of capture dictates that production belongs to the owner of the subdivided part upon which the producing well is located. That the subdivided tracts are subject to a single oil and gas lease does not change the result because there is nothing in typical leases inconsistent with the rule of capture. The owners of the subdivided tracts are presumed to know of the rule of capture and to intend its application. The non-apportionment rule apparently is followed in Arkansas, Colorado, Illinois, Indiana, Kansas, Kentucky, Louisiana, Nebraska, New Mexico, Ohio, Oklahoma, Texas and West Virginia.

b. The Apportionment Rule

The minority view, the apportionment rule, treats royalties like rents. In *Wettengel v. Gormley*, 28 A. 934 (Pa.1894), the landmark case stating the apportionment rule, the Pennsylvania Supreme Court presumed that oil was producible equally from all parts of the subdivided land. It apportioned royalty like surface rents. The apportionment rule has been followed in Pennsylvania, California, and Mississippi, as well as in Ontario.

c. Understanding the Rules

Discussion of the apportionment and non-apportionment rules usually centers around which one is more "fair." In fact, either rule may be inequitable and onerous. Suppose that our example is set in an apportionment jurisdiction and the producing well is drilled on a 10 acre spacing unit in the northeast corner of the east 320 acres. An illustration follows:

LEASE

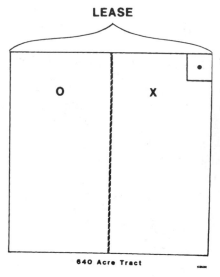

640 Acre Tract

Under such circumstances, it is highly unlikely that any of the oil or gas produced from the well comes from the west 320 acres. Apportionment is unfair. Non-apportionment seems right. If the 640 acre lease composes a single drilling unit with the well located approximately in the middle so that the owner of the 320 acre subdivision upon which the well is not located has no possibility of a well being located on his or her land and drainage is a virtual certainty, however, the apportionment rule seems fair.

The best way to understand the apportionment and non-apportionment rules is to see them as rules of property law developed to make the record-title system more certain. Whenever a property subject to an oil and gas lease is subdivided into separate tracts, an ambiguity arises as to whether or not the grantor and grantee intended that royalties be apportioned. Adopting either the apportionment rule (by analogy to rents) or the non-apportionment rule (by applying the rule of capture) avoids the ambiguity and promotes certainty of title. Because the problem arises every time land subject to a lease is subdivided, it is more important for the legal system that there be a clearly-defined rule than which rule is adopted.

d. Avoiding Conflict With the Rules

Either the apportionment or the non-apportionment rule can be a trap for the unwary or unknowledgeable. The key to avoiding problems is to be familiar with the position taken by your state and to advise clients of the potential for application of the rules.

(1) Modification by Agreement

When the grantor's and grantee's intention to change the applicable rule is clear, the courts will enforce their agreement. Thus, in our example, O and X might agree to apportion royalties by a special provision in the deed transferring title to the east half of the property or by a separate agreement. Such an agreement would be binding upon O and X, although A Company could not actually be required to apportion the royalty payments unless it agreed to modify its lease.

(2) Entirety Clauses

If the owner of property anticipates subsequent subdivision at the time of the grant of the lease, he or she may insert an *entirety clause* in the lease to provide for apportionment of royalties. A common formulation follows:

> "If the leased premises shall [now or] hereafter be owned severally or in separate tracts, the premises nevertheless shall be developed and operated as one lease and all royalties accruing hereunder shall be treated as an entirety and shall be divided among and paid to such separate owners in the proportion that the acreage owned by each such separate owner bears to the entire leased acreage."

Entirety clauses were originally inserted in oil and gas leases by lessees when few states had adopted either the apportionment or non-apportionment rule. They were intended to clarify how royalties were to be paid. In addition, entirety clauses avoided the argument that lessees were required to offset drainage from one subdivided tract to another or to install separate meters and storage facilities where wells were located on different subdivisions subject to the same lease.

Over the years, entirety clauses have fallen into disfavor. One problem has been that subdivision of the leased premises into many small tracts (e.g., as with a residential subdivision) can impose a crushing administrative burden on a lessee. Another has been that where there are several parties with various fractional interests in tracts and not all mineral interests are leased or not all leases include entirety clauses, lessees may be held liable to pay greater royalties than they had anticipated. For example, consider the following problem, based on the facts of a Texas case, *Thomas Gilcrease Foundation v. Stanolind Oil & Gas Co.*, 266 S.W.2d 850 (Tex.1954). Suppose that O, who owns 3/4 mineral interest in Blackacre and 1/4 mineral interest in Whiteacre leases to A Company for a 1/8 royalty with an entirety clause, while X, who owns 1/4 mineral interest in Blackacre and 3/4 mineral interest in Whiteacre, leases to A Company for 1/8 royalty without an entirety clause.

O - 3/4 X - 1/4	O - 1/4 X - 3/4
Blackacre	Whiteacre

If A Company drills a successful well on Whiteacre, O may be entitled to 1/2 of 1/8 royalty by virtue of the literal terms of the entirety clause, while X will be entitled to 3/4 of 1/8 royalty because his lease has no entirety clause.

As a result of problems like these, leases do not often contain entirety clauses. Many leases, however, contain a provision like the following, making clear the lessee's right to operate the lease as a single lease after subdivision but without providing for apportionment of royalties:

> "If the leased premises are now or shall hereafter be owned in severalty or in separate tracts, the premises shall nevertheless be developed and operated as one Lease and there shall be no obligation on the part of the Lessee to offset wells on separate tracts into which the land covered by this Lease may hereafter be divided by sale, devise, descent, or otherwise, or to furnish separate measuring or receiving tanks."

This provision may be mistaken for an entirety clause, but it does not specifically override the rule of capture by providing for apportionment of royalties.

(3) Legislative Provisions

Legislative provisions may also protect drafters from the trap of the non-apportionment rule. In Oklahoma, the oil and gas conservation law provides specifically that all owners of property included in a spacing unit will receive their royalty on all production. In Arkansas, a similar statute apparently requires apportionment of the first 1/8 royalty. It is unclear how royalty in excess of 1/8 is to be handled. In this writer's opinion, the non-apportionment rule probably would be applied. Thus, in our first example, if a 3/16 royalty were provided by the lease, O and X would share 1/8 royalty and X would take the remaining 1/16.

3. TOP LEASING

A *top lease* is an oil and gas lease covering property already subject to an oil and gas lease; a top lease sets on top of an existing lease. A top lease is a partial alienation of the possibility of reverter retained by the mineral interest owner under the original or "bottom" lease.

There are two kinds of top leases. Sometimes a lessee will top lease its own bottom lease to extend the duration of its rights to the property. Such a top lease is called a *two-party top lease*. When development takes place before the bottom lease expires, the parties may disagree about which lease controls. In Louisiana, several cases have applied a novation theory to hold that the top lease terms prevail over those of the bottom lease; as soon as the parties execute the top lease, the top lease replaces the bottom lease. Where a top lease is taken by a person other than the holder of the bottom lease, a *three-party top lease* is created. The top lessee speculates that the bottom lessee will let the bottom lease terminate so that the top lease will become possessory.

At one time, many in the oil industry regarded top leasing as immoral. Rising prices for oil and gas and increased competition for leases changed that perception. Most companies engaged in oil and gas development now take top leases, and so the pitfalls of top leasing are of concern.

a. Obstruction

One pitfall in preparing top leases is the equitable doctrine of obstruction. If a top lease does not refer to the existence of the prior existing lease, some cases have suggested that the title of the bottom lessee is clouded, whether or not the top lease is recorded. The obstruction doctrine suspends the running of time under the bottom lease for the duration of the obstruction or extends the primary term of the bottom lease for a reasonable period of time after removal of the obstruction.

Most top lease preparers attempt to avoid obstructing the bottom lease by providing specifically that the top lease is subordinate to the bottom lease and subject to all of its terms and conditions. In addition, though it should not be necessary, most drafters include a specific undertaking by the top lessor (who is also the lessor of the bottom lease) not to extend the bottom lease or to grant a new lease to the bottom lessee. These devices should be effective to avoid conflicts between the top lease and the bottom lease. There is little definitive precedent, however.

b. The Rule Against Perpetuities

A second top leasing problem is that a top lease may be voided by the rule against perpetuities, an ancient rule of property law that provides that a contingent future interest is void unless it must vest or be destroyed within 21 years of some life in being at its creation. If, to avoid obstruction and to give the lessee the full primary term bargained for, a top lessee modifies the habendum clause of an ordinary oil and gas lease form so that it reads "This lease shall be effective from and after the termination of [description of the bottom lease]," the top lease may be void, since the bottom lease may be extended by operations or production for more than the perpetuities period. The Texas Supreme Court followed similar reasoning in *Peveto v. Starkey*, 645 S.W.2d 770 (Tex.1982), to void a top deed of a nonparticipating royalty. If the interest conveyed in a top lease is considered a possibility of reverter, however, it should not be subject to the rule; the possibility of reverter is a vested interest. In *Hamman v. Bright & Company*, 924 S.W.2d 168 (Tex.App.1996), the court acknowledged that, though it held that a top lease for a primary term beginning "after and subsequent to the forfeiture, or to the expiration" of a bottom lease violated the rule against perpetuities. On the other hand, at common law a possibility of reverter was inalienable. Because of the chance of conflict with the rule against perpetuities, top leases prepared by modifying ordinary lease forms generally are prepared either to become effective immediately or at a specific date within the perpetuities period.

c. Internal Inconsistencies

Drafters frequently create a top lease by modifying a "regular" oil and gas lease form. When they do, there is a high risk that they will create internal inconsistencies. Possible problems include when delay rentals are due, what happens if the bottom lease ends before the end of its primary term, and the scope of the top lease warranty, if any. Such issues have been litigated with varying results. In *Siniard v. Davis*, 678 P.2d 1197 (Okl.App.1984), a lessor who executed a top lease that contained a covenant of general warranty was forced to return the bonus and prepaid delay rentals when the bottom lease was unexpectedly extended. The court refused to imply any modification of the warranty because of the plaintiffs' knowledge of the existing lease. It pointed out that the lessor could have protected herself by striking the warranty or inserting language making it subject to the prior lease. To avoid such issues, many lessees use forms drafted specially for top leasing.

PART III

OIL AND GAS LEASING

CHAPTER 8

ESSENTIAL CLAUSES OF MODERN OIL AND GAS LEASES

A. INTRODUCTORY CONCEPTS

The oil and gas lease is the core legal document of oil and gas development. An oil and gas lease is structured very differently from an ordinary real-property lease. The key to understanding the oil and gas lease is (1) to identify the fundamental goals that a lessee has in leasing, and (2) to bear in mind the nature of the transaction between the lessor and the lessee. The first is important to understanding why leases are structured as they are. Courts often refer to the second in resolving disputes.

First, consider the lessee's goals. There are two:

(a) the lessee seeks the *right* to develop the leased land for an agreed term *without any obligation* to develop;

(b) if production is obtained, the lessee wants the right to maintain the lease for as long as production is economically profitable.

Both goals arise from the economic realities of the petroleum business in the United States. A lessee seeks an option to develop for an agreed term because the lessee does not know when a lease is taken whether there is petroleum under the leased land. Application of modern geological and geophysical techniques increases the odds of finding oil and gas in commercially productive quantities, but there can be no certainty until a well is drilled. Whether it will make sense for the lessee to drill depends upon a variety of economic factors, including the supply and demand for oil and gas, tax structure and incentives, and applicable regulatory policies, which a lessee often cannot assess when it takes a lease. Therefore, a lessee's first goal is to obtain the right to operate without accepting any obligation to drill.

The second goal sought by lessees—the right to maintain a lease as long as it is profitable once production is obtained—is also motivated by economic realities. A lessee wants to maximize its profit from leases upon which it has successfully taken the drilling risk. The right to maintain the lease indefinitely is essential because one cannot predict how long a given well or lease will produce profitably. Profitability is a function not only of the amount of oil and gas in place but also of the porosity and permeability of the structures in which they are found, the technology available to extract hydrocarbons, the supply and demand for energy, and tax and regulatory policies. Therefore, modern oil and gas leases almost always extend for so long as there is "production in paying quantities," "capability of production in paying quantities," or "operations for oil and gas production." In addition, as Chapter 9 discusses, leases typically contain a wide variety of savings clauses.

The nature of the leasing transaction is important because the courts often look to the expectations of the parties in settling disputes over lease terms. Plainly and simply, leasing is a business transaction. Many mineral owners and oil companies speak of their role in maintaining energy security and a strong economy. But an oil and gas leasing transaction is at its heart a contract between a mineral owner, who usually lacks the capital and expertise to explore for and develop minerals, to an oil company, which impliedly or expressly represents that it has the money and talent to develop the leased property. Both the lessor and the lessee are motivated by an expectation of profit from the production that may be obtained from the leased land.

B. THE NATURE OF THE LEASE

A modern oil and gas lease is a unique instrument that fits uneasily into existing legal categories. An oil and gas lease is both a conveyance and a contract, more a deed than a lease, and creates rights that have proved hard to classify.

1. BOTH A CONVEYANCE
AND A CONTRACT

The courts in most states treat an oil and gas lease both as a conveyance of mineral rights from the *lessor* (the mineral owner) to the *lessee* (the oil company) and as a contract between the lessor and the lessee for the development of minerals. The lease is a conveyance because the mineral owner who grants a lease transfers his or her rights to the minerals. It is a contract because the oil company that receives the mineral-rights transfer accepts them with certain conditions and obligations attached.

Louisiana is an exception. Under Article 114 of the Louisiana Mineral Code, a mineral lease is solely a contract under which the lessee is granted the right to explore for and produce minerals. Mineral leases are not subject to prescription for nonuse. The Code provides, however, that a mineral lease may not be continued for more than ten years without drilling, mining operations or production.

2. MORE A DEED THAN A LEASE

As Chapter 5 discusses, oil and gas leases are different from ordinary real property leases in at least three respects: (1) the lessee has the right not only to use the land but to take substances of value from it; (2) the lessee's rights are not limited to a term of years; and (3) the lessee's rights to use the land are not exclusive but must be shared with the surface owner. Therefore, an oil and gas lease is more like a deed of an easement or a mineral deed than a lease of real property.

3. LEGAL CLASSIFICATION

Courts have classified the lessee's interest in an oil and gas lease in a variety of ways. Some states, including Texas, have described the leasehold interest as an *estate* in fee simple determinable in the oil and gas in place. Others, including Oklahoma, California, Montana and Wyoming, have classified the lessee's interest as a *profit a prendre*. Kansas generally treats leases as creating a *license*. Some Appalachian states have classified the lessee's interest under a lease as an inchoate right that becomes a vested tenancy only after production.

4. ESSENTIAL PROVISIONS

The essential provisions of an oil and gas lease are those necessary to make a valid transfer of rights and accomplish the lessee's fundamental goals. Generally, the essential provisions are found in just three clauses; the granting clause, the habendum clause, and the drilling-delay rental clause. We will consider those clauses and issues that frequently arise under them in this chapter.

C. GRANTING CLAUSE

The granting clause of an oil and gas lease spells out the rights that the mineral-interest owner grants to the lessee. The effect is to grant to the lessee the right to search for, develop, and produce oil and gas from the leased premises without imposing any obligation to do so. To be valid, the granting clause must identify the size of the interest granted, the substances covered by the lease, and the land covered by the lease. In addition, most lease granting clauses specifically indicate uses permitted.

1. SIZE OF THE INTEREST GRANTED

A peculiarity of oil and gas leases is that they are structured as if the lessor were leasing 100% of the mineral interest, even though the lessee may know that the lessor owns only a fractional interest. Thus, a lessor of a 1/16 interest in the minerals will be presented with an oil and gas lease completed as if the lessor owned 100% of the mineral rights. This practice grows from the fact that oil companies frequently acquire leases before doing a comprehensive title search. In addition, mineral rights are often split into tiny fractions, many of which become "lost" over the years. The probability is quite high that a lessee will discover after a lease is taken that the lessor had a different portion of the mineral interest than either party thought. As a result, lessees prefer to take leases from all mineral interest owners as if each mineral owner possessed 100% of the mineral interest. The risk to the lessor that this practice will breach the lease warranty clause is discussed below.

2. SUBSTANCES COVERED
BY THE GRANT

Oil and gas wells may produce valuable substances in addition to oil and gas. For example, helium, carbon dioxide, or sulphur may be produced with oil and gas. Lessees generally want the right to anything of value that is produced with oil and gas.

In addition, there has been confusion about the constituents of oil and gas. In the early part of the 20th century, courts in Oklahoma held that casinghead gas (gas produced with oil from oil wells) was neither oil nor gas. Therefore, a lease covering oil and gas only did not entitle the lessee to casinghead gas. More recently, a lessee successfully argued that helium is gas within the meaning of "oil and gas" as used in an oil and gas lease. See *Northern Natural Gas Co. v. Grounds*, 441 F.2d 704 (10th Cir.Kan. 1971).

To avoid disputes, most oil and gas leases cover more than just "oil and gas." For example, the granting clause (paragraph 1) of the Texas lease in the Appendix covers "oil and gas and all other hydrocarbons." The reference is intended to make clear that the lease applies to liquid and gaseous hydrocarbons even if they are not considered to be oil and gas. Other commonly used lease formulations define oil and gas as including "all hydrocarbons and other substances produced therewith" or "oil, gas and all other minerals." Because general references may be ambiguous, specificity is desirable.

3. LAND COVERED BY THE LEASE: THE MOTHER HUBBARD PROBLEM

The standard for sufficiency of the description in an oil and gas lease is the same as that for other conveyances; it must be possible to locate the land. Generally, oil and gas lease descriptions use either the metes and bounds system or the rectangular system discussed in Chapter 5.

In addition to a legal description of the property covered, many leases contain a more general description. Often they provide that the lease is intended to cover all the land owned by the lessor in the area. A common formulation is found in paragraph 1 of the Texas lease form in the Appendix:

"This Lease also covers and includes any and all lands owned or claimed by the Lessor adjacent or contiguous to the land described hereinabove, whether the same be in said survey or surveys or in adjacent surveys, although not included within the boundaries of the land described above."

This language is called a "Mother Hubbard" clause or a "cover-all" clause. It is intended to protect the lessee against inaccuracies in the legal description by covering all the land owned by the lessor even if some of the land is omitted from an erroneous legal description. Frequently, Mother Hubbard clauses will include language covering after-acquired interests in the described land as well.

Occasionally, a case raises the issue of the breadth of the Mother Hubbard clause. Suppose that O, the owner in fee simple absolute of Blackacre, a 640 acre section, grants a lease containing

Mother Hubbard language to A, describing specifically the east 320 acres of the section. An illustration follows:

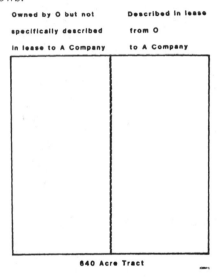

Owned by O but not specifically described in lease to A Company

Described in lease from O to A Company

640 Acre Tract

Suppose further, that A assigns the lease to B, who has no knowledge of the specific intent of O and A. Is B entitled to the 320 acres specifically described or to the whole 640 acres?

If given literal effect, the Mother Hubbard language quoted would subject the full 640 acres to the lease; the west half of the section is "adjacent or contiguous" to the east half. If the purpose of the language were taken into account, however, the lease would be limited to the 320 acres described plus any small tracts that are physically a part of that land but not specifically described in the legal description. On occasion, courts have taken a literal view of the terms of the Mother Hubbard clause. In *Holloway's Unknown Heirs v. Whatley*, 131 S.W.2d 89 (Tex.Com.App.1939), the court held that a Mother Hubbard clause in a deed providing that "if there is any other land owned by me in Liberty County, Texas ... it is hereby conveyed, the intention of this instrument being to convey all land owned by me in said County," conveyed a 1/2 interest in the minerals previously reserved by the grantor. In *Bergeron v. Amoco Prod. Co.*, 789 F.2d 344 (5th Cir.La.1986), a Mother Hubbard clause that was contained in each of three leases covering a total of 330 acres was held to bind the lessors' 2367/2880 interest in a contiguous 40–acre tract. *Smith v. Allison*, 301 S.W.2d 608 (Tex.1956), is probably more representative of the attitude of the courts toward such clauses. There the Texas Supreme Court refused to give literal effect to a Mother Hubbard clause in a deed in circumstances similar to those in the example, limiting application of the clause to small unleased tracts that exist without the knowledge of one or both of the parties. But the same court obscured the role of the Mother Hubbard clause in *J. Hiram Moore, Ltd. v. Greer*, 172 S.W.3d 609 (Tex. 2005). There, a deed described a specific tract, in which it turned out the grantor owned nothing, and then stated that it was the parties' intent to include "all of grantor's royalty and overriding royalty interest in all oil, gas and other minerals in the above named county or counties, whether actually or properly described herein or not." The court rejected the grantee's argument, based on *Holloway's Unknown Heirs v. Whatley*, that the deed unambiguously conveyed not only the specifically described interest but also an additional large royalty interest that the grantor owned in the county. The court said "The deed in effect states that Greer conveys nothing, and that she conveys everything. We cannot construe this deed as a matter of law," and remanded the case for a jury determination of the parties' intent. A well-written and analyzed dissent by Justice Owen [shortly afterward appointed to the Fifth Circuit], criticized the majority for failing to give effect to an unambiguous grant. Because of the likelihood of confusion over the scope of Mother Hubbard clauses, lessors' attorneys generally view them with disfavor, and oil company attorneys hope they will not have to rely on them.

4.   USES PERMITTED BY THE GRANT

a.   General Principle: Lessee's Right to Use Burdens the Surface Interest

An oil and gas lease gives a lessee an implied right to reasonable use of the land surface to locate, develop, and produce oil and gas from the land. The courts have reasoned that since the mineral-interest owner has the right to search for, develop, and produce oil and gas from the premises and since the purpose of the lease is to transfer that right to the lessee, the parties must have intended that the lessee acquire the right to use the surface of the land, even if that is not specifically stated. The commonly stated principle of law is that the lessee has an implied easement to use the surface of the land in such ways and at such locations as may be reasonably necessary to obtain the minerals, as the North Dakota Supreme Court held in *Hunt Oil Co. v. Kerbaugh*, 283 N.W.2d 131 (N.D.1979). The lessee's interest is the *dominant estate*. The surface of the land is *servient* to lessee's right of use.

Courts apply the general principle broadly, giving the lessee discretion both as to the *kinds* of uses and to the *location* of those uses. Specific applications have included the right to conduct seismographic tests, to build roads and construct drilling sites, to erect oil storage tanks and power stations to power pumping units, and to conduct water flood programs to maintain production, even though use of potable ground water was required.

b. Limiting Factors

A mineral lessee's right to use the surface is limited by at least five countervailing principles. The lessee's use must be (1) a reasonable use, (2) in accord with the accommodation doctrine, (3) for the benefit of the minerals under the land leased, (4) in accord with the terms of the lease, and (5) in accord with applicable statutes, ordinances, rules and regulations.

(1) Reasonable Use

All easements are limited to uses reasonably necessary to achieve the purpose of the easement. The purpose of the implied easement for surface use is to enable a mineral owner to develop the minerals. The implied right generally includes the right to conduct seismographic tests, to build well sites, storage tanks, and other structures on the leased land to produce, store, and take care of production, without the lessor's permission and without payment. An easement is *abused* if the use is not necessary or if it is unreasonable in view of the alternatives available. If a lessee uses leased land in a way that is unreasonable or unnecessary, the lessee's liability to the lessor is no different from what it would be under the same circumstances to an adjoining landowner. Thus, lessees have been held liable for damages for negligent pollution and for nuisance for failing to plug abandoned wells and remove equipment and cement foundations. When damages will not be an adequate remedy, a lessor may obtain an injunction to prohibit unreasonable use.

Reasonableness is an important limitation on the right of surface use. It is based upon the conventions and morals of contemporary society. Thus, uses that were considered reasonable in cases considered by the courts a generation ago may no longer be permitted. For example, a greater degree of surface damage was considered acceptable in the 1950s than is acceptable now, because society is more concerned with environmental quality than it was then. Determining what is reasonable depends upon all of the facts and circumstances. Since the facts and circumstances of each case are generally established by a jury, the judicial system quickly reflects changes in contemporary standards of reasonableness.

(2) The Accommodation Doctrine

A lessee's use of the land must also comply with the accommodation doctrine. The accommodation doctrine is a prime example of the responsiveness of the judicial system to changing standards of reasonableness. The accommodation doctrine was first stated as a separate principle from the reasonable use requirement by the Texas Supreme Court in *Getty Oil Co. v. Jones*, 470 S.W.2d 618 (Tex.1971). Jones, the owner of severed surface rights, sought damages from Getty for Getty's interference with his irrigation farming. Jones had drilled water wells and installed rolling irrigators that were elevated approximately 8 feet off the ground and pivoted in a circle. Subsequently, Getty drilled two wells on Jones' property under the authority of a lease from the severed mineral owners. Getty's wells required pumping units. The pumping units installed were substantially higher than the irrigators, so that the irrigators could not function. Jones contended that Getty's use was beyond the scope of its right because it effectively precluded him from farming the land. Getty countered that its pumping units were reasonably necessary to produce the oil.

The Texas Supreme Court held in favor of Jones, concluding that where a severed mineral interest owner or lessee asserts rights to use of the surface that will substantially impair existing surface uses, the mineral owner or lessee must accommodate the surface uses if he has reasonable alternatives available. The court found that Getty could have afforded to sink its pumping units below the surface of the ground to avoid interference with Jones' irrigators.

(a) Rationale of the Accommodation Doctrine

The rationale of the Texas Supreme Court was based upon Professor Eugene Kuntz's manner-of-enjoyment theory, which is discussed in Part B of Chapter 7 in conjunction with the meaning of "minerals." The court reasoned that the intent of the parties when there is a severance of mineral rights from surface rights (or a grant of a lease) is that both the mineral lessee and the surface owner should have valuable estates. Therefore, an oil and gas lessee should be required to accommodate uses of the surface whenever reasonable.

(b) Elements of the Accommodation Doctrine

As Texas Supreme Court articulated it in *Getty Oil Co. v. Jones,* the accommodation principle is limited by three requirements: (1) there must be an existing surface use; (2) the proposed use must substantially interfere with the existing surface use; and (3) the lessee must have reasonable alternatives available. In *Sun Oil v. Whitaker,* 483 S.W.2d 808 (Tex.1972), the court took an even more limited view. There, the court permitted a lessee to deplete a surface owner's ground-water reserves for a secondary-recovery water-flood project even though water could have been purchased at a modest cost from a nearby river. The court held that the reasonable alternatives available to the lessee must be available on the leased premises.

Logically, the accommodation doctrine need not be limited to accommodation alternatives on the leased premises. The premise of the manner-of-enjoyment theory is the probable intent of the parties to a mineral severance or lease of the minerals. It is just as likely that the parties to a mineral deed or lease intend a balancing of the economic consequences of accommodation as that they intend that accommodation be required only when it is available on the premises; their intent is general, not specific. Other courts that have considered conflicts between surface owners and mineral owners or lessees since *Getty Oil v. Jones* and *Sun Oil v. Whitaker* have recognized an obligation on the part of the mineral owner or lessee to accommodate the surface owner's interest without that limitation. The accommodation doctrine has been specifically recognized in North Dakota, Arkansas, Colorado, and Utah, as well as in Texas. In this writer's opinion, it will be generally accepted, probably in a broader form than adopted by the Texas Supreme Court.

(3) For the Benefit of the Minerals Under the Surface

A third limitation to the implied right of a mineral interest owner or lessee to use the surface of the land is that the use must be *exclusively* to obtain the minerals under the land. This is merely an application of the general principle of property law that an easement may not be used for the benefit of any property other than the dominant estate. Use of the land surface for the benefit of adjoining tracts abuses the scope of the easement.

(a) Application of the Limitation

For example, suppose that O, the owner in fee simple absolute in Blackacre, granted an oil and gas lease to A Company. A Company also took an oil and gas lease on Whiteacre, an adjoining tract, from X, owner of Whiteacre in fee simple absolute. A Company now wishes to drill an exploratory well on Whiteacre. May it construct an access road across Blackacre? If the well on Whiteacre is successful, may A Company construct a pipeline across Blackacre to serve the well on Whiteacre? May it erect storage tanks on Blackacre or drill a well to dispose of waste salt water on Blackacre?

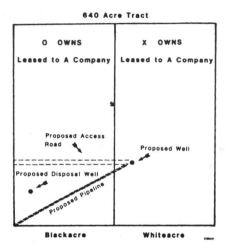

A Company may not use the surface of Blackacre for any of the uses desired. O's lease to A Company grants A Company the right to use the surface of O's land, Blackacre, for the benefit of the minerals under Blackacre. A's use of Blackacre for the benefit of Whiteacre may be enjoined or may result in award of damages to O.

Another question is whether A Company has the right to use the surface of Blackacre in conjunction with operations being conducted by A Company on *both* Whiteacre and Blackacre. Suppose, for example, that A Company drills a well on Blackacre and then wishes to drill a well on Whiteacre and use the access road, pipeline, salt water disposal well, and storage facilities it has erected on Blackacre in conjunction with its operations on Whiteacre. Would such uses be permitted? Here again, the courts take a strict view of the scope of the easement. The lessee has no right to conjunctive uses.

The most difficult question is whether A Company may use the surface of Blackacre in conjunction with Whiteacre when the properties have been compulsorily pooled or included in a spacing unit established by a state conservation agency. When O owns both the surface and minerals, the answer is affirmative because O will benefit from the well drilled. The action of the conservation agency does not deprive O of his property; it protects his correlative rights. But what if O, the lessor, owns only the mineral rights? Can the severed surface owner, who is not benefitted or protected by the state's action, prevent use of the surface of Blackacre in conjunction with Whiteacre? Some courts have held that O cannot because the state action is an exercise of the police power for which the surface owner is not entitled to redress. In addition, pooling protects surface owners as well as mineral owners, for without it the surface could be burdened by over-drilling.

(b) Expanding the Implied Right

A lessee who wishes to use the surface of leased land in conjunction with operations on other leases must obtain express easements. Generally, express easements are conveyed by separate instruments, but occasionally, they are included in the lease granting clause. For example:

"Lessor . . . hereby grants, leases and lets exclusively to lessee the land described below for the purpose of [searching for, developing, and producing oil and gas] ... together with all rights, privileges, and easements *useful* for lessee's operations on said land and *on land in the same field with a common Oil and Gas Reservoir....*" (Emphasis added).

The italicized language expands the scope of the easement generally implied in an oil and gas lease in two ways. First, the language grants the lessee the right to use the land for those purposes that are "useful" as well as for those that are "reasonably necessary." Second, the language gives the lessee the right to use the surface for the benefit of other lands.

Courts generally interpret narrowly language that expands the implied easement for surface use. The right to use the land for purposes "useful" to the lessee may be held to be nothing more than a restatement of the reasonable-use principle. The grant of the right to use the land surface in conjunction with other lands with a common oil and gas reservoir may be held to require that there be producing operations upon Blackacre or that Blackacre be pooled with property upon which producing operations are taking place.

The grant of express easements for surface use is inherently limited when the lease is from a severed mineral-interest owner. A lessor who owns the fee-simple interest in property holds all of the "bundle" of rights. A fee-simple owner may grant specifically to the mineral lessee broader rights than those usually implied in an oil and gas lease. When the lessor is the holder of a severed mineral interest, however, the lessor does not have rights of surface use beyond those normally implied and so cannot grant them.

(4) In Accord With Lease Terms

Modern oil and gas leases frequently contain specific provisions limiting the implied easement for surface use. For example, paragraph 7 of the California lease form in the Appendix provides that the lessee must pay damages for interference with growing crops and must bury pipelines installed on the leased premises. The principle of reasonable use would probably require neither. This commonly encountered lease provision clarifies the parties' intent and limits the lessee's right of surface use.

Many modern leases contain much more extensive and onerous surface use provisions. It is common to see page after page of surface-use limitations and procedures in addenda to leases on large properties. It is important to a lessor that the parties agree to surface use limitations before or contemporaneously with the grant of the lease; otherwise the limitations may fail for lack of consideration. Also, to be binding upon third parties, surface-use restrictions must be reflected on the record, either in an addendum to the lease or (in many states) by reference to an unrecorded agreement. For the lessee, it is important to review surface-use restrictions to make certain that they will allow necessary operations. Although damages or injunction are the usual remedies for an aggrieved lessor, in *Thurner v. Kaufman*, 699 P.2d

435 (Kan.1985), the Kansas Supreme Court found
the lessee's "flagrant" violation of a lease agreement "to maintain ... a high degree of security to
prevent the escape of livestock from fenced areas
at lessee's access point" justified lease forfeiture.

(5) In Accord With Statutes, Ordinances, Rules, or Regulations

Restrictions on the implied right of surface use by
statutes, ordinances, rules and regulations are a
fast-growing phenomena. Requirements that lessees
obtain drilling permits and properly plug and abandon wells have been common since the early part of
the 20th century. Beginning in the 1960s and 1970s
many states set standards for clean-up and restora-
tion of the surface after drilling operations and
upon lease abandonment. State and federal governments use rules and regulations to impose many of
the same kinds of surface-use restrictions that large
mineral-interest owners define in oil and gas leases.
Generally, courts hold such standards valid as legislative or regulatory definitions of reasonable use.

The most recent type of legislative restriction on
surface use, *surface damages acts*, go beyond defining reasonable use. Surface damages acts require
that lessees pay of damages for use of land surface
in oil and gas operations. They reverse the traditional principle of law that the mineral-interest
owner or oil and gas lessee is entitled to reasonable
use of the land surface to obtain minerals without
the landowner's permission and without payment.

The roots of surface damages acts are in the practice of the oil industry. To avoid argument whether a particular use is reasonable, most oil companies pay voluntary "site damages" to surface owners. Landowners have come to regard these payments as their right. Disturbed by what they have regarded as inadequate damage offers and by occasional abuses of the right of reasonable use, they have pressed for surface damages legislation.

Surface damages acts have been attacked on a variety of constitutional grounds, but they have withstood scrutiny. In *Murphy v. Amoco Production Co.*, 729 F.2d 552 (8th Cir.N.D.1984), the court found that the North Dakota statute did not violate the contract clause of the U.S. Constitution because, given the enormous costs of oil and gas development, the additional liability imposed was not a substantial impairment of contract. The court rejected Amoco's arguments that the surface damages act violated the equal protection and due process provisions of the Fourteenth and Fifth Amendments because it found that the classifications of the statute were not arbitrary or unreasonable. Finally, the court found that the statute did not amount to a governmental taking of property because "Amoco's right not to compensate Murphy for unavoidable damage to Murphy's surface estate, if indeed it is 'property' at all, amounts to only a minor strand in the full bundle of rights which constitutes Amoco's mineral estate."

D. THE HABENDUM CLAUSE

The habendum clause of an oil and gas lease, sometimes called the "term" clause, sets the period of time for which the rights given in the granting clause will extend. Modern lease habendum clauses provide for a primary term and a secondary term. The *primary term* of an oil and gas lease is a fixed term of years during which the lessee has the right, without any obligation, to operate on the premises. The *secondary term* is the extended period of time for which rights are granted to the lessee once production is obtained. A common formulation is:

> "[T]his Lease shall be for a term of _____ years from this date, called 'primary term,' and as long thereafter as oil or gas are produced...."

The habendum clause is the explicit statement of the two key goals sought by lessees in oil and gas leases, which are discussed at the beginning of this chapter.

1. THE PRIMARY TERM

The primary term is the option period for the lessee, during which the lessee may hold the lease without drilling. The purpose of the lease primary term is to give a lessee adequate time to acquire additional leases in the area, to do geological and geophysical tests to evaluate whether to drill a test well, and to arrange for financing and support services to drill. The length of the primary term is what the market will bear. It is determined by the bargaining leverage of the parties and the amount of the bonus that the lessee is willing to pay. It may be as long (except in Louisiana and Tennessee where it may not exceed ten years) or short as the parties agree. Ten years was once a common primary term. Ten-year primary terms are still frequently seen in leases in unproven and marginally producing areas. Terms from one to five years are more typical in areas with established oil and gas production.

The lease primary term sets the maximum period of time for which a lessee can maintain its lease rights without drilling. The primary term may be cut short by the lessee's surrender of the lease or if the lessee fails to pay delay rentals properly. The primary term may be extended to the secondary term by production or by one of the constructive production provisions discussed in Part A of Chapter 9.

2.   THE SECONDARY TERM

The purpose of the secondary term is to give the lessee the right to hold a producing lease as long as it is economically viable to do so. The secondary term is an indefinite period of time—"as long thereafter as oil or gas are produced"—because it is impossible to determine how long a lease will be profitable at the time it is granted.

Because the secondary term is not specifically designated, however, disputes frequently arise. Among them are: (a) what constitutes "production" necessary to extend the lease; and (b) when does production cease and the lease terminate.

a. The Meaning of "Production"

Except in a few states, actual production is required to extend an oil and gas lease to the secondary term. The rationale for this view is that the business deal struck by the parties is expressed in the habendum clause, which says that the term will extend as long as there is "production." The literal wording of that clause must be given effect; without actual production, the lease terminates automatically at the end of the primary term, unless some other provision changes that result.

The majority position implicitly requires marketing as well as production. The rationale for the marketing requirement is the economic basis of the leasing transaction. There is no point in producing oil or gas if it cannot be marketed.

A classic case illustrating the strictness of the majority view is *Baldwin v. Blue Stem Oil Co.*, 189 P. 920 (Kan.1920). There the lessee had oil and gas leases with a primary term that ended January 17, 1919. The leases did not provide for extension by operations. Blue Stem Oil Company did not begin drilling operations until December 7, 1918. It did not complete them until after the end of the primary term. Blue Stem attempted to excuse its failure to attain actual production by asserting as affirmative defenses that it had been plagued with troubles such as an inadequate supply of water, flooding, blizzards, shortages of coal, personnel and equipment, and adverse governmental regulation. Despite this impressive list, the Kansas Supreme Court affirmed judgment on the pleadings for the lessor on the grounds that the leases had expired by their own terms. A similar result, under a more conventional lease, is *Stanolind Oil & Gas Co. v. Barnhill*, 107 S.W.2d 746 (Tex.Civ.App.1937), where the court reasoned that a lease creates a fee-simple-determinable interest in the lessee that terminates without action by the lessor when the primary term ends without actual production.

There is a respectable minority view, of which Oklahoma and West Virginia are the main proponents, that an oil and gas lease will not terminate if the lessee discovers oil or gas prior to the end of the primary term; actual production is not necessary to preserve the lease, though "discovery" requires completion and capability of production, and the lessee must make diligent efforts to market. *McVicker v. Horn, Robinson and Nathan*, 322 P.2d 410 (Okl.1958), and *Pack v. Santa Fe Minerals*, 869 P.2d 323 (Okl.1994), state this approach. There are cases in Montana, Wyoming, Kentucky and Tennessee suggesting that the discovery of gas will be sufficient to extend the lease to its secondary term, but that actual production of oil will be required to extend the lease. The rationale of such a distinction is that oil can be produced and stored without actual marketing, while gas cannot be economically stored.

Both minority views interpret "production" in the habendum clause by reference to the essential purposes of the lease rather than to the literal language used. A lessor's major purpose in granting an oil and gas lease is to obtain development of his or her property. That purpose has been substantially served when there is a well capable of production on the lease. A time interval between completion for production and actual marketing is inherent in the nature of the business, particularly when a well produces gas.

b. How Much Production Is Required: "Production in Paying Quantities"

A literal construction of "production" in the habendum clause of an oil and gas lease would mean that small amounts of production would suffice to extend the lease indefinitely. With a few exceptions, however, courts that have considered the issue have concluded that production must be "in paying quantities to the lessee."

The rationale for requiring production "in paying quantities" to extend a lease to its secondary term is convincing. Modern oil and gas leases have an indefinite secondary term to avoid the problem of termination at the end of some arbitrarily fixed term while it is still profitable to produce the leased property. From the viewpoint of both lessees and lessors, the lease is an economic transaction. When it no longer is profitable, a lease should terminate. Otherwise, lessees would be permitted to speculate with lessors' interests.

Logical though the "in paying quantities" standard is, it is difficult to apply in practice. Perhaps the best statement of the standard was made by the Texas Supreme Court in *Clifton v. Koontz*, 325 S.W.2d 684 (Tex.1959):

"[T]he standard by which paying quantities is determined is whether or not under all the relevant circumstances a reasonably prudent operator would, for the purpose of making a profit and not merely for speculation, continue to operate a well. . . .

.   .   .

In determining paying quantities, in accordance with the above standard, the trial court must necessarily take into consideration all matters which would influence a reasonable and prudent operator."

Note that "in paying quantities" does not require that the lessee have a reasonable expectation of recovering the costs of drilling and completing the wells on the lease. Once a lease is put into production, it will make sense to continue to operate it so long as it is marginally profitable—so long as operating revenues are greater than operating costs, even though the costs of drilling and completing will never be recovered. The reasonably prudent operator must make business decisions based upon the facts as they are.

Application of the "in paying quantities" standard is generally a two-step process. First, the court applies a "*litmus test,*" looking to operating revenues and operating costs over a reasonable time period to determine whether operations have been "profitable." If operations have resulted in a profit, however small, the inquiry is ended and the lease is held to be producing "in paying quantities." Second, if the court concludes that operating revenues have not exceeded costs over a reasonable time, it usually applies the *legal test* articulated in *Clifton v. Koontz,* and asks whether there is any reason that a reasonably prudent operator who expected to make a profit from the lease would continue operating it. Only if the answers to both steps of the analysis are negative does the lease terminate.

(1) The Litmus Test

The first step of the analysis is an attempt to quantify the reasonably prudent operator standard of *Clifton v. Koontz.* It may be helpful to think of this step as a "litmus test" because, like its scientific counterpart, it is fallible. A lease may continue to produce "in paying quantities" even if it fails the litmus test; the litmus test is determinative only when it shows that the lease is profitable.

Application of the litmus test requires consideration of at least three factors: (A) what revenues are to be taken into account in determining paying quantities, (B) what expenses are to be considered, and (C) over what period of time the calculation is to be made.

(a) Operating Revenues

Determining lease operating revenues is relatively easy. All revenues from the sale of production are counted in determining paying quantities. Payments that reflect a return of capital rather than operating income (e.g., the sale of an oil storage tank no longer needed) are excluded. Likewise, amounts the lessee paid to mineral-interest owners as royalty under the lease are excluded; the landowner's royalty is not revenue *to the lessee.*

A conceptual problem exists with the treatment of revenues received by a lessee and paid to overriding-royalty owners. As a general rule, the courts take into account the share of operating revenues due to overriding-royalty interests in determining paying quantities; only the landowner's royalty is excluded. The rationale of this distinction may be difficult to understand, for revenues that are paid to overriding royalty interests add nothing to the lessee's profit. But most overriding royalty interests are held by persons who receive them as compensation for their help in structuring ventures. Compensation to such persons would be a capital cost, not an operating cost, if made in cash at the time the services were rendered. Therefore, compensation is treated as capital cost, rather than an operating cost, when paid as an overriding royalty. Equity and public policy may also be a factor. Determination of "paying quantities" is inherently imprecise. Fairness demands that a lessee who has obtained production be given benefit of the doubt. So does the public policy to maximize recovery of oil and gas.

(b) Operating Costs

Much more uncertainty exists about what kinds of expenses are to be taken into account in determining "in paying quantities." Direct operating expenses, such as the wages of the employees who service the well, the cost of electricity to run pumping units, and day-to-day maintenance, are operating expenses to be taken into account. There is substantial dispute, however, whether depreciation and administrative overhead costs should be considered.

Logically, the courts should weigh direct depreciation and administrative expenses as operating costs in the paying-quantities equation. If a pumping unit on a well site is worth $10,000 this month but will be worth only $9,500 next month, the $500 loss in the salvage value of the pumping unit is a real expense factor that an economically oriented lessee will take into account. Likewise, if abandoning an oil and gas lease would permit closing a district office or laying off supervisory personnel, expenses of maintaining those services are logically costs of operating the lease.

Practical considerations may outweigh logic. The Oklahoma Supreme Court decided in *Stewart v. Amerada Hess Corp.*, 604 P.2d 854 (Okl.1979), that depreciation of lifting equipment must be considered an expense in determining paying quantities. That case was followed by a flurry of litigation over what equipment constitutes "lifting equipment" and how lifting equipment should be depreciated. The equitable and public policy principles noted in the discussion of operating revenues also dictate against consideration of such costs. Perhaps for these reasons, the Supreme Court of Kansas in *Texaco Inc. v. Fox*, 618 P.2d 844 (Kan.1980), specifically rejected the Oklahoma position, and the Texas cases, including *Clifton v. Koontz,* suggest that while such costs may be taken into account, a court is not required to consider them.

(c) The Time Factor

The time period over which courts analyze operating revenues and costs in determining paying quantities is equally as important as what revenue and expenses are to be taken into account. The time period is capable of even less precise definition than what constitutes operating revenues and costs.

Before a court will find that a lease has terminated, the history of nonpaying production must be sufficiently long to suggest that the lessee's continued operations are speculative. Few businesses and few oil and gas leases will operate at a profit all the time. The profitability of oil and gas operations is particularly sensitive to seasonal transportation difficulties and changes in market demand. Therefore, production in paying quantities does not cease the first day or the first month that a lease fails to operate profitably. Production in paying quantities ceases only when a lease is losing money and there is no reasonable expectation that it will become profitable.

The cases on the issue are consistent only in that almost all select at least a year as the basis for determination of production in paying quantities. Many consider operating revenues and operating costs over substantially longer periods; eighteen months to three years is common. It is left to the discretion of the court to select a time period that will permit fair assessment of the potential for profitability of the lease in question. Courts frequently take into account equitable factors in determining the appropriate time over which to consider operating revenues and operating costs. Thus, when political or economic conditions are turbulent, a longer history of operating costs and revenues will be considered than will otherwise be the case.

(2) The Legal Test

In a few states, including Kansas, if the economic analysis of the litmus test leads a court to the conclusion that a lease is no longer profitable, the lease terminates without further analysis. In most states, however, the courts will proceed to consider whether there is any other basis upon which a reasonably prudent operator might continue to operate the lease expecting that it would become profitable. The effect is that "in paying quantities" does not operate as a special limitation. *Clifton v. Koontz* admonishes that "all matters which would influence a reasonable and prudent operator" should be considered. In Oklahoma, *Stewart v. Amerada Hess Corp.* and *Pack v. Santa Fe Minerals* say that a "lease continues in existence so long as the interruption of production in paying quantities does not extend for a period longer than reasonable or justifiable in light of the circumstances involved. But under *no* circumstances will cessation of production in paying quantities *ipso facto* deprive the lessee of his extended-term estate."

Any factor that suggests that a reasonably prudent operator might continue to operate its lease, though it is presently unprofitable, may be considered at this stage. For example, in *Barby v. Singer*, 648 P.2d 14 (Okl.1982), the Oklahoma Supreme Court held that 15 months from February 1978 to April 1979 was an appropriate time over which to judge "in paying quantities," but nonetheless overturned a finding that the money-losing lease had terminated. The court concluded that the lessee was acting as a reasonably prudent operator in continuing to operate the lease because the Natural Gas Policy Act, which authorized retroactive price increases for the lease, was pending during that time.

E. THE DRILLING–DELAY RENTAL CLAUSE

The purpose of the lease drilling-delay rental clause is to ensure that the lessee has no obligation to drill during the primary term by negating any implied obligation to test the premises. Before drilling-delay rental clauses became common in oil and gas leases, many courts held that lessees had an implied duty to drill a test well on the leased premises within a reasonable time after the lease grant. The rationale for the implied covenant was that the major consideration for the grant of the lease by the lessor was the expectation that the property would be tested within a reasonable time. Courts' determination of what was a reasonable time ranged from a few months to several years, depending upon the circumstances. Lessees found that they could not rely upon a long primary term alone to preserve their rights.

The drilling-delay rental clause obviates any implied covenant to drill a test well. For example, in *Warm Springs Development Co. v. McAulay*, 576 P.2d 1120 (Nev.1978), the Nevada Supreme Court refused to imply a covenant to test in a geothermal lease for a primary term of 20 years without even considering the amount of bonus paid, even though the delay rentals the lease provided for were only 10 cents per acre per year. The specific right to hold the lease during the primary term by payment of delay rentals disclaims the implied covenant to test.

Lessors do not generally resist drilling-delay rental clauses, in part because the clauses have become customary in lease forms. Lessors commonly enter into leases expecting that development will not occur, if ever, until near the end of the primary term. Lessors who consider the timing of the drilling of the first well important may negotiate for a short primary term or for a specific drilling obligation. But, many lessors look forward to receiving delay-rental payments periodically.

From the lessee's viewpoint, it would be ideal if the option period of the lease primary term could be extended indefinitely. Early in the 20th century, leases giving the lessee the right to extend the term of the lease indefinitely without production were common. They were called *no-term leases* because they could be extended indefinitely by payment of delay rentals. But now, no-term leases are in great disfavor, at least in oil and gas development. Many courts refuse to enforce no-term leases on the grounds that they create a mere estate at will, terminable by either the lessor or the lessee. Other courts have upheld no-term leases, but with the stipulation that the lessee has an obligation to develop or release the lease within a reasonable time. The primary reason for no-term leases disuse, however, is that they are not acceptable in the marketplace; both mineral owners and lessees demand more certainty than no-term leases provide.

1. "UNLESS" v. "OR" CLAUSES

a. The "Unless" Clause

The oil industry uses two polar types of drilling-delay rental clauses. The more common type except in California and Appalachia, is the "unless" clause. An "unless" drilling-delay rental clause is structured so that it automatically terminates the lease *unless* the lessee commences a well or pays delay rentals prior to the date specified. Paragraph 5 of the Texas lease in the Appendix is a typical "unless" provision:

"If operations for drilling are not commenced on said land, or on acreage pooled therewith as above provided for, on or before one year from the date hereof, the Lease shall terminate as to both parties, unless on or before such anniversary date Lessee shall pay or tender to Lessor, or to the credit of Lessor in the _____ Bank at _____ , Texas, (which bank and its successors shall be Lessor's agent and shall continue as the depository for all rentals payable hereunder regardless of changes in ownership of said land or the rentals) the sum of ($_____), herein called rentals, which shall cover the privilege of deferring commencement of drilling operations for a period of twelve months. In like manner and

> upon like payment or tender annually, the commence-
> ment of drilling operations may be further deferred for
> successive periods of twelve months each during the
> primary term hereof...."

The "unless" clause creates a *special limitation* on
the primary term of the lease; it modifies the lease
habendum clause by making periodic commencement of drilling operations or payment of delay
rentals essential to hold the lease during the primary term. Under an "unless" drilling-delay rental
clause, a lease terminates automatically at the end
of the annual period unless the lessee begins drilling operations or pays delay rental.

b.   The "Or" Clause

The less common but increasingly popular "or"
drilling-delay rental clause does not cause a lease to
terminate automatically if the lessee fails to commence drilling operations or pay rentals in a timely
fashion. In contrast to the "unless" clause, an "or"
clause imposes an affirmative duty upon a lessee to
pay the delay rentals:

> "Commencing with the first day of the second year of
> the term hereof, if the lessee has not theretofore com-
> menced drilling operations on said land or terminated
> this lease as herein provided [by surrender], the lessee
> shall pay or tender to lessor annually, in advance as
> rental, the sum of $1 per acre per year for so much of
> said land as may then still be held under this lease,
> until drilling operations are commenced or this lease is
> terminated as herein provided."

Under the terms of an "or" drilling-delay rental
clause, a lessee must either commence drilling *or*

pay rentals *or* surrender the lease prior to the due date. Because the clause affirmatively obligates the lessee to do one of the alternatives, it is commonly referred to as an "or" clause. "Or" clauses are the rule rather than the exception in California and Appalachia. The Appendix includes an example of a California lease with an "or" clause.

c. Forfeiture of "Or" Leases

The lessor's remedy for a lessee's failure to pay delay rentals under a lease with an "or" drilling-delay rental clause is limited to recovery for the amount of the rental payment due, in the absence of a special provision in the lease. A good example of this principle is *Girolami v. Peoples Natural Gas Co.*, 76 A.2d 375 (Pa.1950). There, after making periodic payments for eleven years under an "or" lease that required quarterly payments of delay rentals, the lessee learned of title problems and suspended delay-rental payments for two years. When the lessee resumed payments, the lessor claimed that the lease had terminated or had been forfeited. The Supreme Court of Pennsylvania held that since the lease did not provide for automatic termination or expressly reserve the power of forfeiture to the lessor, the lessor's only remedies were an action in law for recovery of the rentals or an action for recision of the lease on a theory of abandonment. In *Warner v. Haught, Inc.*, 329 S.E.2d 88, 96 (W.Va.1985), however, a court held that a lessee's repeated failure to pay rentals on time under an "or" clause, thereby forcing the lessor to seek relief repeatedly, justified forfeiture of the lease.

Most modern "or" leases contain a *forfeiture clause*. A forfeiture clause gives the lessor the alternative of following procedures to declare the lease forfeited if the lessee does not pay delay rentals. Usually, forfeiture clauses require a lessor to give notice to the lessee and allow an opportunity for corrective action before declaring the lease forfeit. Neither notice nor a chance to correct a failure is a legal essential, however. For example, in *Alexander v. Oates*, 223 P.2d 264 (Cal.App.1950), a California court had before it a commonly used California "or" form with a twenty-year primary term. Its drilling-delay rental terms provided in relevant part:

> "5. Commencing with the Sept. 1, 1945 [sic], . . . if the Lessee has not theretofore commenced drilling operations on said land or terminated this lease as herein provided, the Lessee shall pay or tender to the Lessor semiannually in advance as rental, the sum of One ($1.00) dollars per acre per year for the 1st 18 mo. and 2.00 per acre per yr. for the bal. of 3 yr. period [sic], for so much of said land as may then be held under this lease, until drilling operations are commenced or this lease terminated as herein provided.

> 6. The Lessee agrees to commence drilling operations on said land within three (3) years from the date hereof. . . . *The Lessee may elect not to commence or prosecute the drilling of a well on said land as above provided, and thereupon this lease shall terminate.* (Emphasis added).

. . .

21. *Upon the violation of any of the terms or conditions of this lease by the Lessee and the failure to begin
to remedy the same within 90 days after written notice
from the Lessor so to do, then, at the option of the
Lessor, this lease shall forthwith cease and terminate . . . .*" (Emphasis added).

The lessee did not commence drilling operations
within the three-year period provided in paragraph
6. The lessor contended that the lease had terminated as a result. The lessee disagreed, relying upon
the 90–day notice provided for in paragraph 21. The
court held that the situation was governed by paragraph 6, and that notice was not required under
paragraph 21.

In effect, the lease in *Alexander v. Oates* was an
"or" lease during the first three years of its primary term, requiring the lessor to take affirmative
action to terminate the lease by giving the lessee
notice of the failure to pay delay rentals and time to
correct his oversight. After the initial three-year
period, however, the lease became an "unless" lease
that could not be satisfied by payment of delay
rentals. It could be maintained for the remainder of
its primary term only by periodic drilling. The lease
automatically terminated when the lessee failed to
begin drilling operations.

"Unless" drilling-delay rental clauses and "or"
drilling-delay rental clauses are polar types. Under
the "unless" form, the terms of the drilling-delay
rental clause are a special limitation upon the primary term of the lease that will cut the lease short
if not observed. When the "or" form is used, com-

pliance with the terms of the drilling-delay rental clause is a covenant, and the lessor's remedy for failure to pay is a suit for damages unless forfeiture procedures are provided. Despite some judicial suggestions to the contrary, there is no reason that the parties to a lease should not be able to fashion a hybrid formulation if that more closely meets their goals.

Because the "unless" drilling-delay rental clause is the more commonly used and because most "or" leases contain forfeiture clauses, the drilling-delay rental clause in modern oil and gas leases is a frequent source of dispute and litigation. Typically, problems center upon whether the provisions of the drilling-delay rental clause have been met timely.

2. THE DRILLING OPTION

A lessee who seeks to avoid termination of a lease by complying with the drilling-delay rental clause is presented with a choice of either drilling or paying delay rentals within the period specified. If a lessee chooses to drill, the dispute that most often arises is whether drilling has occurred in a timely manner. Compliance with the drilling option is determined by three factors: (a) the precise language used in the lease, (b) the good faith of the lessee, and (c) the lessee's due diligence.

a. Commencement v. Completion

Modern oil and gas lease forms generally require that a lessee merely "commences operations for drilling" or "commences drilling operations" before the anniversary date to preserve the lessee's rights. Most courts hold that a lessee has complied if the lessee begins preliminary actions usually associated with actual drilling on the premises in good faith, and diligently pursues them to completion.

Compliance is a question of fact, but courts will likely consider sufficient virtually any kind of work at the well site prior to the end of the primary term. In *Breaux v. Apache Oil Corporation*, 240 So.2d 589 (La.App.1970), a court held that the lease was preserved where the lessee built a board road and turnaround, that it was not necessary that drilling equipment be moved to the lease within the primary term. Courts have held that digging a slush pit on the last day of the term, staking a location, delivering material, or erecting a derrick and beginning to drill a water well were sufficient to constitute commencement of operations for drilling. The cases show a clear tendency toward liberality. Any action by a lessee on the premises indicating a clear intent to develop the land will be enough to comply, so long as the lessee diligently pursues development. Some cases have also held that preliminary actions that do not take place on the land, such as setting up a rig on adjacent land for horizontal drilling under the leased land would qualify.

The language of the lease controls. The Kansas Supreme Court held that a requirement in the lease that a well be "completed" required completion rather than mere commencement in *Baldwin v. Blue Stem Oil Co.*, 189 P. 920 (Kan.1920). The court held in *Hall v. JFW, Inc.*, 893 P.2d 837 (Kan.App.1995) that a lease that provided that the lessee must "commence to drill a well within the term of this lease" required actual drilling. In Montana, a court made a distinction between "commencement of operations for drilling" and "commencement of drilling operations," holding that the latter term requires actual spudding. As a general rule, however, courts seem to be willing to take a broad view of what will comply with the drilling option of the drilling-delay rental clause. Their position encourages development and avoids unfairness to lessees who have committed substantial amounts of money or time to development.

b. In Good Faith

The second aspect of the drilling option is that whatever preliminary work the lessee relies upon to comply with the drilling-delay rental clause must be undertaken in good faith. Substance prevails over form. Actions that ordinarily would be considered commencement of drilling operations will be held insufficient if the courts decide that the work was a sham or that there was no intent to complete the well. For example, the Michigan Supreme Court in *Goble v. Goff*, 42 N.W.2d 845 (Mich.1950), held that a well had not been "commenced" where the lessee had not acquired a statutorily required permit and had not executed a drilling contract before the end of the primary term, although the lessee had done substantial work at the well site. The court inferred from the facts before it that the lessee had delayed committing to develop the property until it had an opportunity to review drilling information from an offset well.

No particular action or failure by the lessee short of spudding a well is determinative. Deciding whether operations were commenced in good faith is an application of "gastronomic jurisprudence" to give effect to the parties' bargain.

c. With Due Diligence

The third factor determining compliance with the drilling option of drilling-delay rental clause is the lessee's diligence. Once a lessee commences operations, the lessee must pursue them with due diligence until a well is completed and put into production or plugged and abandoned. Due diligence is determined by the circumstances. The standard's lack of precision gives courts flexibility to protect lessors against overreaching lessees. For example, a lessee who commences drilling operations in a timely manner but removes the equipment from the premises a week after the anniversary date because of a lack of funds to pay the drilling crew probably will lose the lease, because the aborted drilling operations do not benefit the lessor and raise an inference of a lack of diligence or bad faith on the part of the operator. The result should be different if the equipment is removed as a result of a bona-fide contractual dispute between the lessee and the drilling crew, however, even if the force majeure clause (discussed in Chapter 9) does not cover labor disputes. Likewise, when shortages of equipment and crews make it difficult to obtain a drilling rig, substantial periods of time between commencement of preliminary operations on the lease and actual drilling may be permissible.

3.   PAYMENT OF DELAY RENTALS

Beginning performance will not satisfy the lessee's alternative option of paying delay rentals. The option to pay delay rentals rather than to commence drilling operations generally requires perfect compliance. Delay rentals must be paid (a) in the proper amount, (b) on or before the due date, (c) to the proper parties, and (d) in a manner permitted by the lease.

The amount of the delay-rental payment varies. Usually, the payments called for are nominal, running from $1 to $10 per acre per year. The amount of delay rentals is negotiable, however. When leases are in demand, rentals may be substantial.

However nominal the amount of the delay rentals, failure to pay properly generally causes automatic termination of a lease with an "unless" drilling-delay rental clause. Thus, in *Phillips Petroleum Co. v. Curtis*, 182 F.2d 122 (10th Cir.Okl.1950), the court held that a valuable lease had terminated where delay rentals were not paid because a clerical employee mistakenly concluded that the lease was held by production. Similarly, in *Greer v. Stanolind Oil and Gas Co.*, 200 F.2d 920 (10th Cir.N.M.1952), the lessee lost its lease when the lessee made a good-faith mistake about the date the delay-rental payment was due. Underpayment or payment to the wrong person is just as fatal to the lessee as non-payment. In *Young v. Jones*, 222 S.W. 691 (Tex.Civ. App.1920), the lease terminated where a lessee's tender was $2.96 short. The lease from the under-paid owner terminated in *Atlantic Refining Co. v. Shell Oil Co.*, 46 So.2d 907 (La.1950), when the lessee paid delay rentals in the wrong proportions to the co-owners.

A stricter standard is applied to the provisions of the "unless" drilling-delay rental clause relating to payment of delay rentals than to the provisions for commencing drilling operations, possibly for three reasons. First, equities are more with a lessee who seeks the right to spend hundreds of thousands or millions of dollars in drilling than with one who seeks to extend an option to hold a lease by a nominal payment. Second, courts have a deep-seat-ed abhorrence of option agreements and strictly interpret attempts to extend an option. Third, and probably most important, the provisions of the de-lay rental option of the lease are much less open to interpretation than the drilling option. A require-ment that the lessee "commences operations for drilling" is simply easier to interpret broadly than one that the lessee "pay or tender" rentals by a specified date.

a. Protection of the Lessee by the Courts

(1) General Rule: Equity Not Applicable

Ordinarily, equity will not protect a lessee against termination of a lease containing an "unless" drilling-delay rental clause for failure to pay rentals properly. Estoppel and waiver do not apply to termination of an interest subject to a special limitation. Courts use estoppel and waiver to tie the hands of persons who have legal rights in situations in which it is considered unfair that they should exercise them. Termination of a lessee's interest by the special limitation in a lease with an "unless" drilling-delay rental clause requires no exercise of rights by the lessor. The lessee's interest lasts only as long as the terms of the drilling-delay rental clause are met; if delay rentals are not paid, the interest expires automatically by operation of law.

(2) Revivor of the Lease

Revivor is more logically satisfying than estoppel or waiver as a theory to preserve an "unless" lease where a lessee has made an improper payment of delay rentals that the lessor has accepted. Where the lessee has tendered the delay-rental payment incorrectly, the lease automatically terminates. If the lessor accepts the payment tendered, understanding that the lease has terminated, one may argue that the lessor's action has "revived" the lease, if there are actions or a writing sufficient to satisfy the Statute of Frauds. Courts rarely find revivor of a lease, however.

A case that illustrates both the possibilities and the limitations of the theory of revivor is *Brannon v. Gulf States Energy Corp.*, 562 S.W.2d 219 (Tex. 1977). There a lessor complained to her lessee, who had assigned the lease, that her annual lease rental

had not been paid, and the lessee asked the assignee, Gulf States, to make the payment. The Texas
Supreme Court held that the lessor's acceptance of
a check endorsed "lease rental" had revived the
original lease. On this precedent, some attorneys
advise clients that a lease is revived whenever the
lessor accepts a late tender of rentals. That is an
overly broad interpretation. The premise of revivor
is that the parties intended the interest to continue,
even though it had technically terminated. It should
be a precondition to revivor either that the lessor
knows that termination has occurred or that the
facts indicate that the lessor should have known.

(3) Estoppel and Waiver

Notwithstanding the legal theory, there are cases
in most jurisdictions with substantial oil and gas
production that invoke equitable principles to maintain leases with "unless" clauses where there has
been a failure to pay delay rentals properly. Many
reach their pleasing but illogical results with little
reasoning.

The cases that preserve leases after a failure to
pay delay rentals may be divided into at least four
classes:

    (1) those in which the lessor causes late payment or
underpayment;

    (2) those in which payments are inadequate or incor-
rect and the lessor knowingly delays notifying the lessee of his mistake until the anniversary date is past;

    (3) those in which the lessor knowingly accepts a late
payment; and

(4) those in which the failure is due to failure of an independent third party, usually the postal service.

The first two of the four classes is illustrated by *Humble Oil & Refining Co. v. Harrison*, 205 S.W.2d 355 (Tex.1947). There, Harrison gave his lessee, Humble, a copy of an ambiguous mineral-interest deed to support his claim to a portion of delay rentals due under a lease. Humble misinterpreted the title information and deposited incorrect payments for delay rentals due March 1 and May 8 to Harrison's credit. Harrison's bank acknowledged the payments. Harrison took no action to disavow the bank's acceptance of the rentals until June 10. When Humble sued to quiet title, the Texas Supreme Court held that Harrison was estopped to assert that Humble's lease had terminated. The basis of the decision was that Harrison, as a party to the ambiguous deed, had a duty to notify Humble of its mistake in payment so that Humble could correct it.

Cases in which a lessor's acceptance of late delay-rental payments is held to preserve the lease are closely related to *Humble v. Harrison*. Their premise is the contractual principle of cooperation. Parties to a contract are required to act as if they intended to make the contract work. Therefore, when one party has made an obvious mistake, such as underpayment of delay rentals, the other is required to notify the mistaken party promptly of the error so that the mistaken party can correct it. By similar reasoning, a lessor who receives late payment of delay rentals is presumed to know that the lessee tenders payment with the expectation that it will maintain the lease. The principle of cooperation will not permit a lessor to hold delay rentals tendered while speculating whether it would be more profitable to declare the lease terminated or to keep the rentals and honor the lease.

Cases in which the courts have refused to terminate leases containing an "unless" drilling-delay rental clause when there has been a failure of independent third parties turn on a different rationale. In addition to equitable considerations, those cases generally find an implied agreement that use of the services of the third party is appropriate. Most of the cases involve failure of the postal service to deliver properly addressed and stamped letters. Closely related, however, are cases involving the failure of banks to credit deposits properly to lessors' accounts or to honor lessees' checks. In either situation, courts may preserve the leases.

Equity is a flimsy thread upon which to hang a claim to protection for failure to pay delay rentals properly, however. Though equity may prevent a lease's termination, most reported cases hold that equitable considerations are not relevant in the circumstances presented. What circumstances a court will deem appropriate for equity to preserve the lease are so uncertain that equity's protection is of dubious value.

b.   Protection of the Lessee by Lease Clauses

Oil companies do not confront the risk of losing their leases with equanimity; leases are the stock-in-trade of the oil industry. Most oil and gas leases contain provisions drafted to avoid or minimize the risk of premature termination as a result of delay-rental payment disputes.

(1) Payment to an Agent

The typical delay-rental clause anticipates some payment problems. For example, the "unless" clause quoted above specifically permits a lessee to make delay-rental payments to a designated depository bank. This provision is more administratively feasible and more certain than direct payment to the lessor. Bank deposit provides a record of the payment for the lessee, who may be making hundreds or thousands of such payments. Furthermore, a typical clause continues:

> "[P]ayment or tender of rental ... may be made by check or draft of Lessee mailed or delivered to Lessor, or to said Bank on or before the date of payment. If such Bank, or any successor Bank, should fail, liquidate or be succeeded by another Bank, or for any reason fail or refuse to accept rental, Lessee shall not be held in default for failure to make such payment or tender of rental until thirty (30) days after Lessor shall deliver to Lessee a proper recordable instrument, naming another Bank as agent to receive such payments or tenders...."

The provision that payment is effective upon mailing of a check or draft is common. Courts have often been willing to imply the rights to mail and to pay by check or draft, but few lessees are willing to rely upon implication. The final part of the provision, protecting the lessee in the event of default by the depository bank, is also probably unnecessary; typically the lease designates the depository bank as the agent of the lessor.

(2) Notice-of-Assignment Provisions

Most leases also contain a *notice-of assignment clause* to avoid disputes over the effect of an assignment upon delay-rental payments. A notice-of-assignment clause provides that the lessee may rely upon its records in making delay-rental payments. Without such a clause, the lessee risks a finding that it is obligated to review the public property records each year before the anniversary date and to interpret any conveyances found in the record to determine who should be paid delay rentals and in what proportions they should be paid. Typical language is found in the Texas lease in the Appendix:

> "The rights of each party hereunder may be assigned in whole or in part, and the provisions hereof shall extend to their heirs, successors and assigns, but ... no change or division in such ownership shall be binding on Lessee until thirty (30) days after Lessee shall have been furnished with a certified copy of recorded instrument or instruments evidencing such change of ownership...."

Sometimes such language is called a *change-of-ownership clause*. Language like that quoted was a factor in the decision of the court in *Humble Oil & Refining Co. v. Harrison* that equity prevented the lease from terminating where the lessor had failed to notify the lessee of a mistake in payment of delay rentals. The court in *Gulf Refining Co. v. Shatford*, 159 F.2d 231 (5th Cir.La.1947), held that a notice-of-assignment provision protected a lessee even where the lessee received notice prior to the due date of the delay-rental payment, but after the payment had actually been made.

Related problems arise when the lessor dies, or when two or more persons are entitled to delay rentals. Oil and gas leases commonly provide specifically for the payment of delay rentals in such situations. Again, the Texas form in the Appendix is a good example. Its notice-of-assignment clause continues:

"In the event of the death of any person entitled to rentals hereunder, Lessee may pay or tender such rentals to the credit of the deceased, or the estate of the deceased, until such time as Lessee has been furnished with proper evidence of the appointment and qualifications of an executor or an administrator of the estate, or if there be none, then until Lessee is furnished satisfactory evidence as to the heirs or devisees of the deceased, and that all debts to the estate have been paid. If at any time two or more persons become entitled to participate in the rental payable hereunder, Lessee may pay or tender such rental jointly to such persons, or to their joint credit in the depository named herein; or, at the lessee's election, the portion or part of said rental to which each participant is entitled may be paid or tendered to him separately or to his separate credit in said depository; and payment or tender to any participant of his portion of the rentals hereunder shall maintain this Lease as to such participant."

Elaborate notice-of-assignment provisions rarely answer all questions, however. For example, what if the lessee considered the certified copy of a transfer of interest the lessor provided to be ambiguous? Could the lessee ignore it and pay delay rentals as provided in the drilling-delay rental clause of the lease? The notice-of-assignment clause quoted above does not address the issue. The answer is probably "yes," however, *if* the court found, with the benefit of hindsight, that the conveyance really was ambiguous. When the lessor and a transferee create an ambiguity as to how delay rentals are to be paid, the Oklahoma Supreme Court held in *Superior Oil v. Jackson*, 250 P.2d 23 (Okl.1952), that the lessee's rental checks could properly name both the lessor and the transferee. As a practical matter, since delay rentals are usually nominal in amount, lessees often pay delay rentals in full to all possible claimants.

A notice-of-assignment clause can be a double-edged sword, as is illustrated by *Atlantic Refining Co. v. Shell Oil Co.*, 46 So.2d 907 (La.1950). There, a lessee was not given notice of a transfer of a portion of its lessor's rights. A title opinion disclosed the transfer, however, and the lessee paid delay rentals based on the title opinion. Unfortunately for the lessee, the title opinion misinterpreted an ambiguity in the conveyance. The Supreme Court of Louisiana held that the lease had terminated because the lessee had no occasion to rely on the public records. If the lease contains notice-of-assignment provisions, the lessee ignores their terms at its peril.

(3) Notice-of-Incorrect–Payment Clauses

Leases with "unless" drilling-delay rental clauses often contain language to prevent automatic termination in the event of mistake in payment of rentals. A *notice-of-incorrect-payment clause* provides that a lease will not terminate until the lessor gives the lessee notice of the incorrect payment and allows a reasonable time for the lessee to correct the error. A notice-of-incorrect-payment clause effectively converts an "unless" drilling-delay rental clause into a "hybrid" provision; the lease neither automatically terminates if rentals are not paid nor obligates the lessee to pay.

(a) Enforcing Notice-of-Incorrect–Payment Clauses

Courts will strictly construe notice-of-incorrect-payment clauses, like other savings provisions. To work, such a clause should be specifically drafted to apply to delay-rental payments. Even if the notice language refers to payment of delay rentals, a court may refuse to enforce it. In a major Oklahoma case, *Lewis v. Grininger*, 179 P.2d 463 (Okl.1947), the Oklahoma Supreme Court considered a clause that provided:

> "It is agreed that neglect or failure to pay rentals when due shall not operate to forfeit or cancel this lease, until lessor gives lessee notice by registered mail of said failure to pay rental; whereupon lessee shall pay same within 10 days of receipt of said registered letter, or this lease is void."

The Oklahoma Supreme Court refused to give effect to the plain language of the notice clause on the grounds that it was "in conflict" with the "unless" drilling-delay rental clause and indefinite in its terms. Similar decisions are found in Michigan, Montana, West Virginia and Alberta.

The Fifth Circuit Court of Appeals, however, upheld a notice-of-incorrect-payment clause in *Woolley v. Standard Oil Co.*, 230 F.2d 97 (5th Cir. Tex. 1956). There, the following language was added to the delay rental clause:

> "If Lessee shall, in good faith and with reasonable diligence, attempt to pay any rental, but shall fail to pay or incorrectly pay some portion thereof, this lease shall not terminate unless Lessee, within thirty (30) days after written notice of its error or failure, shall fail to rectify same."

The court said that the parties obviously intended to contract against the harsh rule of automatic termination and held that the language saved the lease.

(b) Drafting Notice-of-Incorrect–Payment Clauses

Two problems are presented to the drafter of notice-of-incorrect-payment clauses. The first is to draft the savings language to make it clear that the parties intend the notice-of-incorrect-payment clause to apply. Specific provision that the notice terms are to apply to delay-rental payments and the inclusion of the provision as a part of the delay-rental clause ought to be sufficient. Modifying the "unless" provision itself is also a good idea. In *Kincaid v. Gulf Oil Corp.*, 675 S.W.2d 250 (Tex.App. 1984), the drilling-delay rental clause provided that "this lease shall terminate ... unless, on or before one year from the anniversary date Lessee shall pay or tender (*or shall make a bona fide attempt to pay or tender*) ... delay rentals." (Emphasis added). A notice-of-incorrect-payment provision similar to the one approved in the *Woolley* case followed at the end of the drilling-delay rental clause. The Texas Supreme Court had no difficulty ruling that the lease was preserved despite an incorrect payment. Modifying the "unless" provision as well as inserting a notice-of-incorrect-payment clause should avoid the objection that the savings provision conflicts with the "unless" provision.

The second problem presented to the drafter is to avoid the appearance of overreaching. The notice clause in *Lewis v. Grininger,* if applied literally, would excuse the lessee from making any payments of delay rentals until and unless notice was given by the lessor. Courts may well consider such language unconscionable. A more limited formulation, such as that of *Woolley* or *Kincaid*, where a lessee is excused for paying the wrong amount or the wrong person, but not for neglecting to pay, is more likely to be upheld.

(4) Use of "Or" Leases

The use of leases with "or" drilling-delay rental provisions has become more popular as leases have become more valuable. Under the terms of an "or" lease, a lessee's rights do not terminate automatically for failure to pay delay rentals properly. The lessee has an obligation throughout the primary term of the lease to drill or pay or surrender the lease. If the lessee fails its obligation, the lessor may sue for the rental payment or, under the terms of most leases, institute forfeiture procedures. Generally, "or" lease forfeiture procedures require a lessor to give notice to the lessee and time for the lessee to correct its defaults.

(5) Use of Paid–Up Leases

Another device designed to protect a lessee against loss of a lease for failure to pay delay rentals properly is the "paid-up" lease. A *paid-up* oil and gas lease is one under which all delay rentals bargained for are paid in advance. The lease is held for the full primary term by the initial payment to the lessor.

The choice of a paid-up lease is an economic decision. Factors that increase the likelihood that a paid-up lease will be used are large bonuses, small delay-rental payments, short primary terms, and small acreages or fractional interests. The larger the size of the bonus, the more likely a paid-up lease will be used because the greater will be the potential loss from a failure to pay delay rentals properly. Small acreages or fractions, short primary terms, and modest delay rentals make the paid-up option more affordable.

Sometimes the parties create a paid-up lease by striking out the drilling-delay rental clause and noting in an addendum that delay rentals have been prepaid. That is a dangerous procedure. The drilling-delay rental clause of an oil and gas lease generally is drafted so that it "dovetails" with other clauses of the lease. In the Texas lease in the

Appendix, for example, the shut-in royalty clause (in paragraph 3), the dry-hole clause, and the cessation-of-production clause (both in paragraph 6) refer to the drilling-delay rental clause to make payment of delay rentals a prerequisite for continuation of the lessee's rights under certain circumstances, or to establish the amount of payments due. If one strikes the drilling-delay rental clause from the lease, one may create serious ambiguities.

If one desires a "paid-up" lease, it is preferable to use a lease form drafted for that purpose. Some commonly available forms simply omit the drilling-delay rental clause and conform other provisions of the lease to accommodate the omission. A better formulation is the following, from the American Association of Professional Landmen paid-up lease form for Oklahoma, where paid-up leases are very commonly used:

> "This is a PAID–UP LEASE. In consideration of the down payment, *Lessor agrees that Lessee shall not be obligated,* except as otherwise provided herein, *to commence or continue any operations during the primary term,* or to make any rental payments during the primary term. . . ." (Emphasis added).

This language makes it clear that the lessee can maintain the oil and gas lease for the primary term without drilling an exploratory well on the premises. Without such language, the courts may resurrect the implied requirement that the oil and gas lessee drill an initial test well on the leased premises within a reasonable period of time.

(6) The Dry–Hole Clause

Most oil and gas leases contain a *dry-hole clause*, to clarify the payment of delay rentals after the lessee has drilled a dry hole on the leased premises during the primary term. A dry-hole clause bars the implication of condemnation or abandonment of a lease from the drilling of an unproductive well on the leased premises. Sometimes the clause gives the lessee a free rental period after drilling a dry hole. The clause always specifically affirms the lessee's right to maintain the lease for the remainder of the primary term by paying delay rentals. A common formulation is found in paragraph 6 of the Texas lease in the Appendix:

> "If prior to discovery of oil, gas, or other hydrocarbons on this land ... Lessee should drill a dry hole or holes thereon ... this Lease shall not terminate if Lessee commences additional drilling or re-working operations within sixty (60) days thereafter, or if it be within the primary term, commences or resumes the payment or tender of rentals or commences operations for drilling or re-working on or before the rental paying date next ensuing after the expiration of sixty (60) days from the date of completion of the dry hole...."

Dry-hole clauses were developed to avoid disputes over whether a lessee who drilled a dry hole could maintain the lease for the remainder of the primary term by making delay-rental payments. Before oil and gas leases routinely included dry-hole clauses, lessors successfully argued on occasion that drilling operations resulting in a dry hole constituted an irrevocable election of the drilling option of the drilling-delay rental clause. Thus, the only way the lessee could maintain the lease after drilling a dry hole was by continuing to drill. Lessees convinced other courts that because the essential consideration for the grant of an oil and gas lease was the conduct of drilling operations, the drilling of a dry hole during the primary term should hold the lease for the remainder of the primary term without either payment of delay rentals or further drilling operations. To avoid confusion, the drafters developed the dry-hole clause.

Common problems with dry-hole clauses include (a) what is a dry hole, (b) when a dry hole is completed, and (c) when the payment of rentals is due after a dry hole.

(a) What Is a Dry Hole

How dry must a well be to qualify as a "dry hole"? Must it be a "duster," one that locates no oil or gas, or does the term include a well that is incapable of producing in paying quantities? Courts have divided. Because of the division of authority, many leases define the term.

(b) When a Dry Hole Is Completed

Many dry-hole clauses, like the one quoted, key a lessee's rights to the time of completion of a dry hole. Unfortunately, words like "completion" or "drilled" have no certain meaning. Logic requires that a well should be "completed" or "drilled" as a dry hole when it has been drilled to the depth or formation sought and the lessee has determined in a good faith exercise of its business judgment that the drilling operations were unsuccessful.

(c) When Rental Payment Is Due

A recurring problem of dry-hole clauses is determining when payment of delay rentals is due after a dry hole is drilled. Many early dry-hole clauses were unclear about whether payments were due at the next lease-anniversary date or at the anniversary of the completion of the dry hole. Modern dry-hole clauses clearly specify the date for resumption of delay-rental payments.

Modern dry-hole clauses may present similar difficulties, however. The formulation quoted at the beginning of this discussion of dry-hole clauses illustrates one. It provides that the lessee may continue to maintain the lease after drilling a dry hole by paying delay rentals, but payment is excused on the next delay-rental payment date if the well is completed as a dry hole within sixty days prior to that date. The rationale for such provisions is that it is difficult for oil-company lease administrators to "gear up" to pay delay rentals with less than sixty days notice. But counting the days can be harder than it looks. For example, suppose that the lessee completed a dry hole on the premises on November 4. If the delay rental due date was January 2, is the delay-rental payment excused under the dry-hole clause quoted? The answer is affirmative. Applying accepted contract interpretation principles, the first partial day (November 4) is not counted. Therefore, there are 26 days through the end of November.

December has 31, and both January 1 and January 2 are counted in the total of 59 days. If you had any hesitancy at all in reaching this conclusion, however, the possibilities for miscalculation are apparent.

The interpretation that the parties to the dry-hole clause give to an ambiguous provision may control. For example, in *Superior Oil Co. v. Stanolind Oil & Gas Co.*, 230 S.W.2d 346 (Tex.Civ.App. 1950), the dry-hole clause provided:

> "Should the first well drilled on the above described land be a dry hole, then and in that event, if a second well is not commenced on said land within twelve months thereafter, this lease shall terminate as to both parties, unless the lessee on or before the expiration of said twelve months shall resume the payment of rentals in the same amount and in the same manner as hereinbefore provided."

The delay rental anniversary date was March 3. The lessee completed a dry hole on February 3. On the following January 28, the lessee tendered delay-rental payment to the lessor "in payment of delay rentals for the period of February 3, 1946 to February 3, 1947"; the lessee interpreted the lease provision to require payment twelve months from the completion of the dry hole. In January 1947 and 1948, the lessee made similar payments. After making the 1948 payment, the lessee transferred the lease to an assignee. The assignee tendered payment February 5, 1949, assuming that the twelve month period ran from the lease anniversary. The lessor rejected the tender, and the trial court held that the lease had terminated. An intermediate appellate court upheld the decision, reasoning that the actions of the lessor and the original lessee had amended the terms of the lease agreement. The Texas Supreme Court held that the terms were ambiguous, so that the interpretation of the original lessor and lessee were controlling. As a result of *Superior v. Stanolind*, assignees of leases commonly require that the administrative files of the assignor (which usually contain canceled delay rental checks) be delivered with the assignment.

F. CONCLUSION

The primary goals of the lessee in a modern oil and gas lease are achieved in just three clauses: the granting clause, the habendum clause, and the drilling-delay rental clause. These clauses are essential to the legal sufficiency of the lease, as well as to its practical effect. There is much more to most leases, however, as can be seen from a cursory review of the leases in the Appendix. Chapter 9 will consider several kinds of defensive clauses commonly found in leases, Chapter 10 will examine the lease royalty clause, and Chapter 11 will explore implied lease covenants.

CHAPTER 9

OIL AND GAS LEASE SAVINGS CLAUSES

Oil and gas leases are generally interpreted strictly against lessees, unlike real property leases. Appellate courts justify strict interpretation by the rules of construction that ambiguities in a written instrument are to be interpreted against its drafter, that an instrument is to be construed against the party owing performance under it, and that an option is to be construed against its holder, as well as by the public policy in favor of freeing property to be developed by another. In trial courts, strict interpretation against the lessee may be explained on the mundane basis that disputes over lease provisions usually go to trial in the county where the lessor lives, before judges and juries residing in the area.

Lessees have countered strict interpretation by lacing oil and gas leases with defensive language. Modern leases contain lengthy and complicated savings clauses to protect what lessees regard as their legitimate interests. This chapter will examine those clauses and their interpretations.

A. CLAUSES THAT PROVIDE FOR CONSTRUCTIVE PRODUCTION

Lessees have added several important clauses to oil and gas leases to modify the general rule that a lease terminates at the end of its primary term unless there is production in paying quantities. These clauses extend the lease term without production in stated circumstances. They provide for *constructive production* in the context of the lease. This group of defensive clauses includes: (1) operations clauses, (2) pooling and unitization clauses, (3) force-majeure clauses, (4) shut-in royalty clauses and (5) cessation-of-production clauses.

1. OPERATIONS CLAUSES

Most oil and gas leases include an *operations clause* to protect the lessee against expiration of the primary term while drilling operations are in progress. As Chapter 8 discusses, jurisdictions generally require either actual production or a capability of production at the end of the primary term to extend a lease. Neither test is met when drilling operations are proceeding. Some states, including Kentucky, Kansas, Oklahoma, and Montana, have held that since the lessee has the right to commence operations at any time during the primary term, once a lessee commences operations, the lease will be extended so that the lessee can finish what it has begun, if it acts with due diligence.

To avoid dispute, most modern leases contain a provision specifically extending the lease while oper-

ations begun during the primary term are in progress. A common operations-clause formulation follows:

> "If at the expiration of the primary term, oil, gas or
> other mineral is not being produced on said land, but
> lessee is then engaged in drilling or reworking opera-
> tions thereon, this lease shall remain in force so long as
> operations are prosecuted with no cessation of more
> than thirty (30) consecutive days, and if they result in
> the production of oil, gas or other mineral so long
> thereafter as oil, gas or other mineral is produced from
> said land. . . ."

The operations clause makes drilling operations the
equivalent of production for purposes of the habendum clause. It provides for constructive production
when there is neither actual production nor a capability of production.

a. Well–Completion v. Continuous–Opera-
tions Clauses

In *Rogers v. Osborn*, 261 S.W.2d 311 (Tex.1953),
the Texas Supreme Court reasoned that the operations-clause language quoted above providing that
the lease will extend "so long as operations are
prosecuted" must refer back to the reference to
"drilling or reworking operations thereon" that
triggers the clause, so that the clause permits a
lessee to complete drilling operations begun before
the end of the primary term, but not to commence
additional operations. A lessee cannot complete a
well begun prior to the end of the primary term as a
dry hole and then spud another well. The lease
terminates when the drilling operations commenced

during the primary term are completed, unless some other language of the lease (such as the dry-hole clause) extends the lease. An operations clause that permits only completion of the operations begun before the end of the primary term, is often called a *well-completion clause.*

A slight modification of the operations-clause language will create what may be called a *continuous-operations clause,* an operations clause not restricted to completion of a well in progress at the end of the term:

> "This lease shall continue in force so long as drilling or reworking operations are being continuously prosecuted on said land ...; and drilling or reworking operations shall be considered to be continuously prosecuted if not more than sixty (60) days shall elapse between completion or abandonment of one well and the beginning of operations for the drilling or reworking of another well."

This language permits a lessee to commence a well before the end of the primary term, abandon it after the end of the primary term, and continue to hold the lease by starting another well within sixty days. This result can also be obtained by modifying the habendum clause so that it provides that the lease will extend for "so long thereafter as oil or gas are produced ... or drilling or reworking operations are conducted...." The essential difference between a continuous-operations clause and a well-completion clause is that the former extends the lease so long as *any* operations take place, whether for a well in progress at the end of the term or another, while the latter extends the lease only until operations begun before the end of the primary term are completed.

Sunac Petroleum Corp. v. Parkes, 416 S.W.2d 798 (Tex.1967), illustrates just how crucial the distinction between a well-completion clause and a continuous-operations clause can be. There the clause in question provided:

"5. If prior to discovery of oil or gas on said land Lessee should drill a dry hole or holes thereon ... this lease shall not terminate if Lessee commences additional drilling or re-working operations within sixty (60) days thereafter.... If at the expiration of the primary term oil, gas or other mineral is not being produced on said land but Lessee is then engaged in drilling or re-working operations thereon, *the lease shall remain in force so long as operations are prosecuted* with no cessation of more than thirty (30) consecutive days, and if they result in the production of oil, gas or other minerals so long thereafter as oil, gas, or other mineral is produced from said land." (Emphasis added).

Sunac commenced a well shortly before the end of the primary term of the lease on land that had been pooled with the lease for gas only. The well was completed after the end of the primary term as an oil well. Recognizing that an oil well on the pooled unit would not satisfy the lease terms, Sunac immediately began a second well, this one located on the leased land, and completed it as a producing oil well. Sunac contended that it was entitled to protection either under the dry-hole clause (the first sentence of the quoted paragraph) or under the second sentence of the quoted paragraph, which Sunac contended was a continuous-operations clause. The

Supreme Court of Texas rejected Sunac's argument, holding that the lessee was not entitled to the protection of the dry-hole clause because a well that produced oil was not a dry hole, and that what Sunac termed to be a continuous-operations clause was only a well-completion clause because there was no reference to "additional operations." Therefore, Sunac lost its lease and the producing well.

b. Delay Between Completion of Operations and Production

If one reads the operations clause literally, a lease extended beyond the primary term by operations will terminate upon the completion of operations unless production follows immediately. Since a substantial delay often occurs between completion of operations and actual production, a literal interpretation is contrary to the purpose of the operations clause. Accordingly, some courts have held that an operations clause extends the lease by inference beyond the time that drilling operations are completed for so long as the lessee exercises due diligence in completing, equipping, and producing the well and marketing its production.

Sword v. Rains, 575 F.2d 810 (10th Cir.Kan. 1978), provides an example of the application of the inference. Rains commenced a test well on Sword's land near the end of the primary term. The lease was extended beyond the primary term under the terms of its well-completion operations clause. Rains completed the well and made it ready for a pipeline connection approximately two weeks later.

But more than eight months passed before Rains
sold gas. Sword sued Rains contending that the
lease had expired. The U.S. district court and the
Tenth Circuit Court of Appeals rejected the contention. They held that operations under a well-completion clause will extend the lease as long as the
lessee diligently pursues putting the lease into actual production.

The conclusion reached by the courts in *Sword v.
Rains* seems logically unassailable. There will always be a delay between completion of drilling
operations and inception of production. The delay
may be only a few days for oil production or for
production from a gas well located close to a gas
pipeline. It may extend for months or years in the
case of gas wells not serviced by pipelines or in
times of economic recession. If an operations clause
in an oil and gas lease is to have practical meaning,
it should extend the lease so long as the lessee is
making diligent efforts to produce and market.

2.   POOLING AND UNITIZATION
PROVISIONS

People in the oil industry often use "pooling" and
"unitization" synonymously. *Pooling*, however, is
defined as bringing together small tracts or fractional mineral interests for the drilling of a single
well for primary production on a spacing unit. In
contrast, *unitization* generally refers to combining
leases and wells over a producing formation for
field-wide operations. Unitization is almost always

associated with pressure maintenance or with secondary or tertiary recovery operations rather than with primary recovery operations. Pooling and unitization clauses in leases give a lessee authority to commit the lease property to pooling and unitization and adjust the rights of the lessor and lessee accordingly.

Without the lessor's approval, a lessee generally may not affect the lessor's rights under the lease by pooled or unitized operations. A lessee who accepts a lease without the pooling power cannot extend it to its secondary term without drilling a well on the leased property, even if spacing rules do not permit drilling or geological evidence suggests drilling would be unsuccessful. Furthermore, if a lessee pools its interest under a lease without a pooling clause with that of other property owners and drills a well on the leased premises, the lessee must account to the lessor for the full lease royalty on production from the well, though its pooling agreement allocates to it only a portion of production from the well. Without agreement of the lessor, either in the lease or by separate agreement, the lessee cannot affect the lessor's rights.

The general rule that pooling or unitization by the lessee cannot affect the rights of the lessor under the lease does not fit business realities. Operations combining two or more leases are frequently a legal or economic necessity. For a lessee to seek the lessors' approval on a case-by-case basis is not practicable because of the administrative costs involved and because of the likelihood that the lessors will demand extra compensation. In states where compulsory pooling or unitization is not easily achieved, lessees typically seek the right to pool or unitize in the lease.

a. Community Leases

One way for a lessee to obtain the flexibility it desires is to join all of the mineral owners of the relevant property in a single lease. A single lease covering two or more separately owned tracts of land or fractional mineral interests is called a "community lease." In Texas, execution of a community lease creates a strong presumption that the parties intended to pool their interests, with royalties being apportioned on the basis of the number of acres each lessor has contributed to the community lease. In Oklahoma, execution of a community lease merely raises a rebuttable inference that the parties intended to pool their interests, while in New Mexico it creates no inference at all.

b. Pooling Clauses

The most common way that lessees obtain the right to pool their lessors' interests is by a pooling clause in a lease. An example from a Kansas lease follows:

> "Lessee at its option, is hereby given the right and power to voluntarily pool or combine the lands covered by this Lease, or any portion thereof, as to oil and gas or either of them, with any other land, lease or leases adjacent thereto, when in Lessee's judgment it is necessary or advisable to do so in order to properly develop and operate said premises, such pooling to be into units

not exceeding eighty (80) acres for an oil well plus a tolerance of 10%, and not exceeding six hundred and forty (640) acres for a gas well plus a tolerance of 10%, except that larger units may be created to conform to any spacing or well unit pattern that may be prescribed by governmental authorities having jurisdiction. Lessee shall execute in writing and record in the County records an instrument identifying and describing the pooled acreage. The entire acreage so pooled into units shall be treated for all purposes, except the payment of royalties, as if it were included in this Lease, and *drilling or re-working operations* thereon, *or production of oil and gas* or other hydrocarbons *therefrom* or the completion thereon of a well as a shut-in gas well, *shall be considered for all purposes,* except the payment of royalties, *as if such operations were on or such production were from,* or such completion were on *the lands covered by this Lease,* whether or not the well or wells be located on the premises actually covered by this Lease. In lieu of royalties elsewhere herein specified, including shut-in gas royalties, *Lessor shall receive from a unit so formed only such portion of the royalty stipulated herein as the amount of his acreage placed in the unit,* or his royalty interest therein, *bears to the total acreage so pooled."* (Emphasis added).

A typical pooling clause grants the lessee a power of attorney to pool the lessor's interests. The pooling clause changes the result that would otherwise occur under the lease in two ways addressed by the italicized language in the clause quoted. First, the pooling clause modifies the habendum clause of the lease by providing that production or operations anywhere on the unit formed will be considered to be production or operations on the leased premises; the pooling clause provides for constructive production. Second, the pooling clause obligates the lessor to accept royalty proportionate to the amount of the leased land included in the pooled unit, protecting the lessee against having to make double payments of royalty. Thus, the pooling clause substantially increases a lessee's flexibility.

c. Unitization Clauses

Where the need for eventual enhanced recovery operations is apparent when the lessor and lessee negotiate the lease, the lease may include a unitization clause, as well as a pooling clause. As Part C of Chapter 2 discusses, drainage of oil and gas by enhanced recovery operations may not be protected by the rule of capture. In addition, successful unit operations require cooperation of all the owners, and voluntary cooperation may not be easy to obtain. Unitization for pressure maintenance or for secondary or tertiary-recovery operations generally benefits all owners in the long run, because it may increase the total amount of production obtained from the property. In the short term, however, it may be in the interest of some or all of the owners to refuse to agree to unitize and to continue to operate with primary recovery methods. Furthermore, the difficulty of obtaining voluntary agreement is compounded where there are many owners.

While the unitization power may be as important to lessees as the pooling power, unitization clauses in oil and gas leases are relatively uncommon for three reasons. One is that historically unitization has been economically justified and technologically feasible only in relatively few situations. Dramatic increases in oil and gas prices have increased the number of those situations, however, and provided an important stimulus to technological improvement. Another reason for the rarity of lease unitization clauses is that the focus of lessees when leases are taken is upon primary production. Unitization for secondary or tertiary recovery may be important in the long run, but the long run seems far away when lessees negotiate leases. Third, mineral interest owners object to unitization clauses even more than they object to pooling clauses; the market will not generally bear unitization clauses.

Nonetheless, some oil and gas leases contain unitization clauses. A Colorado lease includes the following:

"Lessee may at any time or times unitize all or any part of said land and Lease, or any stratum or strata, with other lands and Leases in the same field so as to constitute a unit or units whenever, in Lessee's judgment, such unitization is required to prevent waste or promote and encourage the conservation of Oil and Gas by any cooperative or unit plan of development or operation; or by a cycling, pressure-maintenance, repressuring or secondary recovery program. Any such unit formed shall comply with the local, State and Federal Laws and with the orders, rules, and regulations of State or Federal regulatory or conservative [sic] agency having jurisdiction. The size of any such unit may be increased by including acreage believed to be productive, and decreased by excluding acreage believed to be unproductive, or where the owners of which do not join the unit, but any such change resulting in an increase or decrease of Lessor's royalty shall not be retroactive. Any such unit may be established, enlarged or diminished and in the absence of production from the unit area, may be abolished and dissolved by filing of record an instrument so declaring, and mailing or tendering to Lessor, or to the Depository Bank, a copy of such instrument. Drilling or re-working operations upon, or production from any part of such units shall be considered for all purposes of this Lease as operations or production from this Lease. Lessee shall allocate to the portion of this Lease included in any such unit a fractional part of production from such unit on any one of the following basis' [sic]: (a) the ratio between the participating acreage in the unit; or, (b) the ratio between the quantity of recoverable production from the land in this Lease in such unit and the total of recoverable production from all such unit [sic]; (c) any basis approved by State or Federal authorities having jurisdiction. Lessor shall be entitled to the royalties in this Lease on the part of the unit production so allocated to that part of this Lease included in such unit and no more."

Like its pooling counterpart, a unitization clause gives a lessee authority to bind the lessor's interests to a unitization plan. The unitization clause amends the lease habendum clause by making production or operations anywhere on the unit the equivalent of production or operations on the lease. It also amends the lease royalty clause by giving the lessor a royalty calculated on the production from the unit that is allocated to the unit under the unitization agreement rather than on actual production from the leased premises.

d. Problems Under Pooling and Unitization Clauses

Pooling and unitization clauses frequently give rise to disputes between lessors and lessees. Among the issues are (1) whether the power has been exercised in good faith, (2) whether the power has been exercised in accord with the lease terms, (3) whether the lessee has a duty to pool, (4) whether exercise of the power cross-conveys property interests, (5) whether non-operating interest owners have the right to ratify the exercise of the power, and (6) whether the power conflicts with the rule against perpetuities.

(1) Exercise in Good Faith

Courts have implied a requirement that a lessee exercise the pooling or unitization power in good faith. The purpose of the clauses is to give a lessee flexibility to operate efficiently, so the power to pool is limited by that purpose. A lessee should not be able, for example, to pool a portion of one leased property with another leased property solely for the purpose of maintaining two leases by the drilling of one well unless the action is pursuant to plan of development.

A Texas case, *Amoco Production Co. v. Underwood*, 558 S.W.2d 509 (Tex.Civ.App.1977), illustrates the point. The lessors contended that the lessee had "gerrymandered" a drilling unit of 688 acres which, under the terms of the leases, would extend eight leases covering a total of approximately 2,250 acres. The lessee had formed the unit approximately two days prior to the end of the primary terms of several of the leases. The lessors alleged that the lessee had included some clearly nonproductive property in the unit and excluded some clearly productive property. A jury found that the unit was established in bad faith, and the trial court canceled the unit and declared that some of the leases had terminated. On appeal, the appellate court held that good faith is an issue of fact, and that the jury had properly decided that the lessee had acted in bad faith on the basis of the configuration of the unit and the timing of the designation.

One should not assume that all multi-lease poolings near the end of the primary term of one or more of the leases are defective. A lessee's duty is to act in good faith, not to act as a fiduciary. Under general principles of contract interpretation, a pooling or unitization clause should be (and generally is) interpreted broadly. The issue of good faith or bad faith is a question of fact, and the burden of proof is upon the lessor who asserts bad faith.

(2) Exercise in Accord With Lease Terms

A second common problem encountered under pooling and unitization clauses is whether a unit is properly formed. For example, the timing of the unit designation may be questioned. Clauses often provide that pooling or unitization will be effective when the lessee records a unit designation or gives notice of it to the lessor. When the pooling or unitization clause imposes a duty on the lessee to record or give notice, the lessee's intent to pool and good faith are not enough; formal action is required.

Courts strictly interpret pooling and unitization clauses. *Jones v. Killingsworth*, 403 S.W.2d 325 (Tex.1965), is an example. The lease pooling clause provided that the lessee could pool the lease into units that were not larger than 40 acres for oil wells and 640 acres for gas wells. The clause also provided that "should governmental authority ... *prescribe or permit*" larger units, units created under the lease pooling power "may conform substantially in size with those *prescribed* by governmental regulations." (Emphasis added). The Texas Railroad Commission set an 80–acre minimum unit size for oil wells, but encouraged operators to establish 160–acre units. Accordingly, the lessee designated a 160–acre drilling unit. The Texas Supreme Court held that the lease pooling clause meant what it said, that it could not be used to establish a drilling unit greater than 80 acres, since that was the area *prescribed* by Railroad Commission rules.

(3) Duty to Exercise the Power

Several cases suggest that lessees have a duty to pool in appropriate circumstances. As Chapter 11 will discuss in conjunction with covenants implied in leases, courts generally hold lessees liable to lessors for drainage of leased property only where lessors show that an offset well would be profitable. Some cases suggest that a lessee may be liable even if the well is not profitable, if the lessee fails to seek to protect the lessor by pooling the lease with the draining property. By this line of reasoning, a failure to pool may be a breach of the lessee's implied covenant to protect against drainage.

The presence of a lease pooling or unitization clause makes it more likely that a court will impose a duty upon a lessee to act to protect its lessor. Though a lessee is not a fiduciary, the lessee is required to exercise the powers it has received from the lessor in good faith and with prudence. Because the lessee has taken from the lessor the right to decide whether to pool or unitize, the lessor can no longer act to protect himself. Therefore, courts are likely to find that the operator was imprudent or acted in bad faith in situations that are not clearcut.

(4) Cross–Conveyance Theory

In Texas, and probably in California, Mississippi, and Illinois, the effect of a community lease or a voluntary pooling or unitization, whether by a separate agreement or by the exercise of the lessee's rights under the pooling clause, is to *cross-convey* interests in the property among the various interest owners. In other words, each person whose interests are affected by the pooling acquires a proportionate property interest in the land of the others. The theory has been specifically rejected in Oklahoma, and probably in Kansas, Louisiana, Montana, and West Virginia. In those states, pooling creates contract rights in the various parties affected.

Application of the cross-conveyance theory may have profound effects. Owners of pooled interests become necessary parties to suits involving the land pooled or unitized. Consent of all persons who have either operating or non-operating interests in the property covered is necessary to a pooling or unitization agreement. In addition, cross-conveyancing theory may cause application of the Statute of Frauds, conveyancing statutes, and the rule against perpetuities to unit agreements, and may affect the choice of venue.

As a result of these problems, pooling or unitization agreements and designations in Texas and other states where the cross-conveyance theory may apply commonly include express provisions disclaiming cross-conveyancing. Though such devices have a "boot strap" quality about them, they should be given effect where the intention is clear.

(5) The Right of a Non–Executive Owner to Ratify

A fifth common problem with pooling or unitization and community leases is whether the owner of a royalty (or some other non-executive interest) in a part of the tract can ratify. Inevitably, the problem arises after a producing well has been completed upon a pooled tract in which the royalty interest owner has no interest. If the royalty owner has the right to ratify, the royalty owner will become entitled to a share of the production. If the royalty owner cannot ratify, he or she will take nothing.

The problem is a variation of the issue of whether the executive right includes the power to pool non-executive interests, which Chapter 6 discusses. Texas courts have held it does not. If the non-executive right is not affected by pooling, its owner may ratify or reject the action of an executive-interest owner that has purported to affect the royalty. In several Texas cases, courts have permitted ratification of a community lease or a pooling agreement by a royalty owner when the royalty owner has acted promptly. *Ruiz v. Martin*, 559 S.W.2d 839 (Tex.Civ.App. 1977), is an example. There, nonparticipating royalty interest owners had rights only to a portion of the land covered by the lease. Ruiz owned the mineral interest in that portion of the land and the fee interest in the remainder of the property covered by the lease. Martin's predecessor granted a single oil and gas lease covering both portions. Subsequently, the lessee completed a gas well on the portion of the leased property in which the royalty owners had no interest. The royalty owners promptly recorded a written ratification of the lease. The Texas appellate court held that the lease by the mineral owner covering both the property in which the royalty owner had an interest and the property in which the royalty owners had no interest amounted to a proposal to pool. Ratification of the lease by the royalty owners with an interest in part of the land had the effect of pooling their interest on an acreage basis in the whole property. They became entitled to share in royalties even though the well was drilled on a portion of land not subject to their royalty interest.

The underlying rationale of cases embracing the ratification theory, such as *Ruiz v. Martin*, *Montgomery v. Rittersbacher*, 424 S.W.2d 210 (Tex.1968), and *London v. Merriman*, 756 S.W.2d 736 (Tex.App. 1988), is that unless a non-executive owner has the right to ratify, the non-executive's interest will be subject to manipulation by the executive owner so that the value of the interest will be lost; e.g., the shape of the unit or the location of the well may be "rigged" to minimize or cut out entirely the royalty interest. The contrary view, adopted in Louisiana, is that the self-interest of the executive and the power of the courts to intervene to protect the non-executive against bad faith or imprudent exercise of the executive right will be sufficient to protect the non-executive.

(6) Conflict With the Rule Against Perpetuities

Occasionally, a lessor advances the argument that a lease pooling or unitization clause is void because it does not satisfy the rule against perpetuities. The argument is that a lease is potentially without end, so that the pooling or unitization power may be exercised after the end of all lives in being at its creation. That argument has been rejected by the Fifth Circuit Court of Appeals applying Utah law on the grounds that a pooling clause creates contract rights rather than property rights. It has also been rejected by the Supreme Court of Kansas on the basis that the lease creates a vested present estate that is not subject to the rule. The result is not clear in many states, however, so some pooling or unitization clauses impose a 21-year limit upon exercise of the pooling or unitization power. Paragraph 13 of the California lease in the Appendix contains such a limit.

e. Pugh Clauses or Freestone Riders

Lessors often resist including pooling or unitization clauses in oil and gas leases. A mineral interest owner may view a pooling clause as giving the lessee a dangerous amount of discretion to preserve the lease and affect the amount of royalties. As discussed above, typical lease pooling or unitization provisions provide that operations anywhere on the unit established, even though not on the leased premises, will extend the lease to its secondary term. The provisions also allow calculation of the lessor's royalty only on the portion of production allocated to the lease, even where the well is located on the leased premises.

Lessees need the power to pool, however. If a lessee lacks the power to pool, the lease may be lost or economically wasteful actions may be required to preserve it. The lessee will have to go to the time and expense of negotiating (and probably paying for) the lessor's approval each time pooling is desired. Further, since most leases in current use contain pooling provisions, leases without pooling provisions are difficult to market.

A compromise often struck between lessors and lessees over the power to pool is what is commonly called a *"Pugh" clause* or, in Texas, a *Freestone rider*. A Pugh clause modifies usual pooling language to provide that drilling operations on or production from a pooled unit will not preserve the whole lease. There are many variations. A simple formulation follows:

> "Notwithstanding anything to the contrary herein contained, drilling operations on or production from a pooled unit or units established under the provisions of paragraph 4 [the pooling clause] hereof or otherwise

embracing land covered hereby and other land shall maintain this lease in force only as to land included in such unit or units. The lease may be maintained in force as to the remainder of the land in any manner herein provided for, provided that if it be by rental payment, rentals shall be payable only on the number of acres not included in such unit or units."

A Pugh clause compromises the objections of the mineral-interest owner with the needs of the lessee. It gives the lessee the flexibility to make pooling decisions, but limits the effect of decisions to that portion of the lease included in the pooled unit. The lessor's royalty is proportionate to the amount of his or her property included in the unit, but unit operations do not affect the remainder of his or her land. A Pugh clause takes away much of the incentive that lessees might otherwise have to try to hold large tracts of land by creation of small, multi-lease units.

3. FORCE MAJEURE CLAUSES

a. In General

"Force majeure" literally means superior force. Most oil and gas leases include a force-majeure clause to enable a lessee to preserve the lease when circumstances beyond its control prevent it from operating or producing. The clause makes defined events that cause a lessee to fail to perform specific actions a substitute for production. Paragraph 11 of the Texas lease in the Appendix contains a typical formulation:

"Should Lessee be prevented from complying with any expressed or implied covenant of this Lease, from conducting drilling, or re-working operations thereon or from producing oil and gas or other hydrocarbons therefrom by reason of scarcity of, or inability to obtain or use equipment or material, or by operation of force majeure, or because of any federal or state law or any order, rule or regulation of a governmental authority, then while so prevented, Lessee's obligations to comply with such covenant shall be suspended, and Lessee shall not be liable in damages for failure to comply therewith; and this Lease shall be extended while and so long as lessee is prevented by any such cause from conducting drilling or re-working operations on, or from producing oil and other hydrocarbons from the leased premises; and the time while Lessee is so prevented shall not be counted against the Lessee, anything in this lease to the contrary notwithstanding."

This language excuses failure to perform because of factors beyond the lessee's control. It would maintain the lease if drilling operations were not possible, and it would excuse any breaches of express or implied covenants caused by the factors identified.

b. Precise Terms Important

The operative factor in force-majeure clauses is the breadth of the exculpatory language. Analytically, a force-majeure clause will provide constructive production to maintain an oil and gas lease if (1) the event complained of is defined as a force-majeure event by the language of the clause, (2) production is excused by the event defined as force majeure, (3) there is a causal relationship between the event defined as force majeure and the failure of production, and (4) the lessee gives timely notice, if the clause requires it. Not all clauses are so broad as the one quoted above. A more narrow example follows:

> "Whenever, as a result of any cause reasonably beyond Lessee's control, such as fire, flood, windstorm, or other act of God, decision, law, order, rule, or regulation of any local, State or Federal Government or Governmental Agency, or Court; or inability to secure men, material, or transportation, and Lessee is thereby prevented from complying with any express or implied obligations of this lease, Lessee shall not be liable for damages or forfeiture of this Lease, and Lessee's obligation shall be suspended so long as such cause persists, and Lessee shall have ninety (90) days after the cessation of such cause in which to resume performance of this Lease."

This language might not protect a lessee against loss of a lease for failure to begin drilling operations before the end of the primary term. Though its language identifies inability to obtain men and material as a force-majeure event, the clause does not expressly provide for extension of the lease without operations or production. The reference to suspension of expressed or implied covenants is not broad enough to protect the lessee, because an oil and gas lease imposes no obligation upon a lessee to obtain production on the premises; operations or production is a special limitation to the lease, rather than a covenant.

Perlman v. Pioneer Limited Partnership, 918 F.2d 1244 (5th Cir.Tex.1990), illustrates the strictness with which courts are likely to interpret force-majeure clauses. Perlman obligated himself to spend $1,500,000 exploring lands in Wyoming and Montana or to pay the difference. Subsequently, the state shut in another of Perlman's operations in Wyoming because it produced too much water. Perlman then refused to perform his contract with Pioneer, asserting the force-majeure clause of the lease as a defense. The Fifth Circuit Court of Appeals rejected the defense in part because the government regulation that Perlman claimed constituted force majeure presented no actual hindrance to his operations on the Pioneer property; he failed to prove the causation element.

4. SHUT–IN ROYALTY CLAUSES

The problem of delay between completion and production presented to the court in *Sword v. Rains,* discussed above in conjunction with operations clauses, is a recurring problem. It is common for a well to be completed and ready for production but shut in waiting for a market. The majority rule is that a lease terminates at the end of the primary term or any time thereafter that production ceases, even though there is a capability of production; actual production and marketing are required to maintain a lease in a majority of states.

For this reason, most modern oil and gas leases contain a shut-in royalty clause providing that the lease will be maintained if a well capable of producing is shut in. A shut-in royalty clause provides for constructive production, typically in the form of shut-in royalty payments. A common formulation follows:

"While there is a gas well or wells on the land covered by this Lease or acreage pooled therewith, whether it

be before or after the primary term hereof, and such
well or wells are shut in, and there is no other production, drilling operations or other operations being conducted capable of keeping this Lease in force under any
of its Provisions, Lessee shall pay as royalty to Lessor
(and if it be within the primary term hereof such
payment shall be in lieu of delay rentals) the sum of a
one dollar ($1) per year per net mineral acre, such
payment to be made to the depository bank hereinafter
named on or before the anniversary date of this Lease
next ensuing after the expiration of ninety (90) days
from the date such well or wells are shut-in, and
thereafter on the anniversary date of this Lease during
the period such wells are shut-in, and upon such payment it shall be considered that this Lease is maintained in full force and effect."

The effect of the shut-in royalty clause is to provide
for a substitute for production under the habendum
clause.

a. Effect of Failure to Pay

Failure to make a shut-in royalty payment properly is likely to result in termination of the lease, at
least in states that follow the majority rule that
"production" as that term is used in the habendum
clause requires actual production in paying quantities. In *Greer v. Salmon*, 479 P.2d 294 (N.M.1970),
the shut-in clause provided that "on gas, ... a
royalty of $50.00 per year on each gas well from
which gas only is produced while gas therefrom is
not sold ... and *while said royalty is so paid,* said
well shall be held to be a producing well." (Emphasis added). The lessee failed to make the payment,
and the New Mexico Supreme Court held that the

lease had terminated. The court ruled that the language of the shut-in clause made proper payment a condition of maintaining the lease. Texas has many cases to the same effect, including *Freeman v. Magnolia Pet. Co.,* 171 S.W.2d 339 (Tex. 1943).

The analysis of *Greer v. Salmon* and *Freeman v. Magnolia* is consistent with that suggested at the beginning of this chapter. The shut-in royalty clause is a lease provision for constructive production. If the lease is in its secondary term so that "production" is required by the habendum clause to maintain it, if there is no actual production and the state does not consider a shut-in well "producing," then the shut-in clause defines constructive production.

The precise terms of a shut-in royalty clause should determine whether a failure to pay causes lease termination in a state, like New Mexico or Texas, that defines term clause "production" as actual production. When the shut-in royalty clause makes the proper payment of shut-in royalty the constructive production—as did the lease in *Greer v. Salmon* and as does the clause quoted at the beginning of this section—then, if the lessee does not make the shut-in payment, there is neither actual production nor constructive production to maintain the lease. When the shut-in royalty clause defines constructive production as the existence of a shut-in well on the premises, however, the lease should not terminate if the lessee does not make the shut-in payment, because constructive production is still present. For example, the following shut-in royalty language should preserve a lease even if the lessee does not make proper payment:

> "Where a well capable of producing gas is shut-in for lack of a market at the well, or of an available pipeline outlet in the field, or by reason of force majeure, this lease shall nonetheless be considered to be producing within the meaning of paragraph 2 above [the habendum clause], and the lessee shall be obligated to pay annually on the anniversary date thereafter shut-in royalties of $1.00 per net mineral acre covered by this lease."

States that define "production" under the habendum clause to mean a capability of production will likely take a more forgiving approach. In *Gard v. Kaiser*, 582 P.2d 1311 (Okl.1978), the Oklahoma Supreme Court indicated that it would find that a lease had terminated for failure to correctly pay shut-in royalties only if the lease clearly indicated that termination was the parties' intent. The court reasoned that since a capability of production in paying quantities is sufficient to maintain a lease as producing in Oklahoma, it was illogical that the parties intended that a failure to pay would cause termination.

Louisiana courts apparently will reach a similar result, but for a different reason. In *Acquisitions, Inc. v. Frontier Explorations, Inc.*, 432 So.2d 1095 (La.App.1983), a court of appeal reasoned that under the Louisiana Mineral Code a shut-in royalty is a "royalty," so that a court may not terminate a lease unless the lessor has given notice of the failure to pay to the lessee and allowed time for proper payment.

b. Scope of the Clause: Gas, or Oil and Gas

Shut-in royalty clauses are usually limited to gas. For example, the language quoted above applies only to "gas wells." Such a limitation results historically because it is not likely that an oil well will be shut in for lack of market. There are still some parts of the country in which the distances are so great and the terrain so rough that oil wells are shut in periodically, however. Furthermore, conservation commissions sometimes prohibit the flaring of natural gas when there is no available market, causing oil wells to be shut in until gas marketing or recycling can be arranged. Finally, the distinction between a "gas well" and an oil well or an oil and gas well is unclear. Shut-in royalty clauses should be drafted to apply to both oil and gas.

c. Problems of Interpretation and Administration

(1) What Is a "Shut–In" Well

Can a lessee use the shut-in clause to maintain a lease upon which drilling operations have discovered gas if operations are not finished, or must a well be completed and capable of production in paying quantities before a lessee can claim the clause's protection? Courts have consistently recognized that the shut-in royalty clause's major purpose is to substitute payment of the shut-in royalty for actual production when there is no market. It follows that a lessee may not maintain a lease by the terms of the shut-in royalty clause unless there is a well on the lease, or on land pooled with the lease, capable of producing in paying quantities. This rule may be criticized, however, because some geologic formations may be damaged if wells are completed and shut in; the accepted practice is not to complete wells drilled to such formations until actual production is imminent. A lessee should not have to act imprudently to comply with the shut-in royalty clause.

(2) When Is a Well "Shut–In"?

Freeman v. Magnolia Petroleum Co. held that when a shut-in royalty clause does not specify the time that the shut-in payment is due, payment is due before the well is shut-in. Many clauses provide a grace period after shut-in for the payment; for example, the clause quoted at the beginning of this discussion specifies that payment is due "ninety (90) days from the date such well or wells are shut-in." In either circumstance, the time that a well becomes "shut-in" is important. When a well is actually producing, it is shut-in when the control valves at the wellhead are turned to stop production. If a well has never produced, however, it is uncertain when shut-in occurs. The earliest likely date, and the conservative choice for lease administrators, is the date at which testing of the well first suggested that production in paying quantities would be possible.

(3) Shut–In for Reasons Other Than Lack of Market

The question frequently arises whether a shut-in royalty clause can be used to maintain a lease from which there is no production for reasons other than lack of a market. For example, assume that current gas prices are below the replacement cost of the well's reserves. May a lessee maintain the lease by shut-in payments while waiting for prices to rise? Some shut-in royalty clauses are specifically limited to lack of a market. If the clause's language does not limit its use—by referring to lack of market or pipeline connections, for example—the clause should be held to apply whatever the cause of the shut-in so long as the lessee acts for a good-faith business purpose. In *Tucker v. Hugoton Energy Corp.*, 855 P.2d 929 (Kan.1993), however, the court held that a shut-in royalty clause may be relied upon to provide constructive production to hold a lease *only* when no market exists for the gas produced. The court concluded that the clause could not be invoked where a market, even though it was a market at a low price, was available for the gas.

(4) How Long May Payments Be Made

The length of time for which shut-in royalty payments may be substituted for production is a common problem. The underlying issue is whether a provision for shut-in royalty payments relieves the lessee from the implied obligation to market within a reasonable time. It probably does not. Chapter 11 discusses this issue in conjunction with the implied covenant to market.

5. CESSATION–OF–PRODUCTION CLAUSES

a. Temporary–Cessation-of-Production Doctrine

Inevitably, oil and gas wells stop producing from time to time. Equipment must be repaired or replaced. Chemical reactions in the wellbore may require that the well be "reworked." Few oil or gas wells produce constantly over their lives.

A temporary cessation of production will not cause a lease to terminate, despite the literal provisions of the habendum clause that the lease extends only so long as there is "production." Because of the obvious inequity of termination for a temporary stoppage, courts have looked to the facts to determine whether cessation is "temporary" or "permanent." When a lessee moves diligently and promptly to reestablish production or where circumstances excuse inaction, loss of production for substantial periods of time may be termed temporary. For example, in *Saulsberry v. Siegel*, 252 S.W.2d 834 (Ark.1952), the Arkansas Supreme Court held that a cessation of production for more than four years as the result of a fire at the well was temporary.

The distinction between temporary cessation and permanent cessation of production is a question of fact. The courts consider three factors. First, the duration of cessation is clearly important. The longer the period, the more likely it is that a cessation will be considered permanent. *Saulsberry v. Siegel* probably sets the outer limits of a temporary cessation. Second, the cause of the cessation is relevant. When cessation results from circumstances beyond the lessee's control, for example, a long cessation is more likely to be considered temporary than when the lessee could have kept the well producing with diligent actions. Third, courts take into account a lessee's efforts to restore production. If a lessee is slow to act, the cessation is likely to be treated as permanent. All of these factors were considered in *Wagner v. Smith*, 456 N.E.2d 523 (Ohio App.1982), where a court held a lease that had failed to produce for three years because of water in the borehole had permanently ceased to produce.

b. Lease Provisions

Many oil and gas leases contain provisions intended to give lessees more certainty than is given by the temporary-cessation-of-production doctrine. Usually, such provisions take the form of a cessation-of-production clause, a provision in the lease that states that the lease will be maintained so long as production does not cease for more than an agreed period of time, usually sixty to ninety days. Paragraph 6 of the Texas lease in the Appendix contains a common cessation-of-production formulation combined with a dry hole clause:

"6. If prior to discovery of oil, gas, or other hydrocarbons on this land, or on acreage pooled therewith ... production ... should cease from any cause, this Lease shall not terminate if Lessee commences additional drilling or reworking operations within sixty (60) days thereafter, or if it be within the primary term, commences or resumes payment or tender of rentals or commences operations for drilling or reworking on or before the rental paying date next ensuing after the operation of sixty (60) days from the date of ... cessation of production."

So long as more than sixty days does not elapse without operations on the property, the lease will not terminate even though there is no production. This language replaces the "reasonableness" standard of the temporary-cessation-of-production doctrine with the certainty of a definite time. Some courts have held that the clause completely replaces the doctrine. Thus, in *Samano v. Sun Oil Co.*, 621 S.W.2d 580 (Tex.1981), the court held that a lease that contained a 60–day cessation-of-production clause terminated where there were no operations for 73 days after production ceased.

B. ADMINISTRATIVE CLAUSES

Another group of savings clauses in lease forms is intended to liberalize the legal rules that define the relationship between the lessor and lessee. Lessees *could* function without such provisions, but including them simplifies administration and helps avoid problems arising from strict lease interpretation.

1. PAYMENT OF DELAY RENTALS

Most modern oil and gas leases contain provisions relating to payment of delay rentals that make it easier for a lessee to comply with the drilling-delay rental clause. Such provisions include nominating a bank as the lessor's agent to accept payment, providing that payment is made when mailed, and providing that a lessee may pay by check. These provisions are noted in the discussion of the drilling-delay rental clause in Chapter 8.

2.   WARRANTY CLAUSES

In several states, a mineral lessor impliedly warrants the right to quiet enjoyment of the interest leased unless warranty is expressly excluded or limited. In Texas and some other states, covenants of title may be implied from the use of such words as "grant" or "convey" in the granting clause. But most oil and gas leases contain a specific covenant of title from the lessor to the lessee. Paragraph 10 of the Texas lease in the Appendix contains a typical lease warranty: "Lessor hereby warrants and agrees to defend the title to said lands...."

The language quoted creates only a *covenant of warranty*, a promise to defend the lessee against future lawful claims and demands. There is no breach until the lessee is physically or constructively ousted from the property. A lessor does not extend the present covenants of seisin, right to convey, and no encumbrances because they would expose the lessor to liability for the grant of the lease, itself; an oil and gas lease is ordinarily completed so that a lessor grants 100% of the mineral interest even if the lessor owns only a fractional interest, and existing easements and mortgages are not usually excepted from the warranty. Some courts, however, have treated the warranty clause of an oil and gas lease as creating full general warranties.

A warranty clause permits a lessee to recover damages from the lessor for a failure of title. In most states, the limit of a lessor's liability will be the lessee's actual damages up to the amount of the compensation the lessor has received under the lease plus interest. A warranty clause in a lease also protects a lessee by making available the after-acquired-title doctrine; if the lessor subsequently acquires an additional interest in the leased land, that interest will automatically become subject to the lease.

The practice of completing lease forms as if the lessor owns 100% of the minerals, discussed in Chapter 8 in connection with the granting clause, places a lessor in jeopardy of a breach of warranty; technically, if O grants a lease on Blackacre, in which O owns 50% of the mineral rights, without limiting the grant to the 50% O owns or excepting 50% of the minerals from the warranty, and thereafter O's lessee takes a lease from X, the owner of the other 50%, the necessity for the second lease is an ouster of the lessee and a breach of O's warranty. The issue rarely arises, however, because lessees' customarily pay a bonus only for the fractional interest owned and do not expect to obtain full rights. In view of the industry practice, a claim for breach of warranty is not within the intention of the parties. The reasoning of *McMahon v. Christmann*, 303 S.W.2d 341 (Tex.1957), discussed in

Chapter 7, refusing to apply the *Duhig* rule to leases, supports this conclusion.

Lessors frequently strike warranty provisions from oil and gas leases or disclaim them in addenda. These practices result from increased competition for leases. At one time, most oil and gas leases were taken after only a cursory review of title. Rapidly rising lease bonuses led to more careful title searches before leases are taken, which has made the warranty clause less essential. Moreover, many lessees have felt that suits against lessors for title defects (unless the defects were directly caused by the lessors) are an unproductive business practice.

3.   LESSER–INTEREST CLAUSE

Drafters added the lesser-interest clause (sometimes called the proportionate-reduction clause) to oil and gas leases to protect the lessee against the possibility of being required to pay twice for the same mineral interest. The provision in the Texas lease form in the Appendix is in paragraph 10:

"[I]t is agreed that if Lessor owns an interest in the oil, gas, or other hydrocarbons in or under said land less than the entire fee simple estate, then the royalties and rentals to be paid Lessor shall be reduced proportionately."

The effect of the lesser-interest clause is to permit a lessee to reduce lease benefits to the lessor to the extent that the lessor owns less than the full mineral interest described in the lease. The lesser-interest clause has also been applied to reduce lease benefits to the lessor by the amount of outstanding nonparticipating royalty interests.

The warranty clause and the lesser-interest clause are mutually supporting. The warranty clause authorizes the lessee to sue the lessor for breach of warranty of title. The lesser-interest clause authorizes the lessee to proportionately reduce future lease benefits to the extent that the lessor's title fails.

The lesser-interest clause must be carefully applied. In *Texas Co. v. Parks*, 247 S.W.2d 179 (Tex. Civ.App.1952), a court held that a lessee's failure to apply literally a clause identical to the one quoted above caused the lease to terminate. The lease described the land covered as an "undivided one-half interest" in a described tract, probably because the lessors were concerned about the risk of breaching the lease's warranty if they purported to convey more than they owned. Texas Co. applied the lesser-interest clause to delay rental payments. The court held that the lease terminated for failure ato pay delay rentals properly because the reference in the lesser interest clause to "said land" referred back to the half interest described in the granting clause.

4. SUBROGATION CLAUSE

A lease subrogation clause empowers a lessee to protect its interest by paying taxes or mortgages encumbering the property and then stepping into the shoes of the former creditors. The subrogation clause is combined with the warranty clause and lesser interest clause in paragraph 10 of the Texas lease in the Appendix:

> "Lessor ... agrees also that Lessee at its option may discharge any tax, mortgage or other liens upon said land either in whole or in part, and in the event Lessee does so it shall be subrogated to such lien with the right to enforce same and apply rentals and royalties accruing hereunder towards satisfying same."

This language is overly broad, since it literally would give a lessee the power of subrogation even though liens on the property were not in default. Some lessors limit it to encumbrances "that are now or hereafter in default." Oil and gas lessees are not usually interested in acquiring security interests in real property, however, and there is a possibility that a court would limit the lessee's discretion under the clause by taking into account the purpose of the parties in including it.

5. EQUIPMENT–REMOVAL PROVISIONS

Most modern oil and gas leases contain a clause permitting removal of equipment and fixtures after the expiration of the lease. Paragraph 7 of the Texas lease in the Appendix provides that "Lessee shall have the right at any time during or after the expiration of this lease to remove all property and fixtures placed on the premises by Lessee, including the right to draw and remove all casing." The purpose is to give the lessee the broadest possible discretion to determine when to plug and abandon wells and to protect against a finding that the lessee has abandoned equipment left on a lease.

The courts have generally permitted lessees to recover equipment left on leases after termination even without authorizing lease language. Moreover, equipment-removal provisions have been restrictively interpreted. The weight of authority will not interpret such a clause to permit plugging and abandoning a well capable of commercial production. Likewise, despite the clause's reference to "at anytime," the lessee must recover its property from the premises within a reasonable time after lease termination.

6. NOTICE–OF–ASSIGNMENT CLAUSE

As Chapter 8 discusses in connection with the drilling-delay rental clause, most leases contain notice-of-assignment provisions to protect the lessee against the possibility that it will be held to have had constructive notice of an assignment by the lessor and thus be required to check the public records before making delay rental or other payments. The effect of such a clause is to permit a lessee to rely upon the identity of the lessor designated in the lease until the lessee is provided with proof that ownership rights have changed.

7. NO–INCREASE–OF–BURDEN PROVISIONS

Modern oil and gas leases contain provisions to obviate the possibility that an assignment by a lessor may increase the burden of the lessee's duties under the lease. For example, when the lessor subdivides leased property, is a lessee obligated to provide separate measuring devices and receiving tanks for the production? Paragraph 8 of the Texas lease in the Appendix contains language to negate this possibility:

> "No change or division in the ownership of the land, rentals or royalties, however accomplished, shall operate to enlarge the obligations, or diminish the rights of Lessee...."

8. SEPARATE–OWNERSHIP CLAUSE

Closely related to the no-increase-of-burden provision in an oil and gas lease is the separate-ownership clause, which addresses problems that arise when a lessee makes an assignment. When a lessee assigns the lease interest covering a separate portion of the tract leased, failures of the assignee may cause the lessee to lose the whole lease. Paragraph 8 of the Texas lease in the Appendix contains a typical provision attempting to change that result:

> "In the event of an assignment hereof in whole or in part, liability for breach of any obligation issued hereunder shall rest exclusively upon the owner of this Lease, or portion thereof, who commits such breach."

Whether the quoted language would save a lease from termination if a partial assignee failed to pay rentals is problematic; payment of rentals under the Texas lease in the Appendix is a special limitation, not an obligation.

9. SURRENDER CLAUSE

Another problem that occurs where leased property is divided arises when a lease covers a large tract of land, but geological or geophysical evidence indicates that only a portion is potentially valuable. In that circumstance, a lessee may wish to surrender the lease to the extent that it covers land thought to be unproductive. General real property principles will not give the lessee that right; the lease is a whole and cannot be severed at the lessee's whim. Modern oil and gas leases modify the general rule by specific provision such as that found in the last sentence of paragraph 5 of the Texas lease in the Appendix:

> "Lessee may at any time or times execute and deliver to lessor or to depository above named, or place of record a release covering any portion or portions and be relieved of all obligations as to the acreage surrendered, and thereafter the rentals payable hereunder shall be reduced in the proportion that the acreage covered hereby is reduced by said release or releases."

10. NOTICE–AND–DEMAND, NOTICE–BE-FORE–FORFEITURE, AND JUDICIAL–ASCERTAINMENT CLAUSES

Many modern oil and gas leases contain clauses drafted to protect a lessee against lawsuits by requiring the lessor to give the lessee notice of alleged breaches and an opportunity to correct them. A broad version of such language may be called a *notice-and-demand* clause:

"In the event lessor considers that lessee has not complied with all its obligations hereunder, both express and implied, lessor shall notify lessee in writing, setting out specifically in what respects lessee has breached this contract. Lessee shall then have sixty (60) days after receipt of said notice within which to meet or to commence to meet all or any part of the breaches alleged by lessor. The service of said notice shall be precedent to the bringing of any action by lessor on said lease for any cause, and no such action shall be brought until the lapse of sixty (60) days after service of such notice on lessee."

In *Texas Oil & Gas Corporation v. Vela*, 429 S.W.2d 866 (Tex.1968), the court gave limited effect to such language. It reasoned that the reason for providing in a lease that a lessor must give the lessee notice before suing is to protect the lessee against a forfeiture for breach of an implied or express obligation, so that a lessor's failure to give notice may be grounds for abating a suit, but does not bar a lessor from pursuing his or her rights.

A variation may be called a *notice-before-forfeiture* clause. Typical language is found in the first sentence of paragraph 9 of the Texas lease in the Appendix:

"The breach by Lessee of any obligations arising hereunder shall not work a forfeiture or termination of this Lease nor cause a termination or reversion of the estate created hereby nor be grounds for cancellation hereof in whole or in part unless Lessor shall notify Lessee in writing of the facts relied upon in claiming a breach hereof, and Lessee, if in default, shall have sixty (60) days after receipt of such notice in which to commence the compliance with the obligations imposed by virtue of this instrument. . . ."

Judicial-ascertainment clauses are closely related to notice-before-forfeiture clauses, but they give even more protection to lessees. Typically, judicial-ascertainment clauses provide that the lease may not be forfeited or declared terminated until the lessor has proved the alleged breach in court and then, after judgment, the lessee has been given a reasonable time to comply. Most lessors' attorneys will reject judicial-ascertainment provisions in leases they review, and some courts have held them unenforceable as a matter of public policy, since they would deprive the courts of their powers.

CHAPTER 10

THE LEASE ROYALTY CLAUSE

The royalty clause is the main provision in an oil and gas lease for compensation for the lessor. A lessor typically receives a *bonus* payment for granting a lease. During the primary term of a lease, the lessor may receive periodic payments of delay rentals. If production is obtained, the lessor receives *royalty*, usually stated as a percentage of production, or the value, or proceeds of its sale, free of the costs of production.

Stating royalty as a percentage of production, or value, or proceeds of its sale, is a hedge against uncertainty. Both the existence and the quantity of oil and gas that may be produced from a lease are uncertain until someone drills a well on the lease. If there is no production, the percentage royalty is worthless; if there is prolific production, the percentage royalty will be extremely valuable. A percentage royalty balances the interests of the lessor and lessee against the inherent risks of exploration.

Until the 1970s, the "standard" lease royalty in the United States was 1/8, except in California where it was generally 1/6. One still sees 1/8 royalty percentages in "wildcat" leasing and marginal production areas, but 1/6, 3/16, or 1/5 are more common. Lessors and lessees negotiate royalty amounts up to 40% where there is potential for prolific production or competition is intense.

A. COMMON LEASE ROYALTY PROVISIONS

The lease royalty usually is a fixed percentage, but it need not be. Leases sometimes contain sliding-scale royalties, increasing the royalty percentage if production is at high levels. Other leases include provisions for an increase of the royalty percentage after the lessee has recovered its costs or provisions for stated minimum royalties. The economic rationale of all royalty clauses, however, is that the lessor's compensation after production is obtained should vary with the amount of production.

A common formulation is the language of the Texas lease in the Appendix:

> "The royalties to be paid by Lessee are as follows: On oil, one-eighth of that produced and saved from said land, the same to be delivered at the wells or to the credit of Lessor into the pipe line to which the wells may be connected. Lessee shall have the option to purchase any royalty oil in its possession, paying the market price therefore prevailing for the field where produced on the date of purchase. On gas, including casinghead gas, condensate or other gaseous substances, produced from said land and sold or used off the premises ... the market value at the well of one-eighth of the gas so sold or used, provided that on gas sold at the wells the royalty shall be one-eighth of the amount realized from such sale."

The provisions for oil royalty assume that the lessor will be paid royalty *in kind*, while the provisions for gas royalty assume that the lessee will dispose of production and then compensate the lessor *in cash* with a percentage of value or the proceeds of the sale. The difference in structure reflects both the physical and economic differences between oil and gas. It is generally feasible to store oil on the leased premises and sell it periodically. It is generally not practicable, however, to store natural gas at the well. Furthermore, no matter who is the purchaser or what is the length of the contract, the general rule is that the more gas one is able to commit to a contract, the better price one is able to obtain (or in a time of gas surplus, the more likely one is to obtain a purchaser). Therefore, gas royalty provisions in oil and gas leases commonly provide that the lessor will receive royalty in cash rather than in kind because that is to the benefit of both lessee and lessor.

B. NATURE OF THE LESSOR'S ROYALTY INTEREST

Except in a few states, including Louisiana, the lessor's royalty interest under a lease is classified as an interest in real property. After they are taken from the ground, however, both oil and gas are personal property. Therefore the lessor's rights may be different if the lessor has the right to take production in kind rather than a right to a share of value of production or the price for which it is sold.

When a lessor has a right to a percentage of production as royalty, an in-kind royalty, the royalty right is a reservation from the lease grant, so that the lessor retains title to the royalty share of oil or gas as it is produced. In contrast, when a lease merely gives a lessor the right to a share of value or proceeds, the lessor's interest is a contract right against the lessee. Important economic realities may turn upon the distinction. For example, if the lessee's creditors attach a tank load of oil with a judgment lien, the attachment may not affect the lessor's royalty share of that oil because the lessor typically retains title to oil as it is produced. Attachment of the lessee's checking account before it disburses gas royalty to a lessor, however, likely will leave the lessor with merely a contract claim against the lessee. Many states have legislation intended to make those entitled to royalty, whether in kind or in cash, secured creditors under the Uniform Commercial Code.

C. ROYALTY DISPUTES

A key to understanding royalty disputes is to note that a lessor's royalty is due at the well (where the product of development is captured) while oil and gas—particularly gas—are often sold "downstream" from the well. Where royalty is due to the lessor in kind in the field, as is generally the oil royalty, or where a lessee sells to an unrelated third party at the well, there are relatively few disputes. Where royalty is in cash and must be calculated based upon a hypothetical "market value" or by working back from the proceeds of a downstream sale price, however, disputes between lessors and lessees are almost inevitable. The restructuring of the market-place that occurred when oil and gas markets were deregulated in the 1980s exacerbated the situation, because it resulted in the development of market centers or "hubs" that may be many miles away from the place that production occurs.

How courts approach royalty disputes depends in large part upon how they view the royalty clause language.

D. THE MARKET VALUE/PROCEEDS PROBLEM

The market value/proceeds royalty problem was one of the most widely-litigated disputes of the oil and gas industry in the 1970s and early 1980s. The issue was whether "market value" could be greater than a lessee's proceeds received under a long-term contract. Courts in several states held that common royalty-clause language entitled lessors to royalties on natural gas calculated on its market value at the well when produced, although that price was substantially more than the price for which the gas was actually sold. Falling gas prices in the latter half of the 1980s quieted the dispute.

1. THE BASIS OF THE MARKET
VALUE/PROCEEDS DISPUTE

The market value/proceeds controversy arose from attempts by lease drafters to make clear the right to deduct costs of compression, transportation and processing in calculating royalty where production is sold away from the lease. The best way to understand the issue is to consider the language that has caused the problem:

> "The royalties to be paid by lessee are as follows: . . . *on gas* . . . produced . . . and *sold or used off the premises* . . . the *market value at the well* of one-eighth of the gas so sold or used, provided that *on gas sold at the wells* the royalty shall be one-eighth of the *amount realized* from such sale." (Emphasis added.)

The language refers to two methods of calculating gas royalty, which led to disputes over the meaning of the alternative references.

The drafters' intent probably was that when gas is sold at the wellhead the lessor should receive royalty calculated on the lessee's proceeds received under the terms of its gas sales contract. When gas is not sold at the well, however, either because there is no market for gas at the well or because there is a better market elsewhere, the drafters' intended that the lessee should have the right to deduct the lessor's proportionate share of additional costs involved to "work back" to the value of the gas at the wellhead. "Market value at the well" of natural gas then would be the amount the lessee realized from the sale of the gas less the lessor's share of the costs of moving the gas and marketing it, such as the costs of transportation, dehydration, compression, and cleaning and processing. When new long-term contract prices escalated faster than the price-adjustment provisions of old contracts, however, as occurred during the energy shortages of the 1970s and early 1980s, the stage was set for litigation.

2.   DIVISION OF THE CASES

Courts in several states interpreted language like that quoted with a twist that lease drafters had not expected. They held that the plain meaning of "market value" or "market price" imposed an obligation on the lessee to pay royalties based upon the market value of natural gas produced, less costs subsequent to production, rather than upon the amount realized less costs subsequent to production. Since both the economics of the gas industry until the early 1980s and the federal regulatory scheme required that gas be sold under long-term contracts, gas often was sold under "old" contracts at prices substantially less than the current market value at the time of production and sale. Therefore, the market-value royalty decisions exposed the industry to potential liabilities of billions of dollars.

The Texas Supreme Court's decision in *Exxon Corp. v. Middleton*, 613 S.W.2d 240 (Tex.1981), is a good example of the reasoning of these courts. In that case, Exxon and Sun Oil Company gathered natural gas from leases in the Anahuac field near Houston, processed the natural gas at a cleaning plant located in the field, and then sold the gas "at the tailgate" of the plant under a long-term contract. The contract price for the gas was approximately 52 cents per MCF. The market price for new deliveries of gas in the area when the case came to trial was more than $2.00 per MCF. The royalty clause of the Middletons' lease was similar to the one quoted above. The lessors contended that because the natural gas was sold off the leased premises they were entitled to royalties on the market price, rather than the contract price. Reasoning that the plain language must be given effect, the Texas Supreme Court sustained the position of the landowners.

Courts in Oklahoma, Louisiana, and Arkansas rejected this analysis. A leading case in this line of reasoning is *Tara Petroleum Corp. v. Hughey,* 630 P.2d 1269 (Okl.1981), where the Oklahoma Supreme Court held a royalty clause providing for royalties based upon "market price at the well" was "freighted with inherent ambiguity when it is remembered that gas must be sold by long term contracts in which buyers have been able to obtain schedules of prices almost certain to get out of line with contemporary contracts. . . ." The court reasoned that since the implied covenant to market imposed upon lessees the "necessity" of contracting at the market price available, an arms-length long-term contract established market value.

A Louisiana case, *Henry v. Ballard & Cordell Corp.,* 418 So.2d 1334 (La.1982), also treated "market value" as ambiguous. The Louisiana Supreme

Court rejected the "plain terms" cases because they gave "practical and economic necessities ... little or no consideration." That court resolved the ambiguity by embracing Professor Thomas A. Harrell's characterization of an oil and gas lease as a "cooperative venture" between a lessor and lessee that gives rise to a lessee's implied obligation to market. On this basis, it concluded that lease parties typically intend that lessors will receive royalty based on the lessee's contract price.

The market value/proceeds issue was never determined in many states. In addition, important subsidiary issues have never been fully resolved in the states where the market value at the well of natural gas sold can be greater than the price for which it is sold. Among these issues are when the market value royalty is due and how market value is to be determined.

3. WHEN MARKET VALUE ROYALTY IS DUE

Many royalty clauses, like the one quoted from the Texas lease at the beginning of this section, give a lessor the right to market value royalty only when gas is sold "off the premises." When gas is sold "at the wells," they award royalty on the amount realized. The meaning of "off the premises" and "at the wells" is thus thrown into issue. In *Exxon v. Middleton*, the Texas Supreme Court held that the terms referred to the point at which title passed. When gas is sold outside the leased premises, market value is the royalty measure. When the sale takes place on the leased premises, royalty is due on proceeds. This interpretation makes it possible for a lessee to avoid the market value problem by structuring the gas contract so that title passes on the lease.

In contrast, the court in *Piney Woods Country Life School v. Shell Oil Co.*, 726 F.2d 225 (5th Cir.Miss.1984), held that "at the well" refers to quality as well as location. The court said that gas is sold "at the well" when "the price paid is consideration for the gas produced but not for processing or transportation." When the sale price reflects value added by transportation or processing, however, the sale takes place "off the premises" regardless of the point at which title passes. The Fifth Circuit reasoned that "to interpret the leases otherwise would place the lessors at the mercy of the lessee."

A related issue is whether a lessor who is entitled to a market value royalty when the market value is higher than the amount realized by his lessee must accept a market value royalty when market value falls below the price set by the lessee's contract. *Yzaguirre v. KCS Resources, Inc.*, 53 S.W.3d 368 (Tex.2001), held that "market value" must be given its plain meaning, whether it is higher or lower than contract price.

4. HOW TO DETERMINE MARKET VALUE

When the market value of gas at the well is not limited by the amount realized from sale, market value or market price cannot be determined by "working back" from the contract price. Therefore, the courts must address how to determine market value at the well. The Fifth Circuit in *Piney Woods Country Life School v. Shell Oil Co.* stated a pragmatic approach: "Market value is a question of fact.... [T]he point is to determine the price a reasonable buyer would have paid ... at the well when produced." In *Texas Oil and Gas Corp. v. Vela*, 429 S.W.2d 866 (Tex.1968), the first of the market value royalty cases, the Texas Supreme Court held that the market value of gas was to be established by reference to comparable sales, "sales of gas comparable in time, quality, and availability to marketing outlets." If there are no comparable sales, market value or market price is determined by "working back" from downstream sales to the wellhead value.

The hierarchy of royalty-valuation methods is intuitive. "Value" is what a willing buyer and willing seller would agree upon under the circumstances. Where gas is actually sold at the wellhead as it is produced in a transaction negotiated at the time of sale, all elements of the definition and the transaction are in congruity unless the sale is not at arms length or the parties act unreasonably; thus, an actual sale at the wellhead is the best evidence of value. Comparable sales are strong evidence of value because comparable sales illustrate an available market at or near the well. But the circumstances of comparable sales will never be exactly the same as the circumstances at the wellhead. The workback method is still harder to use accurately because it begins further from the wellhead; there are likely to be more variables to take into account.

The "comparable sales" standard too may be difficult to apply. There have been disputes over what period of time and from what area contracts should be considered as "comparable." Generally these issues have been treated as questions of fact within the discretion of the trial judge. Thus, in *Exxon v. Middleton,* the court considered evidence drawn from more than 30,000 gas contracts covering natural gas sold over a substantial portion of the Texas Gulf Coast. It accepted expert testimony that the quarterly average of the three highest prices for gas sold in that area was the market value of the gas at the well. Another issue, during the time that gas prices at the wellhead were federally regulated, was whether a court could consider sales of gas of one regulatory classification in determining the market value of gas in another regulatory classification. The Texas courts held that whether quality is comparable requires consideration of the legal characteristics of gas, but the Kansas courts held that federal price-regulation limits are no obstacle to "market value." A third issue has been whether a judge or jury can consider an existing long-term contract in determining current market value. When *Piney Woods* was retried, the district court held that the royalty owners had failed to establish that the market value of the gas in question was at any time greater than the amount that Shell received under its sales contract and determined value by working back from Shell's contract price. The court of appeals held that reliance on the contract price was "within its discretion" in *Piney Woods Country Life School v. Shell Oil Co.*, 905 F.2d 840 (5th Cir.Miss.1990). When the relevance of a long-term contract to current market value was challenged in *Yzaguirre v. KCS Resources, Inc.*, 53 S.W.3d 368 (Tex.2001), however, the court said: "The gas was not free and available for sale, and its price was negotiated in 1979, not contemporaneously with the deliveries. Under these circumstances, the GPA [Gas Purchase Agreement] price is not evidence of market value, and the trial judge properly excluded it."

E.   WHAT IS THE "AMOUNT REALIZED"?

"Amount realized" royalty provisions became the subject of similar analysis ten years after the market value/proceeds disputes in litigation over whether royalty should be paid on take-or-pay benefits. Take-or-pay provisions are generally associated with long-term gas sales contracts, and from the time that interstate pipelines were constructed in the 1930s until the mid–1980s, long-term contracts were the norm. A gas-contract take-or-pay clause obligates a purchaser to pay for a percentage of the gas that the producer can produce, whether or not the purchaser actually takes it. It may be very simply worded:

> "Subject to all the other provisions of this Contract, Seller agrees to sell and deliver and Pipeline agrees to purchase and receive, or pay for if made available hereunder but not taken, a daily contract quantity of gas ... equal to seventy-five percent (75%) of the maximum quantity of gas that Seller's wells can deliver to Pipeline."

The clause provides a producer with a guaranteed minimum cash flow in return for dedicating a gas supply to the purchaser; once a well's production is dedicated, a producer cannot sell it elsewhere even if the purchaser does not take the gas. To economists, take-or-pay clauses provide for a type of "demand charge," a charge for reserving an option to use. Producers have historically viewed take-or-pay clauses as a guarantee of a minimum cash flow and a protection against the risk that purchasers will "bank" contracted gas in the ground. When the federal government regulated gas prices at the wellhead, pipelines saw take-or-pay clauses as a non-price premium for gas commitment; they paid nothing so long as they took the gas they expected to need.

The supply shortages that caused rapidly-rising prices for natural gas in the 1970s led some pipelines to compete for additional supplies by offering to take or pay for high percentages of well delivery capacity. Take-or-pay percentages increased from as low as 25 percent of well delivery capacity in the early 1970s to as much as 90 percent at the height of the gas boom in the late 1970s. When gas demand in the United States declined sharply in the early 1980s, the gas boom became a litigation boom. The total potential liability of interstate and intrastate pipelines was probably in the range of sixty to seventy billion dollars, and settlement costs were probably in the range of twelve to fifteen billion dollars. The take-or-pay judgements and settlements between producers and pipelines then led to a wave of royalty litigation over whether the take-or-pay benefits were part of the "amount realized" by producers for the sale of gas.

Courts generally decided those disputes by applying the same analytical approaches that they had used in considering the meaning of "market value." One line of cases, including *Killam Oil Co. v. Bruni*, 806 S.W.2d 264 (Tex.App.1991) and *TransAmerican Natural Gas Corp. v. Finkelstein*, 933 S.W.2d 591 (Tex.App.1996), reasoned that "production" is the prerequisite for royalty, so take-or-pay benefits were not generally subject to royalty because they were in lieu of production. The premise of those cases was that the lease royalty clause expresses the "plain meaning" of the parties and "production" or "sale"—the terms usually found in the royalty clause—should be given their usual meaning, just as was "market value." This reasoning led to the conclusion that royalty was not due on take-or-pay payments or settlements, except to the extent that they related to gas actually produced.

Some decisions, such as *Harvey E. Yates Company v. Powell*, 98 F.3d 1222 (10th Cir.N.M.1996), made a distinction between payments associated with contract *buy outs* and *buy downs*. A payment to a lessee to settle a take-or-pay dispute by buying out and terminating the contract, would not be subject to royalty because the payment was not for "production." But a payment a lessee received for agreeing to lower the contract price or "take" requirements so that the contract could continue, would be subject to royalty; the payment would be amortized over the future production sold under the contract and royalty paid as production occurred.

Other cases, in Louisiana and Arkansas, however, held that royalty was due on take-or-pay benefits. *Frey v. Amoco Production Co.*, 603 So.2d 166 (La. 1992), reasoned that the lease royalty clause is but a statement of the general expectations of the parties. The court said that a lessor and a lessee are parties to a "cooperative venture," as it had previously determined in *Henry v. Ballard & Cordell Corp.*, 418 So.2d 1334 (La.1982), its decision that "market value" cannot exceed the long-term contract price. It concluded that if a lessee develops minerals successfully, the lessor should share proportionately in all the benefits that follow. Thus, if a lessee received take-or-pay payments or settled a claim for such payments for a lump sum, the lessor would be entitled to the royalty share.

A major difficulty with the cooperative-venture cases is determining how far the venture extends in the context of types of payments other than take-or-pay benefits. What about payments indirectly associated with the sale of production, such as *producer-demand charges*—monthly payments from purchasers to producers compensating the producers for committing to supply a stated amount of gas each month—or marketing fees or "supply bonuses." Or what about investment devices such as hedges, trades, and swaps of future production? It is unclear from the cases awarding royalty on take-or-pay benefits whether or not such receipts are a part of the "amount realized" from the sale of production.

F.   DEDUCTIONS IN CALCULATING ROYALTY

The sale of natural gas, in particular, may involve substantial costs after the gas comes out of the well. A lessee will often choose to transport gas produced away from the lease to a pipeline, to a market center, or even to an end user. In addition, natural gas often must be dehydrated, cleaned, processed, or compressed before it can be sold. These operations may be very expensive. They may also substantially increase the value of the natural gas.

Where a lease royalty clause calls for royalty *at the well*—whether the measure is value or proceeds—and the sales upon which the royalty is based are downstream from the lease, rather than in the field, both economic logic and fairness require that the downstream sales prices must be adjusted. Most courts have distinguished between *costs of production* and *costs subsequent to produc-*

tion. A lessee is obligated to pay all costs of production, but the lessor shares proportionately in costs subsequent to production since they are incurred after production and ordinarily increase the value of production.

While the basic principle that royalty is subject to costs subsequent to production is almost unanimously accepted, there are many disputes about what specific costs fall within that class. The legal issue is when "production" has occurred for purposes of calculating royalty. There are two general rules, each with variations from state-to-state.

1. THE CAPTURE–AND–HOLD RULE

The conventional analysis has been that "production" occurs for royalty-calculation purposes when oil or gas is captured and held—at the wellhead or on the lease. By this view, the costs of transporting, compressing, and processing or cleaning, as well as severance and gross-production taxes, are charged proportionately against the royalty interest where gas is sold or valued "downstream" from the lease.

Piney Woods Country Life School v. Shell Oil Co., 726 F.2d 225 (5th Cir.Miss.1984), is a classic statement of this analysis. Shell produced sour gas (containing hydrogen sulfide). To put the gas in marketable condition, Shell transported it away from the field to a processing plant, where it was treated to recover "sweet gas"—dry methane—and elemental sulfur. The court concluded that when royalty is to be calculated "at the well," a lessor is entitled to "royalty based on the value or price of unprocessed or untransported gas. On royalties 'at the well,' therefore, the lessors may be charged with processing costs, by which we mean all expenses, subsequent to production, relating to the processing, transportation, and marketing of gas and sulfur."

The rationale of the *Piney Woods* court was the lease language: "We emphasize, however, that processing costs are chargeable only because, under these leases, the royalties are based on value or price at the well." Other courts have relied on basic economic principles; the value of any commodity depends upon its proximity to market, and the value of oil or gas normally increases as it is moved closer to the place it is used. Thus, costs such as compression, transportation, and processing or cleaning tend to increase the value of the product and must be deducted from the downstream sales price or value to obtain an accurate valuation "at the well." Yet others have stated the result in equitable terms; to calculate royalty on a downstream price without deducting such costs would unjustly enrich a royalty owner whose royalty was due at the well.

2. THE MARKETABLE–PRODUCT RULE

But there is another view that has gained majority support in recent years. What has come to be called the *marketable-product rule*, adopted in somewhat different terms by courts in Oklahoma, Kansas, Colorado and West Virginia, as well as by the federal government by regulations, holds that "production" is not complete until a lessee has both captured and held the product, and made it marketable. What these cases have in common is their reliance upon the implied-covenant to market; their underlying premise is that the lessee has an implied duty to the lessor not only to seek a market for production, but to make production marketable.

One of the leading marketable-product cases is *Garman v. Conoco, Inc.*, 886 P.2d 652 (Colo.1994), a dispute over calculation of an overriding royalty. There, the Colorado Supreme Court held that "the relationship between the parties specifically provides for a 'free ride' on costs incurred to establish marketable production." The court based its decision on the implied covenant to market. There is an obligation upon the lessee as the party charged with lease development, it reasoned, to complete all operations necessary to market gas produced from the leasehold. Thus, costs "such as compressing, transporting and processing" required to transform raw gas into a marketable product, which the court defined as product "sufficiently free from impurities that it will be taken by a purchaser," may not be deducted as an expense in calculating royalty.

In fact, both rules present problems of application. An issue that courts in the marketable-product rule states have answered differently is what does it take for gas or oil to become a "marketable product"? In *Rogers v. Westerman Farm Company*, 29 P.3d 887 (Colo.2001), the Colorado Supreme Court held that gas was not a marketable product until it was both in a marketable physical condition and had been brought to a commercial marketplace. Under this test, a producer's transportation costs of moving gas to the first available market are part of the costs of producing and it is up to a jury to determine when that test has been satisfied. *Tawney v. Columbia Natural Resources, LLC*, 633 S.E.2d 22 (W.Va. 2006) reached a similar result. In contrast, the Kansas Supreme Court, in *Sternberger v. Marathon Oil Co.*, 894 P.2d 788 (Kan.1995) and the Oklahoma Supreme Court, in *Mittelstaedt v. Santa Fe Minerals, Inc.*, 954 P.2d 1203 (Okla.1998), adopted rules that a lessee must make production marketable in quality, but concluded that later costs to move gas to market were chargeable to both parties.

Another application problem is how specific the agreement of the parties must be to override the "default" rule? Will an express provision that royalty is due "at the well" permit a lessee to deduct compression, transportation, and processing or cleaning costs in a marketable-product jurisdiction? The Colorado Supreme Court rejected the idea that "at the well" permitted deduction of downstream costs in *Rogers v. Westerman Farm Company*, reasoning that "adopting the view that the 'at the well' language determines which costs are deductible from royalty payments fails to acknowledge that deductibility of costs is determined by whether gas is marketable...." The West Virginia Supreme Court of Appeals, in *Wellman v. Energy Resources, Inc.*, 557 S.E.2d 254 (W.Va.2001), suggested in dicta that it would permit a lessee whose royalty obligation was "at the well" to deduct transportation costs, but in *Tawney v. Columbia Natural Resources, LLC*, 633 S.E.2d 22 (W.Va. 2006), that court held that language such as "at the well," "at the wellhead," or "net all costs beyond the wellhead," or "less all taxes, assessments, and adjustments" is "ambiguous" and not sufficient to permit a lessee to deduct any portion of the costs incurred between the wellhead and the point of sale. The West Virgina court held that lease language intended to allocate between the lessor and lessee the costs of marketing the product and transporting it to the point of sale must expressly provide that the lessor shall bear some part of the costs incurred between the wellhead and the point of sale, identify with particularity the specific deductions the lessee intends to take from the lessor's royalty, and indicate the method of calculating the amount to be deducted from the royalty for such post-production costs.

Just how far the logic that "at the well" authorizes deduction of costs in calculating royalty might be taken is illustrated by *Heritage Resources, Inc. v. NationsBank*, 939 S.W.2d 118 (Tex.1996). *Heritage* involved a dispute over leases with royalty clauses that stated royalty as a percentage of "market value at the well," but which provided also in the same clause that "there shall be no deductions from the value of Lessor's royalty by reason of any required processing, cost of dehydration, compression, transportation, or any other matter to market such gas." Heritage sold gas off the premises and deducted the royalty owner's proportionate part of transportation costs in calculating the royalty due. Nationsbank objected, but conceded that the charges were reasonable and that the sales price of the gas "reflected its market value at the point of sale." A fractionalized Texas Supreme Court held 7–2 in two opinions that the deductions were appropriate because of the literal language of the royalty formulation: where the royalty owner receives "value at the well," downstream transportation costs are not a "deduction from the value" of the lessor's royalty.

As Chapter 11 discusses, the extremes of the dispute over the specificity required if one wishes to disclaim the default rule appear to rest upon the view each jurisdiction takes of whether implied covenants are implied in fact or in law.

Which costs are considered costs of production and which are treated as costs subsequent to production is of crucial importance to both the lessor and the lessee because the amounts of money in dispute may be enormous. The trend is for lease clauses to provide specifically. For example:

> "For gas (including casinghead gas) and all other substances covered hereby, the royalty shall be one-eighth (⅛) of the proceeds realized by lessee from sale thereof, *less a proportionate part of the costs incurred by lessee in delivering or otherwise making such gas or other substances merchantable . . . .*" (Emphasis added).

G. DIVISION ORDERS

An ongoing issue is the extent to which a division order may affect a lessee's royalty obligation. As Chapter 14 discusses, a *division order* is a statement executed by all parties who claim an interest in proceeds of production sales, stipulating how funds are to be distributed. Division orders protect purchasers of production and those who distribute proceeds by requiring those who are paid to warrant title to production transferred and indemnify those who make the payments.

In the market value royalty litigation, oil companies were generally unsuccessful in urging that division orders amended the conflicting terms of the royalty clause; courts like the Kansas Supreme Court in *Maddox v. Gulf Oil Corp.*, 567 P.2d 1326 (Kan.1977), held that division orders were not "true" contracts supported by consideration. Several courts also ruled that royalty owners need not sign division orders as a condition of receiving royalty payments; a lessor's royalty right is based on the underlying lease. Many jurisdictions have statutes barring enforcement of division-order terms that conflict with lease terms.

But other issues remain unresolved. One is the effect of division-order statutes, which are often obtusely drafted. The Texas statute, for example, provides that a division order "shall not change or relieve the lessee's specific, expressed or implied obligations under an oil and gas lease," but "may be used to clarify royalty settlement terms in the oil and gas lease."

Another issue is the effect of payments made by a lessee while a division order is in place. *Exxon Corp. v. Middleton*, 613 S.W.2d 240 (Tex.1981), held that division-order language that stated that the lessors would accept the amount realized by the lessee in settlement of royalty, rather than the market value provided by the royalty clause, barred the lessors from recovering market value royalties for periods before they revoked the division orders. Five years later, in *Gavenda v. Strata Energy, Inc.*, 705 S.W.2d 690 (Tex.1986), a dispute over a "one-half nonparticipating royalty interest" that Strata translated in a division order to a 1/16th nonparticipating royalty, the same court held that a lessee may not rely upon an erroneous division order where reliance would result in unjust enrichment. The court distinguished *Exxon v. Middleton*, on the dubious grounds that Exxon was not unjustly enriched by paying proceeds royalties rather than market value royalties. But then, in *Cabot Corporation v. Brown*, 754 S.W.2d 104 (Tex.1987), the court again held binding a division order that conflicted with an underlying lease provision, this time barring a lessor who signed a division order providing for royalties based upon interstate regulated prices from claiming settlement on higher intrastate prices.

The effect of division orders on oil royalties is also an unresolved issue. Oil royalty is usually due in kind, rather than in cash, so a lessor owns the royalty percentage of oil production as it is captured. Often, however, lessors sign division orders containing language of sale and calling for payment for the oil sold at the "posted price," a price the buyer sets to give notice of what it is willing to pay. In the mid–1990s, dozens of class actions claimed that big oil companies had breached their royalty obligations by failing to set posted prices at a fair market value. Most of those suits were settled. But *Shell Oil Co. v. HRN, Inc.*, 144 S.W.3d 429 (Tex. 2004), subsequently held that the Uniform Commercial Code's "good faith" requirement for unilaterally set prices imposes merely an objective duty to observe reasonable commercial standards, and not a subjective duty of honesty in fact, as well.

H. FAILURE TO PAY ROYALTIES

In general, a lessor's remedy against a lessee who fails to pay royalties is to sue for the royalty plus interest at the statutory rate. Courts are reticent to terminate or cancel a lease for nonpayment of royalty, for two reasons. One is the structure of the royalty clause. In contrast to the drilling-delay rental clause, the royalty clause is structured as a covenant from the lessee to the lessor; the usual remedy for a breach of promise is a suit for damages. Second, damages equal to the royalties due, plus interest, are adequate to make the lessor whole. On this basis, the Oklahoma Supreme Court in *Cannon v. Cassidy*, 542 P.2d 514 (Okl.1975), refused to cancel a lease although the lessee had failed to pay royalties for three months. The court reasoned that the lessors had a remedy at law (damages, plus interest) that would fully compensate them.

The general principle that courts will not terminate leases for nonpayment of royalties is limited by the inherent equitable power of the courts. The courts do not lack the power to terminate leases for nonpayment of royalties; they merely refrain from exercising it. If, for example, a lessee knowingly withheld lessors' royalties for speculative purposes, a court might properly decide to exercise its power.

The courts' power to cancel leases for nonpayment of royalties is explicit by statute in North Dakota and Louisiana. A North Dakota statute specifically authorizes a court to determine "that the equities of the case require cancellation" if royalties are not paid or are improperly paid. In Louisiana, prior to the 1975 Mineral Code, cancellation of leases for nonpayment of royalties was common where an appreciable period of time had passed without payment of royalties and no justification for the delay was shown. The Louisiana Mineral Code (Articles 137–142) limits the availability of cancellation to situations where the lessor has been defrauded or where the court finds cancellation necessary to do equity. It also seeks to provide a meaningful remedy for the lessor short of cancellation, prescribing damages of double the amount due plus attorneys' fees.

Courts may also cancel leases for a lessee's failure to pay royalties when the lessor and the lessee have specifically agreed upon that remedy in the lease. Occasionally, oil and gas leases negotiated by lessors with strong bargaining power will contain cancellation clauses. Such clauses will be strictly construed—equity abhors a forfeiture—but they will be enforced. In *Hitzelberger v. Samedan Oil Corp.*, 948 S.W.2d 497 (Tex.App.1997), for example, the court held that a lessee's failure to pay a timely royalty caused a lease to terminate where the lease habendum clause provided for a three-year primary term and a secondary term for "as long thereafter as oil and gas, or either of them, is produced in paying quantities from said land or lands with which said land is pooled hereunder *and the royalties are paid as provided.*" (Emphasis added.)

The pressure for lease cancellation has been alleviated to some degree by the adoption in many states of statutes calling for lessees to pay interest on overdue royalty payments and by the willingness of courts to act to assess interest even in the absence of specific statutes.

CHAPTER 11

IMPLIED COVENANTS IN OIL AND GAS LEASES

Modern oil and gas leases usually are drafted and prepared by lessees to protect their interests; printed-form leases generally are industry oriented. Often, however, courts hold that lessees are bound by implied terms in addition to those that are written in the leases. *Implied covenants* in oil and gas leases are unwritten promises that generally impose burdens on lessees and protect lessors. This chapter examines the basis and application of common implied covenants.

A. THE BASIS OF IMPLIED COVENANTS

1. IMPLIED IN FACT OR IN LAW?

There has been loud debate whether implied covenants are implied in fact or in law. Those arguing that covenants are implied in fact do so on the basis that the lease does not state the entire agreement of the parties. As Chapter 8 discusses, the main purpose of the structure of an oil and gas lease is to give a lessee the right to hold the lease during the primary term without development and to permit the lessee to maintain the lease after production for as long as it is profitable. There is little in a typical lease dealing with any other issue. Lease forms do not usually set standards for operation of the property or for marketing after initial development. On that basis, some have concluded that where implied covenants are recognized, they reflect the unexpressed intention of the parties, that the covenants are implied in fact, to fill in gaps.

The alternative view, forcefully expressed by the late Professor Maurice Merrill, is that implied covenants are implied at law to correct an imbalance of bargaining power. Though the parties to the lease may not have agreed specifically upon the terms of the implied covenants—indeed they may not even have considered the potential issues—implied covenants impose duties upon lessees because those duties are necessary to achieve a fair, equitable and just result. By this view, implied covenants are legal fictions imposed by law to level the playing field.

Courts have not often addressed directly the implied-in-fact/implied-in-law issue. Implicit in most decisions on implied covenants, such as the leading case of *Brewster v. Lanyon Zinc Co.*, 140 F. 801 (8th Cir.Kan.1905), is the premise that they are implied in fact to "fill in" the agreement of the parties. Other cases, such as the Supreme Court's statement in *Sauder v. Mid–Continent Petroleum Corporation*, 292 U.S. 272, 281 (1934), that implied covenants arise "from the relation of the parties and the object of the lease" seem more consistent with an implied-in-law theory.

Professors Howard Williams and Charles Meyers suggested a synthesis of these theories. They argued that covenants are implied both in fact and law from the contract-law principle of cooperation, which requires that parties to a contract cooperate to achieve its purposes. Because an oil and gas lease is a contract as well as a conveyance, the principle of cooperation requires certain conduct of the parties both as a matter of public policy (implied in law) and because the conduct was probably intended by the parties when they formed the contract (implied in fact). Others have explained implied covenants as a manifestation of the relational-contract nature of an oil and gas lease. The relational-contract theory is that, because leases are long-term and subject to complicated contingencies and unforeseen risks, the parties seek to establish a relationship for mutual benefit, and the lease contract becomes a framework for negotiation and resolution, rather than a discrete and complete agreement.

2. SIGNIFICANCE OF THE DISTINCTION

Whether implied covenants are implied in fact or in law may affect their scope. The source of the covenants also bears upon important procedural aspects. Which statute of limitations is applicable, whether the original lessee is liable for breaches that occur after it has assigned the lease, and where an action should be filed for breach (the venue) may depend upon whether covenants are implied in fact or in law.

Perhaps most important, if covenants are implied in fact rather than in law, parties may more easily disclaim or alter them. Promises implied in fact concern issues that the parties probably thought about but did not directly address in their contract. If parties address particular issues in their agreement, then it would be improper to imply covenants related to those issues, because the implied covenants would duplicate or conflict with express covenants. Likewise, if parties have specifically agreed that there will be no implied covenants or that certain covenants will not be implied, their agreement should stand if they understood the terms of the disclaimers. On the other hand, if covenants are implied at law to achieve a fair, equitable and just result, specific disclaimers of implied covenants should not be given effect; to do so would conflict with the basic rationale for recognizing the covenants.

In fact, however, no jurisdiction follows this logic completely. Even those decisions that sound most strongly based "at law" typically state that a clear express agreement of the parties will modify or override an implied covenant. But some jurisdictions clearly require more specificity than others to disclaim implied covenants. Recent cases from Texas, Colorado, and West Virginia illustrate the dichotomy. *Heritage Resources, Inc. v. NationsBank*, 939 S.W.2d 118 (Tex.1996), held that royalty clauses that stated royalty as a percentage of "market value at the well," permitted a lessee to deductions for transportation costs from the well to a downstream market, reasoning that:

> "There is an express agreement in this case as to how and where royalty will be determined. The implied duty to market gas cannot override that agreement. The words 'at the well' should be given their straightforward meaning. Market value 'at the well' means the value of gas at the well, before it is transported, treated, compressed or otherwise prepared for market."

In *Rogers v. Westerman Farm Company*, 29 P.3d 887 (Colo.2001), however, the Colorado Supreme Court rejected the idea that "at the well" permitted a lessee to deduct downstream costs in calculating royalty. Alluding to the unequal bargaining power of lessors and comparing the relationship of lessees and royalty owners to insurance companies and their customers, the court held that "at the well" was "silent with respect to allocation of costs" so that the implied covenant to market triggered Colorado's "marketable-product" rule for calculating royalties. And in *Tawney v. Columbia Natural Resources, LLC*, 633 S.E.2d 22 (W.Va. 2006), the West Virginia Supreme Court of Appeals held that language that indicates merely that royalty is to be calculated "at the well," or "at the wellhead," or similar language is "ambiguous" and not sufficient to permit a lessee to deduct costs incurred between the wellhead and the point of sale.

B. THE REASONABLY PRUDENT OPERATOR STANDARD

Underlying all implied covenants is the reasonably prudent operator standard—sometimes referred to as the "reasonable prudent operator" standard or "prudent operator" standard. This standard requires a lessee to conduct itself as would a reasonable and prudent operator under the same or similar circumstances. The standard arises from the nature of the leasing transaction. A grant of an oil and gas lease is an economic transaction entered into by the parties in the expectation of profit. The lease transfers the lessor's right to search, develop and produce oil and gas to the lessee. The main consideration for the transfer, which is usually on terms proposed by and using a form prepared by the lessee, is the lessor's expectation of royalties. It follows that the lessee should be required to exercise the authority given by the lease as would a reasonable and prudent operator.

The reasonably prudent operator standard was originally formulated to make it clear that a lessee's obligation is less than that of a fiduciary, but more than an obligation to act in good faith. The standard has since developed a life of its own. What it means in a particular circumstance is a question of fact, but it has generally been employed to impose upon a lessee the obligation to act (1) in good faith, (2) competently, and (3) with due regard for the lessor's interests.

Some have suggested that there is in fact only one implied covenant—the implied promise of the lessee to act as a reasonably prudent operator. A unified analysis does not fit the case method by which the courts have developed the various implied covenants. A unified analysis is useful, however, because the reasonably prudent operator standard is the common denominator of all implied covenants.

1. GOOD FAITH

At a minimum, a lessee must act in good faith toward its lessor. A good-faith requirement is implicit in any contract in a business setting, and imposes only a minimal burden upon the lessee. Good faith is presumed; the burden of proving bad faith is upon the lessor. Bad faith is a question of fact. It is difficult to define in general terms, other than as a failure for some speculative purpose to act to advance the mutual goals of the contractual relationship. Courts generally know bad faith when they see it, however. The good-faith requirement is an example of "gastronomic jurisprudence" at its best (or worst).

2. COMPETENCE

A reasonably prudent operator will be reasonable and prudent in matters relating to the technology and operating practices of the oil and gas industry. By acquiring the operating rights under a lease, a lessee represents itself to possess an expertise that

most persons do not have. Failure to operate competently may trigger liability.

The requirement that a lessee act competently
presents problems akin to those of professional mal-
practice. Although the lessee is not an insurer of
operating success, the lessee must conduct itself as
would other members of the industry in similar
circumstances. But is that standard a local standard, or a regional standard, or a national standard? The issue is important because the level of
technological sophistication of oil companies varies
substantially depending on their size and the region
in which they operate. The trend is toward treating
the standard of competence similarly to the professional liability standard, which imposes a regional
or even national standard rather than a local one.

3. WITH DUE REGARD FOR THE LESSOR'S INTERESTS

A reasonably prudent operator must consider the
lessor's interests while pursuing its own. The lessee
does not owe a fiduciary duty to the lessor, and
liability does not necessarily follow from a bad
decision. Indeed, a lessee's decisions may have a
foreseeably adverse impact upon the lessor without
triggering liability. But the duty requires more than
good faith. The lessee must make decisions with due
regard to the interests of the lessor and to the
nature of the long term business relationship between the parties, as well as to the lessee's own
interests. This requirement is based upon business

reality. A prudent business person will take into account the interests of those associated with him or her in transactions, because to do so is conducive to continuing to do business with them.

The reasonably prudent operator standard is objective, but often hinges on negative inferences. If a lessee appears to have acted for the purpose of harming or taking advantage of the lessor, the lessee may be held in breach. If a lessee appears to have speculated with the lessor's interests by using rights granted by the lease to accomplish some goal not related to its business purpose, the lessee may be held liable.

C. COMMON IMPLIED COVENANTS

Whether implied covenants are implied in fact or in law, and whether they exist independently of one another or merely as applications of the reasonably prudent operator standard, courts may articulate new obligations from time to time. Though courts describe the implied covenants differently, there are at least six commonly-encountered implied covenants: (1) the covenant to test, (2) the covenant to reasonably develop, (3) the covenant to further explore, (4) the covenant to protect against drainage, (5) the covenant to market and (6) the covenant of diligent and proper operation.

Generally, the remedy for breach of any of the implied covenants is an award of damages. A minority of jurisdictions hold that damages are the exclusive remedy for breach of implied covenants. A few jurisdictions allow lease cancellation as a remedy in some circumstances, even where a lessor has not first proved that damages would be an inadequate remedy. The majority rule is that lease cancellation may be awarded as a remedy for breach of implied covenants only upon a showing that damages are wholly inadequate.

Courts do not generally award exemplary or punitive damages for breach of implied covenants, whether the terms are implied in fact or in law. Contracts are "private law," and an aggrieved party is made whole if he or she receives the benefit of the contract bargain. Courts make exceptions, however, where there is a "special relationship" between parties to a contract that creates fiduciary duties or where a defendant's conduct would give rise to tort liability independent of the contract—for example, if a lessee negligently burned down one of the lessor's buildings.

1.   THE IMPLIED COVENANT TO TEST

The implied covenant to test arose in the last quarter of the nineteenth century when fixed-term and no-term leases were common. The covenant required lessees to test the leased premises within a reasonable time after the lease grant. Courts justified the implied covenant by describing it as a part of the consideration for the lease.

As Chapter 8 discusses, modern oil and gas leases avoid the implied covenant to test by providing specifically that a lessee may hold the lease for the duration of the primary term without drilling by paying delay rentals. Courts usually have said that if the lease contains a drilling-delay rental clause, it would be inconsistent with that clause to imply a covenant to test.

2. THE IMPLIED COVENANT TO REASONABLY DEVELOP

The implied covenant to reasonably develop is the corollary to the covenant to test. Though no covenant to test arises under modern leases, once a lessee discovers oil or gas, courts recognize an implied obligation to continue to develop reasonably.

What is reasonable development is a question of fact that depends on particular circumstances. The essential concept is that an economically motivated prudent operator will fully develop resources under its control within a reasonable time. Failure to do so deprives the lessor of the use of the royalty that he or she otherwise would have received, prevents the lessor from making other arrangements to develop, and suggests that the lessee lacks the economic motivation of a prudent business person.

a. Elements of Proof of Breach

Since an oil and gas lease gives the lessee the right to make decisions relating to the property, the burden of proof is upon the lessor to show (1) that additional development probably would have been economically viable and (2) that the lessee acted imprudently in failing to develop. In Oklahoma and perhaps a few other states, however, the burden of proof shifts to the lessee when an unreasonable period of time has elapsed after the initial discovery.

(1) Probability of Profit

To prove that additional development should have been pursued, a lessor must show that the lessee probably would have been able to recover its drilling and operating costs plus a reasonable return on investment. A reasonably prudent operator will not drill a well without expecting to make a profit.

A variety of evidence may be relevant to profitability. Geological data may establish probable sites for an additional well. Technological information from nearby existing wells may establish a probability that an additional well would be of productive. Financial analyses of production prices may show the profit potential.

(2) Imprudent Operator

Establishing the second element—that a lessee has acted as an imprudent operator in failing to undertake additional development— is more difficult because that element questions the lessee's judgment about the timing of development. Frequently, a lessee accused of breaching the reasonable-development covenant counters by contending that the profitability of an additional well can be maximized by deferring development for another few years. Judges and juries are loath to set aside a business judgment in technologically complicated high-risk ventures.

The magnitude of the potential profit must be considered in conjunction with imprudence. For example, though a particular well may have only one chance in four of success, a reasonably prudent operator might proceed to drill if it could expect a one-hundred-to-one return in the first year if it were successful. On the other hand, an operator who drills a dry hole on the first try confronts exactly the same odds—one chance in four of success—if it drills a second time.

Each case turns on its facts. Often, findings of liability seem to be based upon an inference that the lessee was incompetent or motivated by speculative purposes. Successful development of nearby properties may suggest a breach. A similar inference may arise from passage of an extended period of time without development. Some courts have given weight to the willingness of other operators to drill, as well. Such decisions usually seem fair on the basis of their facts, but offer few guiding principles.

A case in point is *Waseco Chemical & Supply Co. v. Bayou State Oil Corp.*, 371 So.2d 305 (La.App. 1979). The defendant in *Waseco* had leased approximately 80 acres in 1952. At that time, there were fifty wells on the tract, most of which were producing. Recovery averaged more than forty barrels per day of a heavy, asphaltic, high viscosity oil. The defendant made no capital expenditures on the lease, drilled no new wells, conducted no technical studies, and made no plans for additional development. By 1976, only nine wells were operating and average production from the property had declined to approximately six barrels per day. In canceling the lease, the trial judge noted that over the same period of time other lessees in the same field had drilled hundreds of wells and had substantially increased their production by use of fire-flooding techniques. The court of appeal upheld the decision, referring to a plat map of the area showing the development on adjoining lands and quoting the trial judge, who had suggested that the defendant's management had learned as much about enhanced-recovery operations in the two weeks of trial as in twenty years as operator. The court apparently found a breach of implied covenant based on an inference of incompetence or bad-faith speculation.

b. Stumbling Blocks to Enforcement

(1) Notice to the Lessee

In addition to proving the two elements of breach, a lessor faces additional requirements to enforce the reasonable-development covenant. In most states, a lessor must make a demand for development upon a lessee as a prerequisite to requesting lease cancellation; in a few states, a lessor's demand for additional development is a prerequisite for damages. A second requirement is that a lessee be allowed reasonable time following the notice to take action. Both requirements are based on the principle of cooperation. As the Eighth Circuit Court of Appeals, applying Nebraska law, noted in *Superior Oil Co. v. Devon Corp.*, 604 F.2d 1063 (8th Cir.Neb.1979), only when a lessee indicates by words or conduct that it will not develop further will courts waive the notice requirement.

(2) Disclaimer or Limitation in the Lease

Another stumbling block to enforcement of the implied covenant to reasonably develop may be express lease provisions restricting its scope. For example, the Texas lease form in the Appendix provides in paragraph 9:

> "After the discovery of oil, gas, or other hydrocarbons in paying quantities on the lands covered by this lease, or pooled therewith Lessee shall reasonably develop the acreage retained hereunder, but in discharging this obligation Lessee shall not be required to drill more than one well per eighty (80) acres of area retained hereunder and capable of producing oil in paying quantities, and one well per six hundred forty (640) acres of the area retained hereunder and capable of producing gas or other hydrocarbons in paying quantities, plus a tolerance of ten percent in the case of either an oil well or a gas well."

Oil wells are often developed on tracts smaller than 80 acres and gas wells on tracts less than 640 acres, but many courts would be unwilling to find an implied promise by the lessee to drill on more dense spacing when the lease agreement specifically provides otherwise.

Lease terms may also limit the scope of the implied covenant for reasonable development by implication. A good example of an implied limitation is

Gulf Production Co. v. Kishi, 103 S.W.2d 965 (Tex. Com.App.1937). Kishi asserted that Gulf had breached its implied covenant for reasonable development on leases of 150 acres and 20 acres. Both leases had addenda that stipulated the number of wells to be drilled following a successful discovery well. The addenda called for 12 wells on the 150 acre tract and 4 wells on the 20 acre tract. In fact, Gulf drilled 15 wells on the 150 acre tract and 6 wells on the 20 acre tract, and all but 3 of the 21 wells produced large quantities of oil. Kishi contended that the implied covenant for reasonable development required development beyond the 16 wells stipulated in the leases, and the trial court agreed. On appeal, however, the appellate court reversed on the grounds that the implied covenant arises "out of necessity and in the absence of an express stipulation" for development. The court reasoned that since Kishi's leases provided for development, no implied covenant for reasonable development arose. A lessee's commitment to a development schedule may obviate an implied covenant for reasonable development unless it is clear that the parties intend that the drilling schedule states only a minimum obligation.

An example of a lease with a specific drilling obligation that did not limit the implied covenant is *Sinclair Oil & Gas Co. v. Masterson*, 271 F.2d 310 (5th Cir.Tex.1959). In *Sinclair,* three leases covering more than 40,000 acres contained express agreements to drill six wells. The lessee asserted that because of the express drilling schedule, there could be no implied obligation to drill more. The Fifth Circuit rejected that argument on the grounds that it was not reasonable to conclude that the parties intended that a total of six wells on 40,000 acres would constitute full development. The court interpreted the drilling schedule as a minimum requirement rather than an agreed definition of reasonable development.

c. Remedies for Breach

In general, courts apply one or more of three remedies for breach of the covenant for reasonable development: (1) lease cancellation; (2) conditional lease cancellation; or (3) damages. Favored remedies vary among the states.

(1) Cancellation

Though damages are the preferred remedy at law for breached agreements, damages are not generally the sole remedy for breaches of implied covenants in oil and gas leases. In some states, including Louisiana, lease cancellation is a common remedy. One rationale asserted for not limiting the remedy for a breach of the covenant for reasonable development to damages is that the covenant is a condition of the lease; indeed, development is the reason for the lease. Therefore, cancellation is an appropriate remedy when a lessee is not fulfilling the lease's purpose. More often, courts justify cancellation on the basis of equitable principles; they hold damages are an inadequate remedy where a lessee is found to be incompetent or guilty of speculation.

When courts grant lease cancellation as a remedy, they usually order only *partial cancellation*; they generally except the portions of the lease surrounding producing wells from cancellation. The lessor is complaining about the lessee's failure to drill additional wells, and cancellation of the lease's undeveloped areas will protect the lessor's interests. If the breach of the reasonable-development covenant is blatant, however, a court may cancel the lease outright. For example, the lessee in *Waseco Chemical & Supply Co. v. Bayou State Oil Corp.*, discussed above, lost its lease outright even though it had several producing wells.

(2) Conditional Cancellation

A decree of conditional cancellation is a more moderate remedy than outright cancellation, and thus is viewed with growing favor. Under a decree for conditional cancellation, the lessee is ordered to commence additional development within a stated period or suffer cancellation of the lease.

(3) Damages

Courts may award damages in addition to a decree of cancellation or conditional cancellation. Damages are generally measured by *lost royalties*, those that the court concludes would have been paid had the lessee drilled the additional well. If the evidence shows that a well should have been drilled and that it would probably have produced 100 barrels of oil daily, and the lessor's royalty share was one-eighth, damages would be the value of twelve and one-half barrels per day for the period of the breach.

Several commentators have argued convincingly that unless drainage from the premises has occurred, the lessor's remedy should be interest on the foregone royalties rather than the royalties themselves. Otherwise, the lessor receives a double recovery: damages in the amount of royalties that he or she should have received, plus the royalty itself when the premises are developed and production takes place in the future. Recognizing the double-recovery problem, the West Virginia Supreme Court in *Cotiga Development Co. v. United Fuel Gas Co.*, 128 S.E.2d 626 (W.Va.1962), permitted a lessor to recover damages based on the foregone royalties, but provided in its decree that future royalty payments would be offset by the damages, when and if the lessee secured production.

3. THE IMPLIED COVENANT FOR FURTHER EXPLORATION

The implied covenant for further exploration is similar to the implied covenant for reasonable development in that it imposes obligations on a lessee only after a lessee has secured production. Since the drilling-delay rental clause gives the lessee the right to hold a lease during its primary term without drilling it, there is no implied duty either to reasonably develop or to explore further during the lease primary term.

The implied covenant for further exploration differs from the covenant for reasonable development in the nature of the lessor's complaint. When a lessor complains about lack of further exploration, the lessor argues that the lessee has not explored undeveloped parts of the land or formations under the land, rather than that the lessee has failed to develop known minerals deposits on the land.

There has been considerable debate whether the law recognizes an implied covenant for further exploration separate from a covenant for reasonable development. Charles Meyers first identified the covenant for further exploration as a separate implied promise. His analysis was challenged by a number of writers. Since then, Meyers' analysis has been rejected explicitly by the Supreme Court of Oklahoma and implicitly by the Supreme Court of Texas.

The major focus of the debate is what a lessor complaining of a lessee's failure to explore must prove. As is discussed above, to prove a breach of the covenant for reasonable development, the lessor must show that the development well he or she demands has a probability of profit. If the same degree of probability is required to establish that an exploratory well should be drilled, as cases like *Sun Exploration and Production Co. v. Jackson*, 783 S.W.2d 202 (Tex.1989) say, then there is no separate implied covenant of further exploration, and proof of probable profit will impose a burden on lessors that they will be able to meet only in rare circumstances. Historically, the oil and gas industry in the United States has found hydrocarbons in paying quantities with only approximately 1 in 10 exploratory wells, and only 1 of every 50 exploratory wells has discovered significant reserves.

Those commentators and cases that have rejected the covenant for further exploration as a separate covenant have done so on the premise that showing a probability of profit is the essence of the reasonably prudent operator standard. The reasoning of the Oklahoma Supreme Court in *Mitchell v. Amerada Hess Corp.*, 638 P.2d 441 (Okl.1981), is an example:

> "Failure to recognize the profit motive as an instrumental force in oil and gas leases on behalf of both lessee and lessor is to ignore the very essence of the contract.... Meyers' formulation of the proposed implied covenant ignores the potential for profit.... Can the duties of the lessee be judged apart from the spectre of profit where the activity is judged exploration rather than development? To do so is unwise and unnecessary.... It is simply not realistic to ignore profit as a consideration of the standard of a prudent operator simply because the lessor demands a wildcat be drilled on a productive lease rather than an additional well to a productive formation."

The Oklahoma Supreme Court's reasoning may misstate the argument for the covenant for further exploration. Professor Meyers did not ignore profit potential. He identified a number of factors that bear on whether the operator acquitted itself properly in exploration, such as the feasibility of further exploratory drilling, which takes into account economic factors like the presence of geologic formations likely to contain oil or gas, the costs of drilling, the market for the product, and the size of the block necessary to drill a test well. The cases that recognize a separate implied covenant to explore further, such as *Gillette v. Pepper Tank Co.*, 694 P.2d 369 (Colo.App.1984), look to a broad range of circumstances, including but not limited to the likelihood of profitability, in assessing the reasonableness of the operator's failure to act.

Because of the reasonably prudent operator standard, the law should recognize an implied promise by the lessee to explore further as well as to develop reasonably. A reasonably prudent operator will act to maximize profit in the long run, as well as in the short run. A lessee that drills only "sure-thing" wells will be out of business when known deposits are fully developed. What a reasonably prudent operator will do—and does do in the "real" world—in the interest of long-term profitability, is to devote portions of its drilling budget to exploration, as well as to development.

Of course, the potential for profitability will always be relevant in evaluating a claim for breach of the covenant to explore further. Operators do not drill exploratory wells without a close evaluation of the likelihood that their operations will be successful. Recognizing that the odds are against the success of any particular exploratory well, a reasonably prudent operator will take great care in choosing which exploratory prospects to drill. But drilling exploratory wells is a matter of survival in the long run. Consequently, an acceptable probability of profit is necessarily lower for exploratory wells than for development wells.

a. Elements of Proof

Where the implied covenant for further exploration is recognized as separate from the implied covenant for reasonable development, a lessor has the burden of proving that (1) additional exploration reasonably can be expected to be successful, and (2) that the lessor's operator is behaving imprudently by failing or refusing to explore further.

As has been discussed, proving a reasonable expectation of profitability from further exploration requires a lessor to prove a lesser probability of profit than that required for breach of the covenant for reasonable development. The burden of showing that the lessee is behaving imprudently in failing to explore is usually much heavier, however, than the parallel proof of breach of the covenant for reasonable development. As the risk of unprofitability increases, so does the apparent reasonableness of a lessee who declines to act.

Furthermore, at least in the short or medium term, the covenant to further explore does not require actual drilling. Based as it is on the reasonably prudent operator standard, the implied covenant does not require that drilling be conducted where preliminary measures will decrease the risks of actual drilling. A lessee can satisfy the obligation by geologic exploration or geophysical testing. In the long run, however, courts say that actual drilling of every part of the leased premises is required.

In the long run, a lessee's failure to drill suggests it has no intention to drill on undeveloped portions of the lease. That, in turn, suggests the lessee has a speculative motive in continuing to hold unexplored portions.

b. Stumbling Blocks to Enforcement

(1) Notice to the Lessee

Because the implied covenant for further exploration and the implied covenant for reasonable development are closely related, the stumbling blocks to enforcement are much the same. The lessor who demands lease cancellation because of the lessee's failure to explore further must generally show that he or she has given the lessee notice of the demand and a reasonable time to comply. Notice is crucial because cancellation is usually the remedy the lessor seeks.

(2) Disclaimer or Limitation in the Lease

Likewise, a lessor's right to demand further exploration may be limited either by specific provisions in the oil and gas lease or by implication from lease provisions. Indeed, because the specific actions required by the implied covenant for further exploration are so imprecise, the courts are likely to accept any express definition of the exploration duty, however limited, as reasonable.

One rarely encounters lease disclaimers or limitations of a duty to explore. That may be because lessees who take leases intend to explore and so are not concerned about disclaiming or limiting their obligations. It may also be because limitations are unacceptable in the marketplace.

c. Remedies for Breach

When a lessor proves breach of the implied covenant for further exploration, courts usually order partial cancellation or conditional cancellation of the lease as to the unexplored area. One reason that cancellation is the favored remedy is the uncertainty of any actual damage to the lessor in terms of lost royalties as a result of the lessee's failure to explore; damages are usually an inadequate remedy. In addition, the burden of proving that the operator has been imprudent in failing to explore is so heavy that where a lessor meets it, the lessee's incompetence or speculative intent is usually so apparent that equity demands lease termination.

4. THE IMPLIED COVENANT TO PROTECT AGAINST DRAINAGE

Courts have been quick to recognize an implied promise by the lessee to protect the leased premises against drainage. The covenant to protect against drainage may obligate the lessee to act even though there has been no drilling and the lease still is held by payment of delay rentals. A lessee has a right under the lease to develop or not as it may choose during the primary term, but its discretion does not extend to permitting drainage.

Modern drilling and spacing rules lessen substantially the need for the implied covenant to protect against drainage. If a conservation agency has properly established the size of spacing units, no great drainage should occur between leases. Spacing unit configurations are merely approximations, however. They are usually established on the assumption that drainage will occur in a circle around the well. In fact, the structure of the producing formation may cause drainage in a very different configuration.

The covenant to protect against drainage usually involves alleged drainage directly from one tract to a well on a contiguous tract, but there may be an obligation to protect against indirect or fieldwide drainage. In *Amoco Production Co. v. Alexander*, 622 S.W.2d 563 (Tex.1981), lessors complained that Amoco had permitted drainage from their leases in the lower area of a tilted reservoir, while actively producing from leases in the upper region of the same reservoir.

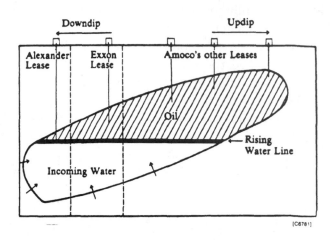

The Alexanders contended that Amoco had in fact accelerated the process by plugging wells on the Alexander leases and increasing production from wells higher on the reservoir. The Texas Supreme Court held that Amoco had an obligation to protect the Alexanders' properties against both local and field-wide drainage. The obligation might require the lessee to drill additional or replacement wells, to rework existing wells, or to seek voluntary or compulsory unitization or other administrative relief to protect the lessors' interest.

The Texas Supreme Court also held that Amoco's obligations to other lessors in the field did not shield Amoco from liability to the Alexanders. Amoco argued that had it acted to protect the Alexanders' property, it would have breached its implied duties to others. The court reasoned that Amoco's conflicts of interest were its own creation, so that

Amoco's obligations to the Alexanders should be determined by reference to the express and implied terms of their lease alone.

a. Elements of Proof: In General

To prove a breach of the implied covenant to protect against drainage, a lessor must show (1) substantial drainage from the leased premises, and (2) a probability that an offset well would be profitable. A lessor has the burden to prove a breach because by granting the lease the lessor has granted to the lessee the right to make operating decisions. There is no reason to change the agreement of the parties unless the lessor proves that the lessee is acting imprudently. Furthermore, if drainage is actually taking place, the lessee has a bigger stake in protecting the property than the lessor, since the lessee's share of production is generally larger than the lessor's royalty. The lessee's self-interest should protect the lessor.

(1) Substantial Drainage

How much drainage is required to be "substantial" is unclear. A few cases suggest that it must be "in paying quantities." "Substantial" drainage ought not be so large. The requirement of substantial drainage prevents a lessor from harassing the lessee by seeking development under the guise of complaining about drainage. Therefore, substantial drainage should be an amount large enough under the circumstances to be reasonably of concern to the lessor; a jury is likely to find that a small measure is substantial.

(2) Probability of Profit

The requirement that a lessor show that the lessee has a probability of profit from a protective well is the key to the implied covenant to protect against drainage. It embodies the reasonably-prudent operator standard. A reasonably prudent operator will not act simply because the leased land is being drained. A prudent operator will drill a protection well only where it appears that a protection well will either prevent the drainage or compensate for it by counter-drainage and produce in quantities sufficient to repay the lessee's cost of drilling, completing and equipping the well, plus a reasonable profit. Without a probability of profit, a reasonably prudent operator will choose to minimize its losses by gritting its corporate teeth and permitting the drainage.

b. Elements of Proof: Where There Is Drainage by the Lessee

A much-discussed issue concerning the implied covenant to protect against drainage is whether a lessor's burden of proof should be modified when the drainage complained of is caused by wells on another property operated by the same lessee. This is called the "common-lessee" situation. For example, suppose that O leases his property to A Company, as does O's neighbor X. Subsequently, A Compa-

ny drills a well on X's property that O contends
drains his property.

O Leases to A Company   X Leases to A Company

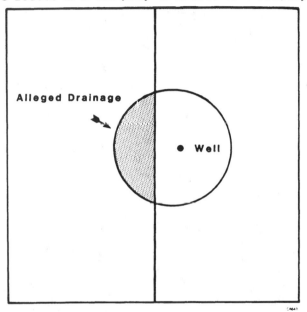

In such a situation, some argue, O ought not have
the burden of proving a probability of profit because
O is not protected by A Company's self interest. It
will not matter to the common lessee if O's property
is drained. A Company will receive the working-
interest share of production whether O's property is
drained from a well on O's property or from a well
on X's property. Indeed, there may be an economic
incentive for A Company to drain O's property from

a well located on X's property, if O's lease provides for a higher royalty percentage than X's lease.

Many courts, like the Texas Supreme Court in *Amoco Production Co. v. Alexander,* discussed above, ignore the conceptual problem and impose the usual burden of proof upon the lessor. Since breach is based upon a finding of the facts of substantial drainage and probability of profit, however, inferences of unfair dealing that may arise from the operator's position as a common lessee may affect the weight a jury gives the evidence.

Some courts have gone further and suggested that when there is a common lessee, the lessor should be relieved of the burden of proving probability of profit. If a lessor can show that his or her land has been substantially drained by a well operated by the lessee on another tract, then the lessor is entitled to a remedy. The common lessee's inherent conflict of interest creates an inference of bad faith when drainage occurs. Such cases have sometimes seen the common-lessee situation as creating another implied covenant. In *Cook v. El Paso Natural Gas Co.*, 560 F.2d 978 (10th Cir.N.M.1977), the Tenth Circuit Court of Appeals recognized an implied covenant of the common lessee to refrain from any action that would injure its lessors' property.

Several commentators have urged that the necessity of showing a probability of profit ought not be waived in the common-lessee situation. The reasonably prudent operator standard is meaningless without reference to a probability of profit. A lessor whose property is drained by a well operated by the lessor's own lessee is in no worse position than he or she would be if the property were being drained by some other operator, so why should the legal standard be different? At most, the procedural rules might be changed in the common-lessee situation so that the burden on profitability would be reversed; where a lessor showed that operations of the lessee on another property were causing substantial drainage from the lessor's property, the lessor would prevail unless the lessee was able to prove that protection probably would not be profitable.

c. **Stumbling Blocks to Enforcement**

(1) Notice to the Lessee

As with other implied covenants, notice of the alleged breach and a reasonable period of time to correct the failure to act are usually prerequisites for the equitable remedy of cancellation. Courts may make an exception, however, where drainage occurs in a common-lessee situation on the theory that the lessee knew or should have known of the lessor's complaint.

(2) Disclaimer or Limitation in the Lease

The implied covenant to protect against drainage can also be disclaimed or limited by agreement of the parties, at least if it is implied in fact. One occasionally sees language that, if applied literally, would obviate the implied covenant. For example:

"In the event a well or wells producing oil and gas in paying quantities should be brought in on adjacent land

and within 150 feet of and draining the leased premises, lessee agrees to drill such offset wells as a reasonably prudent operator would drill under the same or similar circumstances."

Although such language may look at first glance like an express statement of the covenant to protect against drainage, the reference to distance may severely limit the covenant. Ordinarily, spacing rules will not permit a well to be drilled within 150 feet of a property line. Thus, the specific promise is in effect a disclaimer, for it obligates the lessee to protect the premises only in a situation that cannot legally arise.

Courts may refuse to enforce such a provision on a variety of grounds. They may hold it overreaching or unconscionable. They may find it is based upon a mutual mistake of fact concerning the spacing rules. They may enforce it against the lessor where the drainage results from the actions of some other lessee but not where the drainage results from the action of the lessor's lessee. Or, as in *Williams v. Humble Oil & Refining Co.*, 432 F.2d 165 (5th Cir.La.1970), such a provision may be construed as a narrow affirmative statement that does not limit the implied covenant. The possibility that such provisions may be enforced, however, leads many lessors to strike from leases any reference to implied covenants and to affirm specifically in the lease the lessee's obligation to act as a reasonably prudent operator. This approach is based on the premise (which is probably correct) that any reference to implied covenants in an oil company's form lease is likely to be for the purpose of limitation rather than restatement or expansion.

(3) Waiver or Estoppel

A final stumbling block to a lessor in enforcing the implied covenant to protect against drainage is the possibility that a lessor might be found to have waived the right to complain or be estopped from complaining by accepting delay rentals. Several courts have held that a lessor cannot complain of the lessee's failure to protect the premises for any period of time for which the lessor has accepted delay-rental payments. Their theory is that delay rentals are payments for the privilege of maintaining the lease without drilling a well. Because of the possibility of such decisions, lessors who believe their property is being drained should reject delay-rental tenders unless the law of their jurisdiction is clearly different.

Accepting delay rentals ought not bar a lessor from asserting breach of the implied covenant to protect. As Part E of Chapter 8 discusses, oil and gas leases provide for delay rentals to make clear the lessee's right to hold the lease during the primary term without any obligation to test the premises. Lessors are willing to waive the covenant to test because they are compensated by bonus and rentals, and their oil and gas remains in place to be produced later. Neither lessors nor lessees intend that payment of delay rentals will give a lessee the right to let the property be drained. This analysis has been adopted in both Texas and Oklahoma.

d. Remedies for Breach

(1) Damages

Damages are normally an adequate remedy for breach of the implied covenant to protect the premises against drainage. A lessor who is compensated for lost hydrocarbons is made whole. Some courts have measured damages by applying the lease royalty to the amount of drainage. Others have calculated royalty on production that could have been obtained from an offset well. Professors Williams and Meyers have suggested that the measure of damages ought to be the amount of the drainage that could have been prevented by drilling an offset well, but that logical limitation has generally been ignored.

(2) Cancellation or Conditional Cancellation

Lease cancellation or conditional cancellation is also available as a remedy for breach of the covenant to protect against drainage in most states. Courts are unlikely to order lease cancellation, however, unless the lessee has acted in bad faith toward the lessor or unless damages are impossible to ascertain.

5.   THE IMPLIED COVENANT TO MARKET

The implied covenant to market imposes upon the lessee the duty to use due diligence to market oil and gas produced within a reasonable time and at a reasonable price. The reasonably prudent operator is a business person, and will seek to maximize profit. The implied covenant to market requires a lessee to use the diligence of a reasonable and prudent business person in finding a market and negotiating a sale.

Problems with the implied covenant to market usually involve the sale of natural gas rather than oil. One reason is the difference in the physical characteristics of oil and gas. Oil is easily stored, and is sold on a "spot" basis from the storage tank in which it is placed after production. Until the mid-1980s, almost all gas produced was sold into pipelines under long-term contracts. There were often delays of several years between completion of a gas well, negotiation of a gas contract, and extension of a pipeline to take the production. Even today, a significant portion of the natural gas marketed is sold under contracts ranging in duration from a few months to several years, rather than on a true "spot" market. Another reason that most marketing-covenant problems involve gas rather than oil is that lease royalty clauses generally provide for payment of oil royalty in kind, so that an unhappy lessor can make his or her own arrangements for sale. In contrast, gas royalty is usually a percentage of the value of production or the amount realized by the lessee.

a. Within a Reasonable Time

How much time is reasonable for the lessee to find a market will depend upon the facts and circumstances, but it may be a long time. In *Bristol v.*

Colorado Oil & Gas Corp., 225 F.2d 894 (10th Cir.Okl.1955), the court held a delay of nearly eight years before marketing was reasonable because the gas was impure and there was no pipeline available. Even if there is a ready purchaser for gas production, it may be prudent for a producer to wait to get better terms or to deal with another purchaser; decline of demand for natural gas in an economic recession does not fall equally upon all gas purchasers. In addition, gas-contract negotiations historically have been time consuming.

b. At a Reasonable Price

Historically, marketing covenant cases focused on the duty of a lessee to market within a reasonable period of time after discovering oil or gas. More recently, since the U.S. gas-transportation grid has become relatively fully developed, so that it is usually possible to obtain access to markets, disputes have centered upon a second "leg" of the implied covenant; the obligation to market at a reasonable price.

The cases present several issues. One is whether the implied covenant to market should apply equally to both "market value" and "amount realized" royalty provisions—to objective market-driven royalty standards as well as to those within the control of the lessee. The court in *Craig v. Champlin Petroleum Co.*, 300 F.Supp. 119 (W.D.Okl.1969), made no distinction: A "lessee under oil and gas leases . . . has an implied duty and obligation in the exercise of reasonable diligence, as a prudent operator, with due regard for the interest of both lessor and lessee, to obtain a market for the gas produced ... at a prevailing market price...." More recently, neither the Colorado Supreme Court in *Rogers v. Westerman Farm Company*, 29 P.3d 887 (Colo.2001), nor the Arkansas Supreme Court in *SEECO, Inc. v. Hales*, 22 S.W.3d 157 (Ark.2000), nor the Kansas Supreme Court in *Smith v. Amoco Prod. Co.*, 31 P.3d 255 (Kan.2001), distinguished "market value" from "amount realized" in applying the implied covenant. But the Texas Supreme Court in *Yzaguirre v. KCS Resources, Inc.*, 53 S.W.3d 368 (Tex. 2001), held squarely that the implied covenant to market does not apply to a "market value" royalty "because the lease provides an objective basis for calculating royalties that is independent of the price the lessee actually obtains, the lessor does not need the protection of an implied covenant."

A second issue is what is the measure of a lessee's duty under the implied covenant to market? Should a lessee be obligated to sell at the highest possible price, or the best price currently available, or the prevailing-market price, or merely at a price that is reasonable in light of other similar transactions? In *Cabot Corp. v. Brown*, 754 S.W.2d 104 (Tex.1987), the Texas Supreme Court spoke in terms of the "best current price reasonably available." But in *Yzaguirre v. KCS Resources, Inc.*, that court observed that a failure to sell at "market value" was "merely probative" and equated "market value" to the "prevailing market price at the time of delivery." In *Texaco Inc. v. Duhe*, 274 F.3d 911 (5th

Cir.La.2001), the court described the obligation of the implied covenant as being to get the "best price reasonably possible," but observed that "while royalty owners legitimately cannot expect the highest rates of return from their mineral or natural gas interests, they can expect returns consistent with the bargained-for exchange: reasonable rent for the intended use of the land."

A third issue is the effect of transactions among affiliates. Lessees often sell both oil and gas in the field where it is produced to related marketing companies, which then engage in a wide variety of marketing transactions. Lessors often suspect that related companies have negotiated "sweetheart" terms of sale in the field or otherwise manipulated transactions to their benefit and lessors' detriment. Few royalty-dispute decisions have addressed directly the issue of transactions among affiliates, though claims of wrongdoing appear frequently in pleadings. In a footnote to *Tara Petroleum Corp. v. Hughey*, 630 P.2d 1269 (Okl.1981), the court appeared to condemn the practice:

> "Courts should take care not to allow lessors to be deprived or defrauded of their royalties by their lessees entering into illusory or collusive assignments or gas purchase contracts. Whenever a lessee or assignee is paying royalty on one price, but on resale a related entity is obtaining a higher price, the lessors are entitled to their royalty share of the higher price. The key is common control of the two entities."

Most courts—including probably Oklahoma courts—would not go so far. As a Texas court said in *Texas Oil & Gas Corp. v. Hagen*, 683 S.W.2d 24

(Tex.App.1984), as a general principle of corporate law, even the fact that a subsidiary is wholly owned by a parent and there is an identity of management does not justify disregarding the corporate entity of the subsidiary, unless management and operations are assimilated to the extent that the subsidiary is simply a name or a conduit through which the parent conducts its business. It is both inevitable and appropriate, however, that courts will subject transactions between affiliates to closer scrutiny than transactions between unrelated parties. Transactions with an affiliate may place a lessee in a conflict of interest with its lessor, and justify examination of the details of the dealings. But there is no logic to support the proposition that either a lessee's express royalty obligation or its implied duties should be different when it deals with an affiliated entity.

c. Proof of Imprudence

When a lessee is held to have breached its obligations, it is often because of its has failed to deal fairly with the lessor. *Amoco Production Co. v. First Baptist Church of Pyote*, 579 S.W.2d 280 (Tex.Civ. App.1979), is a good example. There, Amoco entered into a long-term gas sales contract in 1969. Market conditions at the time were poor, and to sell its production, Amoco had to commit to the contract future production from undeveloped leases it held. In 1973, Amoco and others drilled a well on a 640 acre unit that included several of the previously undeveloped leases dedicated to the 1969 contract as well as leases that Amoco had not dedicated to the 1969 contract. By that time, gas prices had climbed substantially. Amoco negotiated an amendment to its 1969 contract by which it committed all its leases in the 1973 unit to the 1969 contract and, in return, the purchaser increased the contract price for all gas sold by Amoco under the contract. Though the renegotiated contract was obviously good business for Amoco, several lessors whose leases had been committed to the 1969 contract by the amendment sued, alleging Amoco had breached the implied covenant to market. They presented facts showing that other owners had contracted to sell their gas in 1974 and 1975 on substantially better terms than those obtained by Amoco. The court found breach of the implied covenant because Amoco had obtained a substantial improvement in the price that it received under the 1969 contract by trading-off the interests of the lessors.

The principle of *Amoco Production Co. v. First Baptist Church* has broad application. In Texas, at least, as has been discussed above in connection with *Amoco Production Co. v. Alexander* and the implied covenant to protect against drainage, whether a lessee has met its implied obligation to its lessors is determined on a lease-by-lease basis; a lessee must meet the covenant-to-market standard for the production from *each* of its leases. A court is likely to find a breach of the implied covenant to market whenever a lessee exchanges a benefit that the market or a contract would allocate to its lessor for a benefit to the lessee or some other lessor.

d. Remedies for Breach

(1) Failure to Market Within a Reasonable Time

When the breach alleged is a failure to market production within a reasonable period of time, a lessor will ordinarily claim that the lease has ended. If the claim is brought during the primary term, the lessor will demand that the court exercise equity powers to cancel the lease. If the claim is made after the primary term, the lessor's theory will be that the lease has terminated by its own terms because of the lessee's failure to secure production in paying quantities.

A lessor's demand for lease cancellation or termination for breach of an implied covenant to market within a reasonable time is not likely to fall on receptive ears. Once a lessee has gone to the risk and expenditure of developing a well on leased premises, courts are reticent to find that the lessee's rights have terminated. As a general rule, damages will be the lessor's remedy. But many cases hold that lease cancellation or forfeiture is appropriate because the lessee's failure to market shows that the lessee has abandoned its rights.

(2) Failure to Market at a Reasonable Price

It is particularly likely that damages will be the remedy a court assesses if the breach proved is a sale by the lessee at less than a fair price. When a lessor complains that his or her royalty is not calculated on an adequate price, the lessor can be made whole by damages.

Interesting problems may be encountered in calculating damages due, however. *Amoco Production Co. v. First Baptist Church of Pyote,* discussed above, is an example. There, the gas royalty clause provided that the lessor was to be paid royalty calculated on the basis of the "amount realized" from the sale of the natural gas. Having found that Amoco had marketed the production at less than a fair price, the court awarded the lessors damages based upon the fair market value of the gas when delivered. The court reasoned that since Amoco failed to obtain a "fair" price for the gas it marketed, the amount realized from the sale was inappropriate as a basis for royalty. The result was that Amoco's lessors were able to collect royalty for their share of the natural gas produced on a price higher than that received by anyone else selling gas from the unit. The remedy fashioned probably reflected an attempt by the court to punish Amoco for its abuse. As such, it demonstrates the scope of courts' powers.

e. Stumbling Blocks to Enforcement

(1) Notice to the Lessee

Notice to a lessee of a claimed breach of the implied covenant to market is usually held essential where a lessor asks the court to exercise equitable powers to cancel the lease. Notice may also be required by the contract principle of cooperation wherever the basis for the claim of breach of the implied covenant is the lessee's failure to market the product within a reasonable period of time;

presumably, the lessee can mitigate the lessor's damages by acting promptly after such a notice.

When the lessor's asserted breach is the lessee's failure to sell the production at a fair price, however, notice should not be a prerequisite if the sale is under a long-term contract. Most lease royalty clauses are structured so that the lessee owns all of the natural gas produced, with the lessor's royalty being based upon the price for which the gas is sold. By the time the lessor becomes aware of the sale, there will be no purpose for the notice.

(2) Waiver or Estoppel

A lessor should not be held to have waived or be estopped from asserting the implied covenant to market unless the lessor has knowingly ratified the terms of a gas contract. Merely accepting payments of royalties the lessee tenders should not establish grounds for waiver or estoppel because there is no question but that the amount of royalties tendered is due; the lessor's contention is that *more* is due. The indicated result may not hold, however, where the lessor has executed a division order agreeing to accept the amount of royalty tendered as full payment, as Chapter 10 discusses.

(3) Disclaimer or Limitation in the Lease

When a lessor claims that the lessee has not acted within a reasonable time to market production, some have asserted that the presence of a shut-in royalty clause in the lease should bar the lessor's suit. The lessee has the right under a shut-in royalty clause to maintain the lease without actual production and marketing by paying a shut-in royalty, as Chapter 9 discusses. Arguably, the shut-in royalty clause gives a lessee the option of maintaining the lease either by production or by payment of shut-in royalties.

Courts have rejected this argument. The purpose of the lease shut-in royalty clause is to protect the lessee against lease loss for failure of production where marketing is not possible or advisable, not to relieve the lessee of the duty to market. Nevertheless, payment of shut-in royalty may bear on the reasonableness of marketing delays. A lessor whose lease contains a shut-in royalty provision and who receives a payment simply has a weaker complaint that marketing has not occurred quickly enough.

6. THE IMPLIED COVENANT OF DILIGENT AND PROPER OPERATION

The implied covenant that a lessee will operate diligently and properly overlaps several of the other implied covenants. For example, the decision in *Waseco Production v. Bayou States Oil Corp.,* discussed in conjunction with the implied covenant to reasonably develop above, could have been based on the implied covenant to operate diligently and properly. A reasonably prudent operator is competent, and will use enhanced-recovery techniques where they will be profitable. Likewise, the result reached by the court in *Amoco Production Co. v. Alexander,* discussed in conjunction with the implied covenant to protect against drainage above, may also be seen as an application of the implied covenant to operate diligently and properly. A reasonably prudent operator will seek to protect both its interests and its lessor's interests by seeking voluntary or compulsory pooling or unitization or appropriate administrative action.

As Professors Williams and Meyers noted in their treatise, complaints that the implied covenant to operate diligently and properly has been breached usually are based upon one of four types of objections: (1) that the lessee has damaged the property by negligence or incompetence, (2) that the lessee has damaged the lessor by prematurely abandoning a well capable of producing in paying quantities, (3) that the lessee has failed to use advanced production techniques, or (4) that the lessee has failed to protect the lessor by failing to seek favorable regulatory action.

Such a categorization does not limit the scope of the implied covenant of diligent and proper operation. As is discussed above, all of the implied covenants may be seen as applications of the reasonably prudent operator standard. Courts have been quick and creative in extending implied covenants to protect lessors' interests. Because the implied covenant to operate diligently and properly is the broadest of the six commonly encountered implied covenants, it is likely to be used by courts to remedy future problems even when they do not fall clearly within the categories noted.

D. THE FUTURE OF IMPLIED COVENANTS

Some predict that implied covenants will become less important as lessors become more sophisticated and demand express covenants. Clearly, increasing oil and gas prices, which have led to higher bonuses and royalty percentages cause lessors to pay closer attention to lease terms. To the extent that oil and gas leases are not executed on preprinted forms but are specially negotiated by the parties to fit their particular circumstances, one may expect that they will leave less room for application of implied covenants.

CHAPTER 12

LEASE TRANSFERS

Lease interests are frequently transferred. Leases are considered by oil companies to be inventory, and oil companies frequently trade leases to put together "blocks" that can be more efficiently explored and developed. Promoters often assign fractional working interests to investors who put up the money for drilling. The landman who acquired the lease, the geologist who developed the prospect, or others who were instrumental in structuring the venture may receive overriding royalty or other nonoperating interests as compensation. This chapter will discuss common problems presented by transfers of lease interests.

A. LESSEE'S RIGHT TO TRANSFER

Courts generally treat interests under oil and gas leases like interests in real property. Interests are freely assignable unless reasonable limitations are imposed by the terms of their creation. Therefore, even without provisions in the lease expressly permitting assignment, a lessee may transfer all or any part of its interest.

Most lease forms, however, contain language that specifically permits assignment. An example is the first sentence of paragraph 8 of the Texas lease in the Appendix: "The rights of Lessor and Lessee may be assigned in whole or in part...." The California lease in the Appendix contains similar language in paragraph 9. Leases typically include a specific provision permitting assignment because the nature of the lessee's interest under an oil and gas lease has been described in a variety of ways ranging from a mere license to a fee simple determinable interest in minerals. If common-law doctrines were applied strictly, there would be no implied right to divide the lease in states where the leasehold interest is classified as a profit in gross; although profits in gross were assignable at common law, they were not divisible.

B. EFFECT OF TRANSFER ON THE LESSOR

1. FURTHER RIGHTS AGAINST THE LESSEE

At common law one may assign contract rights but remains bound by contract obligations because of privity of contract. Accordingly, unless a lease provides otherwise, a lessee who assigns the operating rights under a lease remains liable for future breaches. The lessee can protect itself by imposing a specific obligation upon the assignee to indemnify the lessee against such claims. More generally, lessees seek to change the general rule by provisions in the lease. Language from a lease used in North Dakota is typical:

"In case Lessee assigns this lease, in whole or in part, Lessee shall be relieved of all obligations with respect to the assigned portion or portions upon furnishing the Lessor with a written transfer or assignment or a true copy thereof."

Similar language is included in paragraph 8 of the Texas lease and in paragraph 9 of the California lease included in the Appendix. Although the exculpatory terms are not expressly restricted to breaches occurring after the transfer, they are so limited by the courts.

2. FUTURE RIGHTS AGAINST THE TRANSFEREE

a. Lease Covenants Run With the Land

The transferee of a lessee's interest under an ordinary real property lease is bound by provisions that "run with the land." Covenants are held to run with the land where (1) they were intended to do so by the original parties, (2) they pertain to matters that "touch and concern" the land, and (3) there is privity of estate between the original lessor and the transferee. When these elements are present, transferees of leasehold interests are held to be bound by both express and implied provisions of the lease.

Almost without exception, the provisions of oil and gas leases have been held to be covenants that run with the land. Consequently, the transferee of a leasehold interest assumes all of the obligations imposed by the original lease. An assignment may impose additional obligations upon the transferee, but nothing in the assignment can limit the rights of the original lessor against the transferee under the terms of the lease.

b. The Assignment/Sublease Distinction

The obligations of a lease transferee to the lessor may be affected by whether the transfer is an assignment or a sublease. An *assignment* is a transfer of the entire leasehold interest in all or any portion of the property. A *sublease* is a transfer of less than all of the interest. When the transaction is classified as an assignment, the lessor can enforce covenants of the lease that run with the land against the transferee as well as his or her lessee; the lessor will be in privity of estate with the transferee and in privity of contract with the lessee. If the transaction is classified as a sublease, the lessor's rights are against the lessee/sublessor and the transferee's obligations are owed to the lessee/sublessor because no privity of estate exists between the lessor and the sublessee.

Some jurisdictions have applied the assignment/sublease distinction to transfers of oil and gas leases. When the lessee has assigned the lease for less than the entire remaining term or reserving a right to reenter or an overriding royalty interest, some courts have held that a sublease is created rather than an assignment. Louisiana recognizes the distinction routinely. The distinction has been largely ignored by courts, however, because it is not recognized by the customs and usages of the industry.

C.　RIGHTS AND DUTIES OF THE LESSEE AND HIS TRANSFEREE

When the lessee retains rights after the transfer of the lease, whether those rights are to a non-operating interest or to an operating interest in a portion of the leased premises, disputes frequently arise over the relationship of the transferor and the transferee.

1.　PROTECTION OF NON–OPERATING INTERESTS BY IMPLIED COVENANTS

Authority is divided whether a lessee who assigns the working interest retaining an overriding royalty or other non-operating interest is entitled to the protection of implied covenants. Most of the cases suggest that the lessee is not. In *XAE Corp. v. SMR Property Management Co.*, 968 P.2d 1201 (Okl. 1998), the Oklahoma Supreme Court refused to recognize an implied covenant to market protecting an overriding royalty interest, reasoning that implied covenants do not arise from lease assignments "where there was no express agreement in the contract that could form the basis of relief for the breach of an implied obligation." Other cases, such as *Cook v. El Paso Natural Gas Co.*, 560 F.2d 978

(10th Cir.N.M.1977), often assume that the lessee is protected.

The conceptual difficulty is that the original lessee/assignor cannot claim the protection of the covenants implied in an oil and gas lease. Lease implied covenants benefit the lessor and burden the lessee. Thus, if courts are to protect the original lessee/assignor they must imply covenants in the lease assignment. Courts have been reticent to imply covenants in assignments because an assignment is usually a "pure" conveyance and a transaction between sophisticated persons.

Non-operating interest holders should be protected by implied covenants, just as are lessors. With assignments as with leases, a substantial part of the consideration for the transfer is likely to be the expectation of profits from production that the transferee will share with the transferor. The parties will often not think or sometimes be sophisticated enough to draft specific contractual protections for the transferor. Thus, the protection of the usual lease implied covenants can be implied in transfer of non-operating interests either from the facts of the transaction or in law in the interest of fairness.

Extension of the protection of implied covenants to a lessee that transfers its operating rights in exchange for a non-operating interest will not materially affect the obligations of the holder of the lease. The lessee's transferee will have no obligation to test the premises, unless the assignment imposes a specific drilling obligation. The transferee will ordinarily have no liability to the original lessee for letting the lease terminate by failing to pay delay rentals. The transferee will merely have an obligation to the lessee, as well as to the lessor, to protect the premises against drainage, to reasonably develop and explore once production is obtained, and to perform as would a reasonably prudent operator under the circumstances.

2. PROTECTION OF NON–OPERATING INTERESTS AGAINST "WASH OUT"

A frequent problem after a lessee has transferred operating rights in a lease and retained a non-operating interest is the "wash out." If the transferee permits the lease to terminate and then subsequently re-leases the property, should the original lessee's non-operating interest be recognized under the new lease? Not affording the original lessee protection will tempt transferees to maximize profits unfairly by washing out non-operating interests. On the other hand, requiring recognition of the original lessee's non-operating right in lease extensions or replacement leases will hamstring transferees; there may be sound business reasons to permit a lease to terminate and then re-lease the property. The transferee should not be a fiduciary for the transferor.

Some cases, like *Brannon v. Sohio Petroleum Co.*, 260 F.2d 621 (10th Cir.Okla.1958), and *Sunac v.*

Parkes, 416 S.W.2d 798 (Tex.1967), have held that one who transfers operating rights but retains a non-operating interest is not protected against a washout by implied covenants. Others, however, have extended the transferor protection on the grounds that either (a) a constructive trust is created by a special or confidential relationship between the parties as shown by the particular facts, or (b) the facts give rise to an inference of bad faith by the transferee.

As a result of the uncertainty whether a lessee that transfers its operating rights in a lease will be protected against a washout and when such protection will be extended, lease assignments reserving non-operating interests frequently contain specific provisions guaranteeing recognition of the transferor's non-operating interest in lease extensions and renewals. In *Reynolds–Rexwinkle Oil Co., Inc. v. Petex, Inc.*, 1 P.3d 909 (Kan.2000), the Kansas Supreme Court held that a lease assignment reserving an overriding royalty and providing that the overriding royalty would apply to "renewals and extensions" of the lease assigned creates a duty of fair dealing between the parties, so that a lease granted covering the property while the original lease was still in effect was an "extension" lease.

An alternative is to obligate the transferee to offer to reassign the lease before permitting the lease to terminate. The biggest problem with reassignment clauses may be that they *will* be enforced in situations in which the promising party does not expect them to be. *Shore Exploration & Production*

Corp. v. Exxon Corp., 976 F.Supp. 514 (N.D.Tex. 1997), illustrates the point. Shore assigned leases to Exxon, Texaco and Eastern, in separate transactions reserving an overriding royalty. The assignments required the assignees to pay delay rentals or to notify Shore, so that Shore could request reassignment. Subsequently, Texaco acquired the interests of the other assignees. After drilling several dry holes, Texaco assigned the leases, covering over 82,000 acres and subject to Shore's overriding royalty and the reassignment clause, to Eastern. Eastern neither paid the rentals nor gave the notice required by the reassignment clauses. All of the leases were forfeited for failure to pay delay rentals. The court found Texaco liable on a theory of privity of contract for Eastern's failure to give notice.

3. IMPLIED COVENANTS OF TITLE FROM THE LESSEE

Is a lease transferee entitled to protection from covenants of warranty implied in the assignment from the original lessee? The transferee is protected by the covenant of warranty of the lessor found in most oil and gas lease forms, but the language of an assignment generally does not support implied covenants of title. The language of assignments may differ substantially, however, and in some states the use of particular words of grant may imply some covenants. Therefore, assignments of leases often specify whether covenants of title are intended.

4. PERFORMANCE OR FAILURE OF PERFORMANCE BY A PARTIAL ASSIGNEE

Disputes frequently arise about the effect of the transferee's actions or failure to act upon the rights of a lessee who partially assigns operating rights. Suppose, for example, that A Company takes a lease on a 640 acre section of land and subsequently assigns the east 1/2 of the section to B Company:

640 Acre Tract

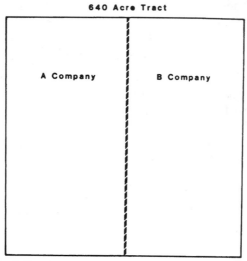

A Company Assigns East 1/2 to B Company

What is the effect of production by B Company? What is the effect of B Company's failure to pay delay rentals?

Both situations are governed by the general principle that the rights and duties of a lessor and a lessee under a lease are set when the lease is originally granted; lease obligations are not divisible, as *Oag v. Desert Gas Exploration Co.*, 659 N.Y.S.2d 654 (N.Y.App.Div.1997), illustrates. The term clause of a lease typically provides that the lease will extend so long as there is production "from the leased premises." If B Company obtains production on the property, the production extends the lease for both the west and the east portions. Even where the lease habendum clause requires "production by the lessee," courts generally have held that the language is satisfied if production is obtained by the lessee's assignee or one to whom the lessee has agreed to assign. On occasion, there has not even been a written agreement to assign.

Likewise, unless the lease provides otherwise, a failure either by A Company or B Company to pay delay rentals properly will cause the lease to terminate upon both the east and west portions of the tract; the lease calls for delay-rental payments to be made covering the whole premises described. Most modern oil and gas lease forms contain specific language to change this result. A typical example is the following from a New Mexico lease form:

> "In the event of an assignment of this Lease as to a segregated portion of said land, the rentals payable shall be apportioned as between the several Leasehold owners ratably according to the surface area of each and default in rental payment by one shall not affect the rights of other Leasehold owners hereunder."

The effect of the language is to make delay rentals divisible where the lease is subdivided by the lessee.

In Louisiana, when the lease contains a clause like that quoted, A Company would be required to establish production on the west half in order to satisfy the term clause as to that portion, even if B Company had obtained production on the east half. Louisiana courts have held that the clause makes the lease divisible so that each portion must be treated as a separate lease.

5. DIVISIBILITY OF IMPLIED COVENANTS AFTER A PARTIAL ASSIGNMENT

Some states recognize an exception to the general rule that lease obligations are not divisible after a partial assignment, at least for the implied covenants to reasonably develop and to explore further. At issue is whether the obligation of the lessee and its assignee is to be judged by reference to the lease as a whole or whether each must stand on its own. As the example above illustrates, production from either portion of a subdivided lease satisfies the lease habendum clause for the whole property. Because the lease is not divisible, both A Company and B Company have an obligation to continue to develop reasonably. The question remains, however, should the diligence of the lessee and his assignee be judged on the basis of the lease as a whole or separately for the two portions? Logic and adherence to the principle that rights and obligations under the lease are set when it is formed indicate that the lease should be considered to be indivisible for the purposes of implied covenants just as it is for express covenants. That is the position adopted in *Kothe v. Jefferson*, 455 N.E.2d 73 (Ill.1983). Several cases, however, such as *Cosden Oil Co. v. Scarborough*, 55 F.2d 634 (5th Cir.Tex.1932), have specifically rejected that conclusion, and others are unclear.

*

PART IV

TAX AND BUSINESS MATTERS

CHAPTER 13

OIL AND GAS TAXATION

Oil and gas taxation is usually covered in a course separate from the basic course in oil and gas law. An understanding of the fundamental rules of oil and gas taxation is essential, however, for any lawyer practicing oil and gas law in the United States, as well as for mineral owners and industry landmen or managers; routine transactions may have important tax implications. This chapter considers taxation of oil and gas operations on a transactional basis.

A. BASIC PRINCIPLES

In most respects, taxation of oil and gas transactions is consistent with general tax principles, which are beyond the scope of this book. There are at least three concepts, however, that are peculiar to oil and gas taxation and are fundamentally important to oil and gas operations. They are (1) the property concept, (2) the intangible drilling cost deduction, and (3) depletion.

1. THE PROPERTY CONCEPT

For oil and gas tax purposes, the term "property" refers to each separate legal interest owned by a taxpayer in each geological deposit, in each separate tract or parcel of land. Treas.Reg. § 1.614–1(a). Thus, "property" has legal, geological, and geographical aspects.

The concept of "property" is important to oil and gas transactions in several ways:

    a. a taxpayer must allocate geological and geophysical costs incurred in the search for oil and gas to a property unit and include those costs as a part of the depletable basis of that property unit;

    b. a taxpayer deducts intangible drilling costs on a property basis and may have to recapture those costs when that property is sold or transferred;

    c. a taxpayer must calculate depletion, whether percentage depletion or cost depletion, separately for each property;

    d. a taxpayer must compute gain or loss from sales separately for each property.

2. INTANGIBLE DRILLING COSTS DEDUCTION

The deduction for intangible drilling costs is an important tax benefit under the Internal Revenue Code. *Intangible drilling costs* are those costs necessarily incurred in drilling wells and preparing them for production of oil and gas that result in no salvage value. Treas.Reg. § 1.612–4.

Were it not for a special provision of the Internal Revenue Code, taxpayers would be required to capitalize intangible drilling costs along with costs of equipment and depreciate them over the lifetime of the well. Subject to strict limitations, however, § 263(c) of the Internal Revenue Code permits taxpayers to deduct intangible drilling costs in the year that they are incurred. The owner of a working interest in an oil and gas property has the option either to deduct intangible drilling costs as expenses in the year incurred or to capitalize them and recover them through cost depletion or depreciation. The intangible drilling cost deduction is limited for integrated oil companies (those with retailing and refining operations) to 70%. The remaining 30% is capitalized and amortized ratably over 60 months.

Most taxpayers elect to deduct intangible drilling costs currently, on the theory that it is better to take tax deductions sooner rather than later. The benefit is not without a price. Intangible drilling costs deducted are an item of tax preference and therefore trigger minimum tax consequences for some taxpayers. Also, intangible drilling costs are subject to recapture under § 1254 when the property is sold or transferred.

An important limitation on a taxpayer's option to "expense" intangible drilling costs is the requirement that a taxpayer must both (a) incur the costs, and (b) own the full share of the working interest for which intangible drilling costs are deducted until production has paid out all of the costs of drilling, equipping, and operating the well. This limitation, which is set out in Rev.Rul. 70–336, 1970–1 C.B. 145, is sometimes referred to as the *complete payout limitation*. Parties to oil and gas transactions carefully structure them to comply with or to avoid the complete payout limitation, because intangible drilling costs often amount to 60% to 70% of the total costs of drilling and equipping a well. A common avoidance technique for a partnership is a special allocation of intangible drilling costs to the partners who contributed drilling funds. A special allocation will be upheld if it has "substantial economic effect," which requires that there be "business logic" to the allocation; i.e., the capital accounts of the partners must reflect the allocations.

3. DEPLETION

Producing a mineral deposit depletes it. In a very real sense, production consumes a taxpayer's capital investment. Some part of every dollar a taxpayer receives from the sale of oil and gas production is a return of a portion of the costs expended in developing the property, rather than a true profit. Therefore, a deduction from current income for mineral depletion is appropriate. Depletion deductions are in turn subject to recapture when a property is sold.

The Internal Revenue Code recognizes two methods for taxpayers to compute depletion: cost depletion and percentage depletion. The law requires a taxpayer to make both calculations and to deduct the larger of the two amounts.

a. Cost Depletion

Under cost depletion, the taxpayer who owns an interest in an oil and gas property deducts the basis in the property from the income as oil and gas are produced and sold. Cost depletion is calculated by a formula set forth in Treas.Reg. § 1.611–2 that can be expressed as follows:

$$B \times \frac{S}{(U + S)}$$

B equals the adjusted basis of the property at the end of the period.

U equals units remaining at the end of the period.

S equals units sold during the period.

This formula relates the recovery of the taxpayer's investment to the proportion that the current unit sales of oil and gas bear to the total anticipated sales from the property. The investment is recovered ratably over the life of the reserves.

b. Percentage Depletion

Percentage depletion is a statutory provision that permits deduction of specified percentages of the gross oil and gas income from a property in lieu of depleting the actual basis. The law excludes from taxation a fixed percentage of each dollar one receives from sales of oil and gas production. Percentage depletion is not limited to the actual capital costs incurred by a taxpayer. Deductions for percentage depletion from a prolific lease may greatly exceed the actual capital costs incurred by the taxpayer in developing the property.

(1) Economic Interest Concept

An important limitation to the availability of percentage depletion is the requirement that the taxpayer own an economic interest in the property to claim percentage depletion. The rationale of the economic-interest limitation is that Congress intended percentage depletion to be an incentive for those who own mineral deposits. As the term "economic interest" has been defined, however, a taxpayer need not own the mineral interest itself. Treas. Reg. § 1.611–1(b) provides that a taxpayer holds an economic interest where a taxpayer acquires any interest in minerals in place and secures, by any form of legal relationship, income from extraction to which the taxpayer must look for return of capital. Royalty interests, net profits interests, and carried interests are all generally recognized as economic interests.

(2) Independent Producers' and Royalty Owners' Limitation

Percentage depletion was originally enacted as a special incentive to promote oil and gas production. For approximately forty years it was broadly available and usually more advantageous for taxpayers than cost depletion. In 1975, at the height of an oil shortage, the Tax Reduction Act of 1975 repealed percentage depletion for oil and gas produced after December 31, 1974. Exceptions to repeal were provided in § 613A, however, one of which is for independent producers and royalty owners. Since 1984, taxpayers qualifying as independent producers or royalty owners have been permitted percentage depletion at a 15% rate for a total of 1,000 barrels of oil or 6 million cubic feet of natural gas per day to the extent of 50% of the taxable income from the property and, with certain adjustments, to the extent of 65% of the taxpayer's taxable income for the year. In 1990, Congress modified the deduction to allow for a higher rate (16–25 percent) of percentage depletion for marginal properties or stripper oil when the price of oil averages below $20 for the prior year. Congress increased the rate of percentage depletion on marginal production by 1 percent for each $1 that the price of oil is below $20, up to a maximum increase in the rate of 10 percent. Congress also increased the taxable income limitation from 50 percent to 100 percent. The primary purpose of the 1990 changes was to encourage the continued production of marginal properties and to limit the effect of significant price drops in the oil markets. Thus, for individual investors and small oil companies, percentage depletion is still an important incentive.

B. TAXATION OF TRANSFERS OF MINERAL RIGHTS

1.   LEASE PAYMENTS

a. Lease Bonus

A mineral owner usually grants an oil and gas lease for a *lease bonus*, a payment from the lessee to the lessor to induce the grant. Although a typical oil and gas lease conveys the lessor's mineral rights to the lessee, the bonus payment is taxable as ordinary income to the lessor. Before the Tax Reform Act of 1986, a lessor could claim percentage depletion on bonus payments. Now, however, percentage depletion cannot be claimed on lease bonus payments, advance royalties, or any other payments that do not relate to actual production.

A lessee must capitalize lease bonus payments as a part of geological and geophysical costs, which are discussed below.

b. Delay Rentals

U.S. Tax law treats delay-rental payments made by a lessee to a lessor during the primary term of a lease as rents from the land. As such, rental payments are taxed to the lessor as ordinary income not subject to percentage depletion. A lessee who pays delay rentals may deduct them as an operating expense. A lessee may also elect to capitalize rentals and recover them through cost depletion.

Because lessees can deduct delay rentals but must capitalize bonus payments, some lessees have attempted to couch bonuses as delay rentals by making them payable in installments. Courts have ruled that for a payment to qualify as a delay rental, the payment must be avoidable by drilling, production, or lease abandonment. Otherwise, the payment is considered a bonus that must be capitalized.

c. Royalty Payments

Royalties received by a lessor are taxed as ordinary income. When the royalty is based on actual production, it ordinarily qualifies for the depletion allowance. The lessee excludes the royalty from its income. Where the royalty is not based upon actual production, the lessee treats the royalty as an operating expense.

2. LEASE TRANSFERS

a. The Sale/Sublease Distinction

The tax rules make an important distinction between a sale and a sublease. When a transaction is classified as a sale, the seller computes gain or loss on the difference between the fair market value of the consideration received and the seller's basis in the property transferred. In contrast, if a transaction is termed a sublease, all consideration the seller receive is treated as ordinary income. Therefore, classification as a "sale" is often more beneficial to the seller than classification as a "sublease" because the seller can deduct basis in computing the gain.

What is the difference between a sale and a sublease? For tax purposes, a sale results (1) when the seller transfers *all* of the interest or an undivided fractional interest that is identical in kind (i.e., working interest, royalty interest, etc.) to that which the seller retains, or (2) when the interest the seller conveys is of a continuing non-operating nature (e.g., an overriding royalty interest conveyed from a working interest), or (3) when the seller conveys the working interest and retains only non-operating rights of a non-continuing nature (such as a production payment). Any other type of transaction is classified as a sublease for tax purposes.

The sale/sublease distinction is particularly troublesome because leases are often acquired for speculative purposes by persons who then trade them to oil companies in return for cash consideration and a retained overriding royalty interest. Though the parties to the transactions are often not aware of it, the tax result is that all of the cash received by the lease transferor is taxable as ordinary income. The theory is that, because the transaction is a sublease in which the transferor conveys less than all that he or she owns, the basis of the transferor is accumulated in the retained overriding royalty interest. Some attorneys believe that the result may be avoided if the transferor retains a fraction of the working interest in addition to an overriding royalty interest, retains a carried or working interest rather than an overriding royalty interest, or transfers the lease to a partnership composed of the transferor and the assignee that provides for benefits similar to those of an overriding royalty interest.

b. Production Payments

Sometimes an owner will transfer a lease in exchange for a production payment. A *production payment* is a share of production from the leased premises that terminates when a specified amount of money has been recovered. An example would be "1/5 of all oil and gas produced and saved from said land, free of cost, until the market value at the well of such production shall aggregate One Million Dollars." For tax purposes, a production payment is treated as a mortgage, and the transaction that creates the production payment is treated as a sale. The transferor recognizes ordinary income or capital gain as the production payment is received. The transferee of the interest capitalizes the amount of the production payment. Special rules may apply, however, where the production payment is pledged for development.

c. Sharing Arrangements

When one transfers an interest in a mineral property to another in exchange for a contribution from the transferee to the cost of acquisition, exploration, or development of the property, a *sharing arrangement* is generally created for tax purposes. The parties to a sharing arrangement are held to have "pooled" their capital and created an informal partnership for tax purposes. As a result, there are no tax consequences of the transfer until the property is abandoned or transferred, at which time the transaction will generally be taxed as a sale. See generally, G.C.M. 22730, 1941–1 C.B. 214.

A farmout, a transfer of an interest in acreage in return for participating in drilling and testing operations on that acreage, is one of the most important sharing agreements. Rev.Rul. 77–176, 1977–1 C.B. 77 establishes an important limitation on such transactions. There, the Internal Revenue Service took the position that a transfer of acreage in addition to that included in the drilling unit was a transfer of separate property not protected from taxation by the pool of capital doctrine. Worse, the revenue ruling concluded that the value of the property for tax purposes should be determined as of the date of the transfer, which usually is after the property has been proved by successful drilling operations. Revenue Ruling 77–176 limits the flexibility of sharing arrangements, and has spawned a variety of creative avoidance devices.

Bottom-hole and dry-hole contributions differ from usual sharing arrangements in that the party drilling does so on its own land and the party contributing support receives geological information to help it evaluate its own property, instead of an interest in the property being developed. The Internal Revenue Service treats such transactions as sales rather than as sharing arrangements. The recipient of the funds recognizes income to the extent of the amount received. The contributing party must capitalize its expenditure as a geological and geophysical cost. See Rev.Rul. 80–153, 1980–1 C.B. 10.

C. TAXATION OF OIL AND GAS DEVELOPMENT

1. FORMS OF OWNERSHIP

Because of its high risk and large capital requirements, oil and gas exploration and development are often conducted by more than one person or entity. Problems then arise as to what form the joint ownership should take.

a. Corporation

Limited liability makes a corporation an attractive business entity for oil and gas development. As a tax vehicle, however, a corporation is generally unattractive. Tax benefits in the form of accelerated deductions (such as intangible drilling cost deductions) or unrecognized income (such as that afforded by percentage depletion) are recognized at the corporate level, and do not pass through to the individuals or entities who own a corporation. Moreover, income earned by a corporation and distributed to its shareholders is doubly taxed, once at the corporate level and again as a dividend upon distribution.

Corporations that have elected to be taxed as partnerships under Subchapter S of the Internal Revenue Code have generally not been used as vehicles for oil and gas development because the technical rules applied have conflicted with important tax incentives. There are at least three reasons that so-called *S Corporations* may not be the optimal form of business organization for an oil and gas venture. First, the tax code places substantial restrictions on the stock ownership of corporations that qualify as S Corporations. S Corporations can have no more than seventy-five shareholders, and foreign investors, non-resident aliens, and "regular" corporations cannot be shareholders of the S Corporation. Second, the owners of an S Corporation cannot specially allocate losses and deductions. Finally, unlike the owners of partnership interests, the owners of S Corporations cannot include liabilities for which they are personally liable in the calculation of the amount considered to be "at-risk"; they cannot operate on borrowed money.

b. Partnership

A partnership is the ideal entity for oil and gas development from a tax viewpoint, because partnerships are not taxed under the Internal Revenue Code. Both profits and losses flow through the partnership to the individual partners, though the benefit of deductions may be limited by "at risk" and "passive loss limitation" rules. Further, partners are permitted to specially allocate losses among themselves, subject to detailed limitations, which may assist a partnership in attracting investment capital to the venture. From a liability viewpoint, however, a partnership is a poor choice. Each partner is liable to the full extent of his or her assets for the torts and contracts of all of the partners. Moreover, preparing and filing an annual tax return makes a partnership entity substantially more expensive than concurrent ownership. For these reasons, partnerships are not usually used in oil and gas development.

Until the Tax Reform Act of 1986, limited partnerships were the preferred form of entity for oil and gas development among small investors. Limited partnerships offered limited partners the guarantee of liability limited to their actual investment, though general partners were subject to unlimited liability. For tax purposes, however, all partners of a limited partner were treated like general partners and entitled to flow through partnership profits and losses.

Limited partnerships were never favored by active participants in the oil and gas industry because limited partners are not permitted to participate in management. Their allure to investors was further tarnished by the Tax Reform Act of 1986, which classified limited partnerships as "passive" investment activities. Under the Tax Reform Act of 1986, losses and tax credits from passive activities can offset only income and taxes from passive activities. Excess passive losses and credits are suspended, and carried forward, but not back. These rules substantially limit the "tax shelter" characteristic that has traditionally made oil and gas investments attractive to investors.

c. Limited Liability Entities

Many states have enacted legislation that permit business persons to form *limited liability companies* and *limited liability partnerships*, both of which combine the corporate characteristic of limited liability and the tax pass-through of a partnership. The personal liability of the owners (typically called "members") is limited to the amount of cash contributed to the entity. Unlike limited partners, members of a LLC or LLP are free to participate in management without fear of being subjected to personal liability. The IRS' "check-the-box" regulations provide that, in determining the federal tax liability of the entity and its members, the LLC qualifies for treatment as a "pass-through" entity. Unlike an S Corporation, the LLC has no restrictions on the number and type of owners that can participate in membership. Members of a LLC can specially allocate profits and losses, and the IRS will recognize allocations in computing the federal income tax liability of the members.

A LLC or LLP, then, offers prospective owners of an oil and gas venture the opportunity to form an entity that will maximize the ability to attract investors. Members enjoy limited liability, but benefit immediately from the deductions available for intangible drilling costs. Members can use the ability to specially allocate deductions to attract non-operators, or "financial" investors. Members can attract capital from foreign investors by offering an ownership interest in the venture without fear of losing pass-through tax status for the entity. In fact, foreign investors may find the LLC favorable merely because the entity is more familiar than partnerships in many countries.

d. Concurrent Ownership

Concurrent ownership is traditionally the favored form of entity for oil and gas operations among those active in the oil and gas industry. When parties jointly own and operate properties, each owns a separate property for tax purposes, and the tax results are approximately the same as if the parties were active partners. The Tax Reform Act of 1986 contained a special provision exempting concurrently-owned working interests in oil and gas from the passive investment rules. On the other hand, liability of the non-operating party is effectively limited to the amount of its investment. The operator is treated as an independent contractor, liable for its own torts and contractual obligations. There are important and apparently growing exceptions to this rule, however, that impose liability upon nonoperators by strict liability theory or by statute.

2. TAXATION OF SEARCH COSTS: GEOLOGICAL AND GEOPHYSICAL COSTS

Expenditures made to obtain data to serve as a basis for the acquisition or retention of oil and gas properties are called *geological and geophysical costs*. "G & G" costs include costs of core drilling and seismographic surveys. Taxpayers must capitalize these costs and recover them by depletion, like leasehold costs. There are substantial accounting problems presented in allocating geological and geophysical costs among properties.

3. TAXATION OF DEVELOPMENT COSTS

a. Intangible Drilling Costs

Costs incurred in preparing a drill site and actually drilling a well can be broken into two classes for tax purposes: intangible drilling costs and equipment costs. Intangible drilling costs are costs incurred that have no salvage value and are incidental to and necessary for the drilling and preparation of wells for the production of oil and gas. Typical intangible drilling costs expenditures include wages, fuel, services, and supplies used in preparing the drill site, drilling the well, and many completion costs. Intangible drilling costs do not include the costs of installing equipment for cleaning, processing, or storage, however.

b. Equipment Costs

Oil and gas producing equipment is treated for tax purposes like the equipment of any other industry. The cost of production equipment must be capitalized and depreciated. Taxpayers can claim accelerated depreciation under the Modified Accelerated Cost Recovery System, subject to recapture upon early disposition. Producing equipment placed in service before 1986 ordinarily qualified for investment tax credits, but the Tax Reform Act of 1986 repealed the provision.

4. TAXATION OF OIL AND GAS PRODUCTION

The value of oil and gas production is taxed as ordinary income to its owners, subject to the deductions for cost or percentage depletion.

CHAPTER 14

OIL AND GAS CONTRACTS

Although oil and gas contracts other than leases are not covered in most courses in oil and gas law, anyone who works in or with the oil and gas industry should be familiar with the types of contracts used in operations. These include:

Support Agreements

Farmout Agreements

Drilling Contracts

Operating Agreements

Gas Contracts

Gas Balancing Agreements

Division Orders

This chapter will provide a functional overview of these commonly-encountered agreements.

All oil and gas agreements are subject to the general rules that govern contracts. A promise becomes a *contract*, a legally binding agreement, only if there has been an offer and acceptance of clear and unambiguous terms pertaining to a subject matter that is not illegal or contrary to public policy, supported by consideration, between two persons or entities with the legal capacity to contract. Generally, oil and gas contracts must meet all the requirements for binding legal agreements.

Most oil and gas agreements are of sufficient duration or involve transfer of an interest in land, so that the Statute of Frauds requires that they be evidenced by a writing. In fact, because of the large amounts of money at stake, the contracts identified above are almost always in writing, whether or not a writing is a legal requirement.

A. SUPPORT AGREEMENTS

Support agreements, sometimes called *contribution agreements*, are contracts used to encourage and "support" drilling operations. The contributing party to a support agreement agrees to contribute money or property in exchange for information. From the contributing party's view, a support agreement is a purchase of geological or technological information. From the viewpoint of the party receiving the support, the support agreement lessens the cost or the risk of drilling operations.

Three commonly encountered kinds of support agreements are:

Dry–Hole Agreement—the contributing party agrees to make a cash contribution if the drilling party drills a dry hole. The drilling party generally agrees to provide geological and drilling information whether or not the well is a dry hole.

Bottom–Hole Agreement—the contributing party agrees to make a cash contribution to the drilling party in exchange for geological or drilling information, if the drilling party drills a well to an agreed depth and provides the information.

Acreage–Contribution Agreement—the contributing party agrees to contribute leases or interests in the area of the test well to the drilling party in exchange for drilling information, if the drilling party drills a well to an agreed depth and provides the information.

With each of these agreements, it is essential that the parties clearly agree (1) what test information must be provided by the drilling party and (2) what conditions the drilling party must meet to earn the contribution. Frequent disputes arise about how dry a well must be in order to be a "dry hole" or what happens if the drilling party cannot reach the total depth agreed in a bottom-hole agreement.

B. FARMOUT AGREEMENTS

A *farmout agreement* is an agreement to assign an interest in acreage in return for the conduct of or payment for drilling or testing operations on that acreage. The *farmor,* the person or entity making the assignment, may use a farmout agreement to maintain a lease by securing production close to the end of the lease primary term, to comply with an implied covenant to develop or offset, or to obtain an interest in production without additional cost. The allure of a farmout agreement to a *farmee,* the person or entity receiving the assignment, is that a farmee may earn acreage not otherwise available or at a lower cost than otherwise possible, or may be able to keep people and equipment gainfully employed. Typically, a farmee will actually conduct the earning operations, but sometimes a farmee will merely agree to pay or share the costs of operations the farmor will conduct.

A farmout agreement is closely related to support agreements. A farmout agreement supports oil and gas operations by spreading risks, costs, and information. A farmout agreement differs from support agreements in that the earning party conducts or pays for operations on the property of the contributing party rather than on the earning party's own property, and the parties end up sharing ownership of developed property.

The most important substantive issues of farmout agreements generally are:

(1) The duty imposed—whether drilling the well is a covenant or a condition;

(2) What must be done in order to earn the right to the assignment; and

(3) What is earned.

The distinction between a drilling *covenant* and a drilling *condition* relates to the liability of the farmee for failure to drill. If the farmee promises to drill a well on the premises, then the farmee may be held liable if it fails to perform the promise. The majority rule measure of damages, adopted in Oklahoma and Louisiana, is the cost of drilling the promised well. In other states, including Texas, the remedy is the usual rule for recovery of damages for breach of contract, the benefit that the farmor would have received had the farmee drilled the well as promised. The Texas approach is often called "lost royalty" rule, because the lost overriding royalty is usually the value of the performance. The "lost royalty" rule places a heavy burden of proof upon a farmor whose farmee has failed to perform, however. *Martin v. Darcy*, 357 S.W.2d 457 (Tex.Civ. App.1962), is a case in point. There, Martin promised to drill a well under an farmout assignment from Darcy but failed to do so, though another person later drilled the well as a dry hole. Darcy sued and recovered $3000 on the theory that the interest that he had retained had possessed a market value of $6000 and that he would have sold half of it before completion of the well had Martin drilled it. The appellate court reversed the award on the basis that, to recover, Darcy would have had to have shown (1) that the profits he claimed had been contemplated by the parties when the agreement was made and (2) that he actually would have sold his interest. Because of the difficulty of satisfying the "lost royalty" rule, the parties to a farmout agreement may either include a stipulation of liquidated damages or agree that the majority rule will apply.

On the other hand, if drilling a test well is a *condition* of earning rights under a farmout agreement—the more common farmout agreement structure in the United States—then a farmee has no liability for failing to drill. A farmee who fails to drill simply earns no rights. Sometimes, farmout agreements make initial drilling a covenant of the farmee but permit the farmee to escape the obligation if it encounters unforseen conditions in drilling.

The terms of the farmout agreement relating to what the farmee must do to earn rights determine the time constraints and the costs the farmee must incur. The number of wells to be drilled, and the number and kind of tests to be conducted are obviously important. Farmout agreements usually require strict compliance by the farmee; to earn rights, generally, a farmee must drill to the depth specified, complete all tests specified, and obtain production sufficient to repay the costs of drilling and return a reasonable profit. Terms are negotiable, however. Sometimes parties negotiate provisions for partial performance or substantial performance or even earning without commercial production.

What a farmee earns by performing a farmout agreement is determined by such variable factors as the number of leases and the percentage in each earned, the depth earned under each lease, the substances covered by the farmout, the size of the nonoperating interest reserved by the farmor, and whether the farmor's reserves a right to convert its nonoperating interest to a working interest. Typically, how much a farmee is able to earn under a farmout reflects the negotiating strengths of the parties. Inattention to detail can make the difference between profit and loss, however, because farmout agreements are complicated and technical.

C. OPERATING AGREEMENTS

An *operating agreement* is a contract between cotenants or separate owners of oil and gas properties being jointly operated. It sets out the parties' agreement with respect to initial drilling, further development, operations, and accounting.

1. PURPOSE

An operating agreement defines the rights and duties of co-owners or cooperating owners. It pools the leases and fractional interests of the parties for operating purposes.

In the United States, the parties generally use one of several "model" forms developed by the American Association of Professional Landmen. Occasionally in the United States and often in Canada, one sees the model form developed by the Canadian Association of Petroleum Landmen. The provisions of the model forms are designed for use in transactions involving companies or persons active in the oil and gas industry. Frequently, the parties substantially modify the terms of the model agreements.

2. COMMON SUBSTANTIVE ISSUES

Although there may be substantial differences in the provisions of operating agreements, all operating agreements must address common substantive issues to accomplish their basic purposes. There are at least three essential issues: (a) the scope of the operator's authority, (b) provision for initial drilling, and (c) additional development.

a. Scope of the Operator's Authority

Someone must be appointed as the operator and empowered by the co-owners or cooperating owners to be responsible for operations on a day-to-day basis. The model-form operating agreements provide for a narrow scope of liability for the operator ("gross negligence or willful misconduct") and a limited basis for removal. The reason for such limitations is that in dealings between companies and persons active in the industry, the operator usually acts as operator as an accommodation, perhaps because it has other operations in the same area. In contrast, many operating agreements cover the relationship of groups of investors with the operator who sold them their interests in the oil and gas property. The operator expects to make a profit from its operations and charges an appropriate fee. In such circumstances, the operator's investors may consider the limiting provisions of the model agreements overly restrictive.

Courts will enforce limitations of liability in operating agreements, but there is disagreement about the scope of the "gross negligence or wilful misconduct" limitation. The 10th Circuit, in *Shell Rocky Mtn. Prod., LLC v. Ultra Resources, Inc.*, 415 F.3d 1158 (10th Cir. Wyo. 2005), held that the disclaimer applies only to an operator's failure to conduct operations in a "good and workmanlike manner," or to its tortious conduct in conducting operations;

it does not apply where an operator has breached express contractual provisions or has failed to perform its administrative duties. Three Texas Courts of Appeals have reached the same result. But the Fifth Circuit Court of Appeals went further in *Stine v. Marathon Oil Co.*, 976 F.2d 254 (5th Cir.Tex. 1992), reasoning that "in the present case, Marathon [the operator] is not liable for any action taken in connection with the completion, testing or turnover, or any well drilled under the provisions of the JOA unless Stine [the nonoperator] can prove that Marathon's actions were grossly negligent or willful.... This protection extends to Marathon's various administrative and accounting duties, including the recovery of costs under the authority of the JOA."

Operating agreements generally spell out in great detail both the obligations of the operator and limitations upon its discretion. Nonoperators are generally not liable for the contracts or torts of operators, because operators are not agents for the nonoperators. Typically, operating agreements impose duties upon the operator to carry certain amounts of insurance, maintain certain kinds of accounts, and hire legal and accounting assistance, as well as operate the property. Operating agreements also place limitations upon an operator's discretion to make certain decisions (e.g., to plug and abandon a well or release a portion of a lease). Most operating agreements, in addition, place a monetary limit on the authority of the operator (e.g., the operator may not undertake projects estimated to involve the expenditure of more than $10,000 without permission of the other owners, except in an emergency).

All of the model agreements take great care to limit the powers of the nonoperators to approval or disapproval of proposed operations—"go no-go" decisions. When nonoperators actively participate in management or have the right to do so, they may be held liable jointly and severally with the operator as *mining partners*, a partnership relationship implied at law. Otherwise, the relationship of the operator and nonoperators is analogous to that of cotenants, so that each is liable only for its own torts and contracts. As the court noted in *Blocker Exploration Co. v. Frontier Exploration, Inc.*, 740 P.2d 983 (Colo.1987), "co-ownership alone does not give rise to a mining partnership." Nonoperators' interests may be subject to mechanics and materialmen's liens, but that is ordinarily the extent of their liability under operating agreements.

b. Initial Drilling

Parties generally enter into operating agreements only after they have decided to drill an initial well. Therefore, the operating agreement almost always directs the operator to drill an initial well on the premises, setting time limits within which work must be commenced (to preserve the leases), and specifying depths to be reached and formations to be tested. Consent of all of the parties is generally required to plug and abandon a well.

c. Additional Development

Operating agreements typically address the possibility of development on the leased premises after initial drilling. Many operating agreements cover substantial tracts of land with room for development drilling. Even if the operating agreement covers only a single drilling and spacing unit, there is always the possibility that it will be desirable in the future to drill again to a deeper depth.

Operating agreements typically deal at length with the possibility that not all of the co-owners will want to participate in additional drilling operations. The model forms provide a system of incentives for those who do participate and disincentives for those who decline. No owner has to participate in additional operations; any owner may "go nonconsent." Those who do participate must advance the share of the costs that those who decline would otherwise have paid. In return, those owners who consent to bear the risk of additional drilling operations obtain the right to receive the share of production attributable to the nonconsenting owners until the consenting owners have recovered the costs that they advanced plus an agreed percentage, which may vary from as low as 50 percent to as high as 1000 percent.

D. DRILLING CONTRACTS

Drilling contracts are agreements for the drilling of a well or wells entered into by *drilling contractors*, who own drilling rigs and associated equipment, and *lease operators*, the persons or entities owning mineral or leasehold rights.

1. KINDS OF DRILLING CONTRACTS

Drilling contracts commonly provide for compensation on a daywork, footage, or turnkey basis. The provision for compensation generally controls the scope of discretion given the contractor and affects the potential liability of the party contracting to have the well drilled.

One form of drilling contract is a *daywork contract*. Under a daywork drilling contract, the drilling contractor is compensated on the basis of the amount of time spent in drilling operations. In essence, the lease operator hires the contractor's drilling rig and staff to work under the operator's direction. The contract gives the operator broad discretion to give instructions to the drilling contractor how to conduct the drilling operations, and the lease operator is subject to broad contractual liability.

Under a *footage contract*, the drilling contractor's compensation is calculated on the basis of the number of feet drilled. The lease operator has less discretion than under a daywork contract to instruct the drilling contractor how to conduct drilling. Consequently, the lease operator's liability is narrower.

Under a *turnkey contract*, the drilling contractor agrees to drill, complete, equip, and deliver a well to the lease operator. The lease operator has little or no discretion to instruct the drilling contractor and little or no contractual liability exposure for the contractor's actions.

2. MODEL–FORM DRILLING CONTRACTS

Parties frequently use one of two sets of model-form drilling contracts. One set of forms is prepared by the International Association of Drilling Contractors, a drilling-industry association. Model forms are also prepared by the American Petroleum Institute, an association composed mainly of large oil companies who must contract with drilling contractors. The form contracts are slanted in favor of the interests of the group that sponsored their preparation. Many drilling contractors and many producers have their own drilling-contract forms, which are usually based upon one of the model forms.

The drilling industry is extremely competitive, and competition has a great impact upon the terms of drilling contracts. In the late 1970s and early 1980s drilling rigs were in high demand. Many drilling contractors refused to consider anything but daywork contracts, which effectively shifted most of the responsibility and risks to the lease operators. By the end of 1982, the drilling industry had experienced a severe recession, and nearly half of the country's drilling rigs were not working. In a period of a few months, drilling contractors' prices dropped 25 to 40 percent and producers found it possible to make substantial revisions to drilling contractors' agreements. Drilling contract terms are what the market will bear.

E. GAS CONTRACTS

A gas contract is an agreement for the sale of natural gas by a producer to a pipeline, a local distribution company, or an end-user.

Although there is wide variety in the terms found in gas contracts, common issues will always be addressed in such agreements: (a) term, (b) price, (c) take obligations, (d) reserves committed, (e) reservations of seller, and (f) conditions of deliveries.

1. TERM

Historically, gas contracts have been for long terms. Terms of 25 years or "life of the well" have been common. In part, long terms reflected regulatory requirements; the Natural Gas Act of 1938 required that gas transported across state lines be subject to a minimum 15–year contract. Economic conditions also demanded long terms. Long-term commitments by producers to gas buyers were a condition of the complex financing arrangements that made possible the construction of interstate pipelines. Further, the security of energy supply is an important factor to many users of natural gas.

More recent gas contracts are for much shorter terms. Contracts for a few months to a year or five years are the norm. Short-term contracts—for a day, a week, or a month—are commonly referred to as *"spot market"* contracts. A short term is often coupled, however, with *evergreen provisions* that extend the contract after its initial term until one of the parties gives notice, perhaps of only a few days or weeks.

In the early years of the spot market sales were conducted using company-drafted forms. More recently, the most common vehicle for a spot sale has been the North American Energy Standards Board (NAESB) contract form. The 2006 NAESB contract is relatively short and even-handed. Parties can either buy or sell in short-term transactions of thirty days or less on pre-agreed terms and conditions.

The term of the contract is the threshold issue of any gas contract. If the term is relatively short, other issues are relatively unimportant; however bad a deal may be, it is easier to tolerate it for a short term than for a long term. The longer is the term, however, the more important are other issues.

2.   PRICE

The price to be paid to a producer for natural gas sold is obviously important both to the producer and to the purchaser. Price is a major factor determining profitability for both.

In long-term gas contracts, there are generally provisions for periodic adjustment of the initial price. Such provisions are referred to as *price-ad-*

justment clauses, and they may provide for adjustment of prices down as well as up. If the price of the natural gas in question is subject to regulatory controls, however, a producer can collect only the maximum regulated price permitted, even if the contract specifies a higher price.

There are several kinds of price-adjustment clauses, more than one of which may be included in the same long-term contract. A *fixed-escalation clause* provides for periodic increases in price of a stated amount or percentage; (e.g., 4 cents per quarter or 1½% per quarter). An *area-rate clause* is one that provides for adjustment to the highest price that is permitted in the area by the appropriate regulatory body. A *most-favored-nations clause* provides for adjustment of the contract price upward if any other producer in the area receives a higher price for gas of similar quantity and quality. A *two-party most-favored-nations clause* adjusts the price only if a higher price is paid by the purchaser with whom the producer has contracted. A *three-party most-favored-nations clause* adjusts the price upward if any purchaser pays a higher price. A *price-renegotiation clause* allows renegotiation of the price periodically so that parties can take into account changed conditions in the market, and an *index-adjustment clause* provides for adjustment of the price in accordance with changes in an index or in some price (e.g., no. 2 or no. 5 fuel oil) the parties have agreed is an appropriate indicator of the value of natural gas. A *net-back clause* provides that the price the seller receives will be determined by netting back the amount received from the final sale, deducting transportation charges and other costs incurred.

Short term, or "spot market" contracts often provide for a fixed price, without adjustment, rather than for complicated adjustments. If market changes make the price unrealistic, the parties renegotiate. If the short-term contract has an evergreen provision, so that it renews periodically, the renewal price likely will be based upon the spot-market price as reported in an industry publication.

3.   TAKE PROVISIONS

The third common issue addressed by most gas contracts is the obligation of the purchaser to buy natural gas, or under some contracts, to pay for gas that it does not purchase. The demand for natural gas is cyclical, dependent upon weather and economic conditions. Therefore, producers sometimes obtain promises from their long-term purchasers that the purchasers will either *take* substantial amounts of gas or *pay* the producer for the amounts not taken. *Take-or-pay* provisions are intended to assure the producer of minimum cash flows. Usually, the purchaser has the right to make up quantities of natural gas paid for but not taken, with payment to the seller for the difference between the price in effect at the time the gas is taken and the price paid.

Both producers and purchasers miscalculated in negotiating take-or-pay clauses during the gas shortages of the 1970s and early 1980s. Pipelines agreed to take or pay for virtually all of the delivery capacity producers would promise. When gas demand and prices declined sharply, many purchasers found themselves confronted with liabilities that totaled billions of dollars. Producers miscalculated also, for they had never dreamed that pipelines would neither take nor pay, which is precisely what happened.

Short-term contracts are not likely to contain take-or-pay clauses. Instead, one frequently sees what may be termed "handshake deal" provisions in the natural gas spot market. For example:

> "Seller shall deliver and sell and Buyer shall purchase and receive such quantity of gas upon which Buyer and Seller agree from time to time ... up to the Maximum Daily Quantity set forth in Appendix A, ... together with any additional quantities upon which the parties may agree. Sales under this Agreement are interruptible by either party, and nothing herein will obligate Seller to sell and deliver or Buyer to purchase and receive any minimum quantity of gas."

The language quoted states no real promise from either party to the agreement, though it is coupled with representations that the seller has gas available and can provide gas up to the maximum amount agreed and with representations that the buyer anticipates needing the quantities stated. There is no promise to buy or sell any amount. Rather there is a "handshake deal" based upon the economic interests of the parties, rather upon the binding terms of the contract. The contract merely sets a framework for sales that the parties may choose to make in the near future. Volumes are fully *interruptible*, which means that either buyer or seller may choose not to perform with no liability.

The NAESB model contract provides for damages for a seller's failure to deliver or a buyer's failure to accept *firm* volumes, based either on the difference between the contract price and the spot price or on the difference between the contract price and the *cover* price—what the buyer had to pay for the volumes it had to buy elsewhere or what the seller could get for the gas the buyer refused.

4. COMMITMENT

The commitment provisions of a gas contract identify the lands, the leases, the wells, and the formations that are covered by the gas contract. In times of gas shortages, purchasers have traditionally wanted as broad a commitment as possible. In the late 1960s it was not unusual to see commitments under long-term interstate contracts of all of the gas that might be produced from all of the formations that might be drilled presently or in the future upon any leases then owned by the producer in an entire county. In times of gas surplus and in areas in which transportation is readily available, purchasers generally seek only very limited commitments or none at all. Spot contracts rarely have any commitment provision.

5. RESERVATIONS

Gas-contract reservations provisions are the other side of the coin of commitment provisions. In a long-term contract, the reservations clause identifies what gas the producer may produce from the committed properties that it need not deliver to the purchaser. Typically, reservations clauses permit a producer to provide their lessors with free gas for domestic and farming purposes if their leases so provide. Typically, also, they permit producers to use gas produced for operations on the lease premises. Reservations clauses may also give producers the right to use gas on or off the premises for oil-lifting or repressuring operations and to process gas produced to remove valuable liquids from the stream before or after delivery to the purchaser. Short-term contracts usually do not include reservations.

6.   CONDITIONS OF DELIVERY

Conditions of delivery include the quality of the gas and the place of delivery. Both issues are important economic factors in any gas contract. Removing impurities from the gas stream can be very expensive, but can increase the value of the gas substantially, as can transportation of the gas to a pipeline. Therefore, contract provisions for conditions of delivery may be the subject of hard bargaining in long-term contracts. Short-term contracts typically merely require gas to be "of pipeline quality" and impose upon the seller the obligation to deliver the gas at a market "hub."

F. GAS–BALANCING AGREEMENTS

1. THE GAS–BALANCING PROBLEM

Gas-balancing agreements address the problem of imbalances in production from a gas well or field. Co-owners frequently sell their share of production to different purchasers on different terms and for different prices; such sales are called "split-stream" sales. Even when co-owners sell to the same purchaser, their contracts are likely to be signed at different times and to have different price and take provisions. Thus, production imbalances are inevitable.

Although ownership of the gas stream may be split, natural gas is fungible, and it is impossible to differentiate between gas owned by different cotenants. As a result, the gas owned by a cotenant who does not wish to sell its share or whose purchaser is not in a position to take its share cannot be physically withheld; whoever buys the gas produced takes gas that is owned not only by its seller but also other cotenants.

The basic law of cotenancy undoubtedly applies. Some courts have found, however, that there is an industry custom to *balance in kind*. From time to time the operator will adjust deliveries from one purchaser to another so that over time gas deliveries of all owners are roughly in balance. Disputes have arisen over what period of time balancing in kind is appropriate, and when *cash balancing* should be ordered and on what basis—on the amount received for the gas when sold, on the value when finally produced, or on some other basis? There are no clear-cut legal answers to these questions.

2.   COMMON SUBSTANTIVE PROVISIONS

With increasing frequency, co-owners of natural gas wells enter into gas balancing agreements to provide for periodic balancing. A typical agreement requires that the operator maintain an account showing amounts overproduced and underproduced. Often, underproduced parties are given specific right to make up in kind, with cash balancing on the basis of amounts actually received by the overproduced parties where it is not possible to balance in kind. In times of surplus, co-owners who fear difficulty in finding a market will prefer frequent cash balancing. There are no "standard" provisions, however.

G.   DIVISION ORDERS

A division order is a statement executed by all parties who claim an interest, stipulating how proceeds of production are to be distributed. Division orders protect purchasers of production and those who distribute proceeds by warranting title to production transferred and indemnifying them for payments they make. Many division orders contain a variety of extraneous and (to those asked to sign them) objectionable provisions, in addition.

Gas division orders are not true contracts, as the Texas Supreme Court noted in *Gavenda v. Strata*

Energy, Inc., 705 S.W.2d 690 (Tex.1986), and so cannot be used to cure title defects or amend leases. Oil division orders have been described as an offer for a unilateral contract that can be accepted by a purchaser who takes oil and sends payment for it. That description does not fit gas division orders as they affect royalty owners, however, for the lessor under an oil and gas lease does not generally have the right to take gas in-kind and so cannot sell it.

Many royalty owners refuse to sign division orders, and courts generally hold that signing a division order is not a precondition for payment of royalty. The lease sets forth the agreement between the lessor and the lessee, and it usually says that the lessee "shall pay" royalty on gas. Oil royalty may be a different matter, however, at least practically. Most leases provide that the royalty owner is to receive oil royalty in kind. If the royalty owner has to market his or her own oil, the royalty owner will find it difficult to find a buyer who will accept the oil without the protection of a division order. Even if the lessee has an implied duty to find a market for royalty oil if the lessor chooses not to take in kind, it would not be inconsistent with the language of the royalty clause to find a concomitant implied obligation of the lessor to cooperate by signing "usual" documents of transfer.

APPENDIX OF FORMS

Mineral Deed.
Conveyance of Nonparticipating Royalty Interest.
Oil and Gas Lease (Texas AAPL Form 675).
California Oil and Gas Lease.

Form 128—Burkhart Printing &
Stationery Co., Tulsa, Okla.

MINERAL DEED

(APPROVED BY MID–CONTINENT ROYALTY OWNER'S ASSOCIATION)

KNOW ALL MEN BY THESE PRESENTS:

That _____
of _____
(Give exact postoffice address)
hereinafter called Grantor, (whether one or more) for and
in consideration of the sum of _____ Dollars, ($_____)
cash in hand paid and other good and valuable considerations, the receipt of which is hereby acknowledged, do
_____, hereby grant, bargain, sell, convey, transfer,
assign and deliver unto _____ of _____,
(Give exact postoffice address)
hereinafter called Grantee, (whether one or more) an
undivided _____ interest in and to all of the oil, gas and
other minerals in and under and that may be produced
from the following described lands situated in _____
County, State of _____, to wit:

containing _____ acres, more or less, together with the
right of ingress and egress at all times for the purpose of
mining, drilling, exploring, operating and developing said

409

lands for oil, gas, and other minerals, and storing, handling, transporting and marketing the same therefrom with the right to remove from said land all of Grantee's property and improvements.

This sale is made subject to any rights now existing to any lessee or assigns under any valid and subsisting oil and gas lease of record heretofore executed; it being understood and agreed that said Grantee shall have, receive, and enjoy the herein granted undivided interest in and to all bonuses, rents, royalties and other benefits which may accrue under the terms of said lease insofar as it covers the above described land from and after the date hereof, precisely as if the Grantee herein had been at the date of the making of said lease the owner of a similar undivided interest in and to the lands described and Grantee one of the lessors therein.

Grantor agrees to execute such further assurances as may be requisite for the full and complete enjoyment of the rights herein granted and likewise agrees that Grantee herein shall have the right at any time to redeem for said Grantor by payment, any mortgage, taxes, or other liens on the above described land, upon default in payment by the Grantor, and be subrogated to the rights of the holder thereof.

TO HAVE AND TO HOLD The above described property and easement with all and singular the rights, privileges, and appurtenances thereunto or in any wise belonging to said Grantee herein, _____ heirs, successors, personal representatives, administrators, executors, and assigns forever, and Grantor does hereby warrant said title to Grantee _____ heirs, executors, administrators, personal representatives, successors and assigns forever, and does hereby agree to defend all and singular the said property unto the said Grantee herein _____ heirs, successors, executors, personal representatives, and assigns against all and every person or persons whomsoever lawfully claiming or to claim the same, or any part thereof.

WITNESS Grantor's hand this _____ day of _____, 19___.

_____	_____
_____	_____
_____	_____
_____	_____

(ACKNOWLEDGMENT)

CONVEYANCE OF NONPARTICIPATING ROYALTY INTEREST

KNOW ALL MEN BY THESE PRESENTS:

That _____, hereinafter called "Grantors," for good and valuable consideration in hand paid, the receipt and sufficiency of which Grantors hereby acknowledge, do hereby grant, bargain, sell, convey, transfer, assign, and deliver unto _____, hereinafter called "Grantee," for the term hereinafter specified, an undivided _____ interest in any and all Royalty (as hereinafter defined) on oil, gas, casinghead gas, distillate, condensate, and any and all other hydrocarbon or nonhydrocarbon substances, whether similar or dissimilar which may be produced or extracted and saved from the following described land situated in _____ County, Oklahoma:

(Description)

or from lands pooled or unitized with any portion thereof, or from lands located within any governmental drilling and spacing unit which includes any portion thereof, together with the right of ingress and egress to the surface thereof for the purpose of taking and receiving the herein granted interest in production.

"Royalty," as used herein, shall mean: (1) Any interest in production or the proceeds therefrom reserved by or granted to Grantors, their successors or assigns, in connection with any present or future lease for the production or extraction of substances from said lands, including, but not limited to, whether royalty, net profits interest, or production payment; (2) any payment so granted or reserved to be paid in lieu of production, including, but not limited to, whether similar or dissimilar, any shut-in well payments or minimum royalty; (3) in the event of the development of any portion of the above described land by Grantors, their successors or assigns, for the production or extraction of any substances, the same interest in production, proceeds, or payment to which Grantee would have been entitled if Grantors, as of the date of commencement of development, had executed a lease providing for a royalty equivalent to that set forth in the succeeding paragraph. As to production or extraction of substances from lands pooled or unitized with the above described land or from lands located within any governmental drilling and spacing unit which includes any portion thereof, "Royalty" shall include only that portion of said production, proceeds or payments attributable to the above described land's interest in said production unit. "Royalty" shall not include any cash bonus received by Grantor at the time of executing any future oil, gas, or mineral lease, nor any rental paid for the privilege of deferring commencement of development under any existing or future lease.

Grantors, their successors and assigns, reserve the exclusive right to execute leases for the production or extraction of substances from the above described land; provided that no lease or contract for the development of said land shall provide for a royalty less than that customarily then being received by lessors in the area, and in no event less than one-eighth (⅛) of all substances produced and extracted, delivered free and clear of all cost and expense except a proportionate part of taxes on production; and provided further that Grantors, their successors and assigns in exercising said leasing power, shall be deemed to owe a fiduciary duty to Grantee.

TO HAVE AND TO HOLD unto Grantee, his successors and assigns, (forever) (for a term of—years from the date hereof, and as long thereafter as oil, gas or other minerals is being produced from, or a shut-in well is located on, or operations are being conducted on, the above described land, or from lands pooled or unitized with any portion thereof, or from lands located within any governmental drilling and spacing unit which includes any portion thereof), and Grantors do hereby warrant title to the herein granted interest to Grantee, his successors and assigns, and do hereby agree to defend all and singular such interest unto Grantee, his successors or assigns, against any person whomsoever claiming or to claim the same or any part thereof; and Grantors, on behalf of themselves, their successors and assigns, do hereby agree to execute such further assurances as may be requisite for the full and complete enjoyment of the herein granted interest.

EXECUTED to be effective as of this _____ day of _____, 19__.

_____   _____

_____   _____

_____   _____

(ACKNOWLEDGMENT)

AAPL FORM 675

OIL AND GAS LEASE*

TEXAS FORM—SHUT–IN CLAUSE, POOLING CLAUSE

THIS AGREEMENT made and entered into the _____ day of _____, 19__, by and between _____, Lessor and _____, Lessee.

WITNESSETH:

1. Lessor, in consideration of the sum of _____ Dollars ($_____), in hand paid, receipt of which is hereby acknowledged, and the royalties herein provided, does hereby grant, lease and let unto Lessee for the purpose of exploring, prospecting, drilling and mining for and producing oil and gas and all other hydrocarbons, laying pipe lines, building roads, tanks, power stations, telephone lines and other structures thereon to produce, save, take care of, treat, transport and own said products, and housing its employees, and without additional consideration, does hereby authorize Lessee to enter upon the lands covered hereby to accomplish said purposes, the following described land in _____ County, Texas, to-wit:

[Legal Description]

This Lease also covers and includes any and all lands owned or claimed by the Lessor adjacent or contiguous to the land described hereinabove, whether the same be in said survey or surveys or in adjacent surveys, although not included within the boundaries of the land described above. For the purpose of calculating rental payments hereinafter provided for the lands covered hereby are

* Approved for use in Texas by the American Association of Professional Landmen.

estimated to comprise _____ acres, whether it actually comprises more or less.

2. Subject to the other provisions herein contained this Lease shall be for a term of _____ years from this date (called "primary term") and as long thereafter as oil and gas or other hydrocarbons are being produced from said land or land with which said land is pooled hereunder.

3. The royalties to be paid by Lessee are as follows: On oil, one-eighth of that produced and saved from said land, the same to be delivered at the wells or to the credit of Lessor into the pipe line to which the wells may be connected. Lessee shall have the option to purchase any royalty oil in its possession, paying the market price therefor prevailing for the field where produced on the date of purchase. On gas, including casinghead gas, condensate or other gaseous substances, produced from said land and sold or used off the premises or for the extraction of gasoline or other products therefrom, the market value at the well of one-eighth of the gas so sold or used, provided that on gas sold at the wells the royalty shall be one-eighth of the amount realized from such sale. While there is a gas well on this Lease, or on acreage pooled therewith, but gas is not being sold or used Lessee shall pay or tender annually at the end of each yearly period during which such gas is not sold or used, as royalty, an amount equal to the delay rental provided for in paragraph 5 hereof, and while said royalty is so paid or tendered this Lease shall be held as a producing Lease under paragraph 2 hereof. Lessee shall have free use of oil, gas and water from said land, except water from Lessor's wells, for all operations hereunder, and the royalty on oil and gas shall be computed after deducting any so used.

4. Lessee, at its option, is hereby given the right and power to voluntarily pool or combine the acreage covered by this Lease, or any portion thereof, as to the oil and

gas, or either of them, with other land, lease or leases in the immediate vicinity thereof to the extent hereinafter stipulated, when in Lessee's judgment it is necessary or advisable to do so in order to properly develop and operate said leased premises in compliance with the Spacing Rules of the Railroad Commission of Texas, or other lawful authorities, or when to do so would, in the judgment of Lessee, promote the conservation of oil and gas from said premises. Units pooled for oil hereunder shall not substantially exceed 80 acres each in area, and units pooled for gas hereunder shall not substantially exceed 640 acres each in area plus a tolerance of ten per-cent thereof in the case of either an oil unit or a gas unit, provided that should governmental authority having jurisdiction prescribe or permit the creation of units larger than those specified, units thereafter created may conform substantially in size with those prescribed by governmental regulations. Lessee under the provisions hereof may pool or combine acreage covered by this Lease, or any portion thereof as above provided for as to oil in any one or more strata and as to gas in any one or more strata. The units formed by pooling as to any stratum or strata need not conform in size or area with the unit or units into which the Lease is pooled or combined as to any other stratum or strata, and oil units need not conform as to area with gas units. The pooling in one or more instances shall not exhaust the rights of Lessee hereunder to pool this Lease, or portions thereof, into other units. Lessee shall file for record in the county records of the county in which the lands are located an instrument identifying and describing the pooled acreage. Lessee may at its election exercise its pooling operation after commencing operations for, or completing an oil or gas well on the leased premises, and the pooled unit may include, but is not required to include, land or leases upon which a well capable of producing oil or gas in paying quantities has theretofore been completed, or upon which operations for drilling of a well for oil or gas have theretofore been commenced. Operations for drilling on or production of oil or gas from any part of the pooled unit composed in whole or in part of the land covered by this Lease, regardless of whether such operations for drilling were commenced or such production was secured before or after the execution of this instrument or the instrument designating the pooled unit, shall be considered as operations for drilling on or production of oil or gas from the land covered by this Lease whether or not the well or wells are actually located on the premises covered by this Lease, and the entire acreage constituting such unit or units, as to oil and gas or either of them as herein provided, shall be treated for all purposes except the payment of royalties on production from the pooled unit as if the same were included in this Lease. For the purpose of computing the royalties to which owners of royalties and payments out of production and each of them shall be entitled upon production of oil and gas, or either of them from the pooled unit, there shall be allocated to the land covered by this Lease and included in said unit a pro rata portion of the oil and gas, or either of them, produced from the pooled unit after deducting that used for operations on the pooled unit. Such allocation shall be on an acreage basis, that is to say, there shall be allocated to the acreage covered by this Lease and included in the pooled unit that pro rata portion of the oil and gas, or either of them, produced from the pooled unit which the number of surface acres covered by this Lease and included in the pooled unit bears to the total number of surface acres included in the pooled unit. Royalties hereunder shall be computed on the portion of such production, whether it be oil or gas or either of them, so allocated to the land covered by this Lease and included in the unit just as though such production were from such land. The production from an oil well will be considered as production from the Lease or oil pooled unit from which it is producing and not as production from a gas pooled unit; and production from a gas well will be considered as production from the Lease or gas pooled unit from which it is producing and not from the oil pooled unit.

5. If operations for drilling are not commenced on said land, or on acreage pooled therewith as above provided for, on or before one year from the date hereof, the Lease shall terminate as to both parties, unless on or before such anniversary date Lessee shall pay or tender to Lessor, or to the credit of Lessor in the _____ Bank at _____, Texas, (which Bank and its successors shall be Lessor's agent and shall continue as the depository for all rentals payable hereunder regardless of changes in ownership of said land or the rentals) the sum of _____ Dollars ($_____), herein called rentals, which shall cover the privilege of deferring commencement of drilling operations for a period of twelve (12) months. In like manner and upon like payment or tenders annually the commencement of drilling operations may be further deferred for successive periods of twelve (12) months each during the primary term hereof. The payment or tender of rental under this paragraph and of royalty under paragraph 3 on any gas well from which gas is not being sold or used may be made by check or draft of Lessee mailed or delivered to Lessor, or to said Bank on or before the date of payment. If such Bank, or any successor Bank, should fail, liquidate or be succeeded by another Bank, or for any reason fail or refuse to accept rental, Lessee shall not be held in default for failure to make such payment or tender of rental until thirty (30) days after Lessor shall deliver to Lessee a proper recordable instrument, naming another Bank as Agent to receive such payments or tenders. Cash payment for this Lease is consideration for this Lease according to its terms and shall not be allocated as a mere rental for a period. Lessee may at any time or times execute and deliver to Lessor, or to the depository above named, or place of record a release covering any portion or portions of the above described premises and thereby surrender this Lease as to such portion or por-

tions and be relieved of all obligations as to the acreage surrendered, and thereafter the rentals payable hereunder shall be reduced in the proportion that the acreage covered hereby is reduced by said release or releases.

6. If prior to discovery of oil, gas or other hydrocarbons on this land, or on acreage pooled therewith, Lessee should drill a dry hole or holes thereon, or if after the discovery of oil, gas or other hydrocarbons, the production thereof should cease from any cause, this Lease shall not terminate if Lessee commences additional drilling or re-working operations within sixty (60) days thereafter, or if it be within the primary term, commences or resumes the payment or tender of rentals or commences operations for drilling or re-working on or before the rental paying date next ensuing after the expiration of sixty (60) days from the date of completion of the dry hole, or cessation of production. If at any time subsequent to sixty (60) days prior to the beginning of the last year of the primary term, and prior to the discovery of oil, gas or other hydrocarbons on said land, or on acreage pooled therewith, Lessee should drill a dry hole thereon, no rental payment or operations are necessary in order to keep the Lease in force during the remainder of the primary term. If at the expiration of the primary term, oil, gas or other hydrocarbons are not being produced on said land, or on acreage pooled therewith, but Lessee is then engaged in drilling or re-working operations thereon, or shall have completed a dry hole thereon within sixty (60) days prior to the end of the primary term, the Lease shall remain in force so long as operations are prosecuted with no cessation of more than sixty (60) consecutive days, and if they result in the production of oil, gas or other hydrocarbons, so long thereafter as oil, gas or other hydrocarbons are produced from said land, or acreage pooled therewith. In the event a well or wells producing oil or gas in paying quantities shall be brought in on adjacent land and draining the leased premises, or acreage pooled therewith, Lessee agrees to drill such offset wells as a reasonably

prudent operator would drill under the same or similar circumstances.

7.   Lessee shall have the right at any time during or after the expiration of this Lease to remove all property and fixtures placed on the premises by Lessee, including the right to draw and remove all casing. When required by the Lessor, Lessee shall bury all pipe lines below ordinary plow depth, and no well shall be drilled within two hundred (200) feet of any residence or barn located on said land as of the date of this Lease without Lessor's consent.

8.   The rights of each party hereunder may be assigned in whole or in part, and the provisions hereof shall extend to their heirs, successors and assigns, but no change or division in the ownership of the land, rentals or royalties, however accomplished, shall operate to enlarge the obligations, or diminish the rights of Lessee; and no change or division in such ownership shall be binding on Lessee until thirty (30) days after Lessee shall have been furnished with a certified copy of recorded instrument or instruments evidencing such change of ownership. In the event of assignment hereof in whole or in part, liability for breach of any obligation issued hereunder shall rest exclusively upon the owner of this Lease, or portion thereof, who commits such breach. In the event of the death of any person entitled to rentals hereunder, Lessee may pay or tender such rentals to the credit of the deceased, or the estate of the deceased, until such time as Lessee has been furnished with the proper evidence of the appointment and qualification of an executor or an administrator of the estate, or if there be none, then until Lessee is furnished satisfactory evidence as to the heirs or devisees of the deceased, and that all debts of the estate have been paid. If at any time two or more persons become entitled to participate in the rental payable hereunder, Lessee may pay or tender such rental jointly to such persons, or to their joint credit in the depository

named herein; or, at the Lessee's election, the portion or part of said rental to which each participant is entitled may be paid or tendered to him separately or to his separate credit in said depository; and payment or tender to any participant of his portion of the rentals hereunder shall maintain this Lease as to such participant. In the event of an assignment of this Lease as to a segregated portion of said land, the rentals payable hereunder shall be apportioned as between the several leasehold owners ratably according to the surface area of each, and default in rental payment by one shall not affect the rights of other leasehold owners hereunder. If six or more parties become entitled to royalty payments hereunder, Lessee may withhold payment thereof unless and until furnished with a recordable instrument executed by all such parties designating an agent to receive payment for all.

9. The breach by Lessee of any obligations arising hereunder shall not work a forfeiture or termination of this Lease nor cause a termination or reversion of the estate created hereby nor be grounds for cancellation hereof in whole or in part unless Lessor shall notify Lessee in writing of the facts relied upon in claiming a breach hereof, and Lessee, if in default, shall have sixty (60) days after receipt of such notice in which to commence the compliance with the obligations imposed by virtue of this instrument, and if Lessee shall fail to do so then Lessor shall have grounds for action in a court of law or such remedy to which he may feel entitled. After the discovery of oil, gas or other hydrocarbons in paying quantities on the lands covered by this Lease, or pooled therewith, Lessee shall reasonably develop the acreage retained hereunder, but in discharging this obligation Lessee shall not be required to drill more than one well per eighty (80) acres of area retained hereunder and capable of producing oil in paying quantities, and one well per six hundred forty (640) acres of the area retained hereunder and capable of producing gas or other hydro-

carbons in paying quantities, plus a tolerance of ten percent in the case of either an oil well or a gas well.

10.   Lessor hereby warrants and agrees to defend the title to said lands and agrees also that Lessee at its option may discharge any tax, mortgage or other liens upon said land either in whole or in part, and in the event Lessee does so, it shall be subrogated to such lien with the right to enforce same and apply rentals and royalties accruing hereunder towards satisfying same. Without impairment of Lessee's rights under the warranty in event of failure of title, it is agreed that if Lessor owns an interest in the oil, gas or other hydrocarbons in or under said land, less than the entire fee simple estate, then the royalties and rentals to be paid Lessor shall be reduced proportionately. Failure of Lessee to reduce such rental paid hereunder or over-payment of such rental hereunder shall not impair the right of Lessee to reduce royalties payable hereunder.

11.   Should Lessee be prevented from complying with any express or implied covenant of this Lease, from conducting drilling, or reworking operations thereon or from producing oil or gas or other hydrocarbons therefrom by reason of scarcity of, or inability to obtain or to use equipment or material, or by operation of force majeure, or because of any federal or state law or any order, rule or regulation of a governmental authority, then while so prevented, Lessee's obligations to comply with such covenant shall be suspended, and Lessee shall not be liable in damages for failure to comply therewith; and this Lease shall be extended while and so long as Lessee is prevented by any such cause from conducting drilling or reworking operations on, or from producing oil or gas or other hydrocarbons from the leased premises; and the time while Lessee is so prevented shall not be counted against the Lessee, anything in this Lease to the contrary notwithstanding.

IN WITNESS WHEREOF this instrument is executed on the date first above set out.

_____   _____

_____   _____

_____   _____

(ACKNOWLEDGMENT)

CALIFORNIA OIL AND GAS LEASE

THIS AGREEMENT, made and entered into as of the
_____ day of _____, 19__, between _____
                                      (and all other parties

_____
executing this lease or any counterpart hereof) hereinafter called "Lessor"

_____
and Chevron U.S.A. Inc., a corporation, hereinafter called "Lessee."

1. Lessor, for and in consideration of one dollar and
other valuable consideration, receipt and sufficiency of
which is hereby acknowledged, and of the royalties and
agreements of the Lessee herein provided, hereby grants,
lets and leases exclusively unto Lessee the land described
and included in paragraph 18 hereof and hereinafter
referred to as "said land" for the purposes of exploring
and prospecting for (by geological, geophysical, and all
other means whether now known or not), drilling for,
producing, saving, taking, owning, transporting, storing,
handling, treating, and processing oil, gas, all other hydrocarbons, and all other substances produced therewith,
collectively hereinafter referred to as "said substances,"
in, on, under or that may be produced from said land, and
hereby grants all rights, privileges and easements useful
or convenient for Lessee's operations on said land, on
adjacent or contiguous lands, and on other lands in the
same vicinity, including, but not limited to, the right to
construct, install, maintain, repair, use, replace, and at
any time remove therefrom, roads, bridges, pipelines,
tanks, pump and power stations, power and communica-
tion facilities and lines, facilities for surface and subsurface disposal of produced water and other substances,

plants and structures to treat, process, and transport said substances and products manufactured therefrom; and the right to drill wells and use Lessee's existing wells including producing wells to inject gas, water, air or other substances into the subsurface zones.

2. This lease shall remain in force for a term of _____ years from the date hereof, called "primary term," and either as long thereafter as any of said substances is produced from said land in paying quantities (being quantities sufficient to pay operating costs) or so long as continuous operations (as defined in paragraph 5 hereof) are conducted on said land or so long as this lease is kept in force under any other provision hereof.

3. The consideration expressed in Paragraph 1 covers all rental for the first _____ year(s) of the primary term. If drilling operations are not commenced on said land on or before _____ year(s) from the date hereof then, subject to the provisions of Paragraph 15 hereof, Lessee shall pay or tender to Lessor or to Lessor's credit in _____ Bank at _____ (which bank and its successors are Lessor's agents and shall continue as depository for all rentals payable hereunder regardless of changes in the ownership of said land or of the right to receive rentals) the sum of _____ dollars ($_____) which shall maintain this lease in force and extend for one additional year the time within which such operations may be commenced. Thereafter, annually and in like manner and upon like payments or tender (all of which are herein called "rentals"), such operations may be deferred for successive periods of one year each during the primary term. Payments or tenders of rental may be made by mailing cash, check, or draft to Lessor or to the depository bank and the date of the mailing shall be considered the date of payment. Payments or tenders of rentals may be made by Lessee or by any person or persons on Lessee's behalf, and may be made jointly to all parties Lessor or to their credit in the depository bank or such

rentals may be tendered or paid separately to each owner or to his separate credit. From time to time during the primary term, if (a) Lessee shall drill and abandon a well as being in Lessee's opinion incapable of producing any of said substances and there is at the time of abandonment no other well so producing, or (b) all production of said substances shall cease, then Lessee may (subject to provisions of paragraph 15 hereof) commence or resume operations (as defined in paragraph 5 hereof), the production of any of said substances or the payment of delay rental and in such event this lease shall remain in full force and effect as though there had been no interruption in operations, production, or rental payments, as the case may be. If abandonment under (a) above or the cessation of production under (b) above occurs more than six months before the next ensuing anniversary date of this lease, Lessee shall have until such anniversary date in which to commence or resume operations, production or rental payments; if such abandonment or cessation of production occurs less than six months before the next ensuing anniversary date of this lease, the Lessee shall have until the second ensuing anniversary date in which to commence or resume operations, production or rental payments; provided, Lessee shall not have the right under this provision to extend the primary term of this lease.

4. The term "agreed share" as used herein means _____. Royalies to be paid by Lessee are: (a) on oil, the value of the agreed share of that produced and saved from said land. It is mutually agreed that the value shall be the price currently offered or paid by Lessee for oil of like gravity and quality in the same field. The volume of oil upon which royalty payments are based may be determined either by metering and sampling or by tank gauges. After such measurement, all or any part of the oil may be transported to locations on said land or other lands and commingled with oil from other lands. Lessor may at any time or times, upon 90 days written notice to Lessee, elect to take Lessor's agreed share of oil in kind, in lieu of

such share in value, provided that such election must be for a period of at least one year, and upon such election Lessor's share shall be delivered at the wells into storage furnished by Lessor or to the credit of Lessor into the pipeline to which the wells may be connected. If royalty on oil is payable in cash, Lessee may deduct therefrom the agreed share of the cost of treating unmerchantable oil produced from the leased land to render it merchantable. In the event such oil is treated elsewhere than on the leased land, the Lessor's cash royalty shall also bear the agreed share of the cost of transporting the oil to the treating plant. Nothing herein contained shall be construed as obligating Lessee to treat oil. If Lessor shall elect to receive the royalty on oil in kind, it shall be of the same quality as the oil removed from the leased land for Lessee's own account, and if Lessee's own oil shall be treated before such removal, Lessor's oil will be treated therewith before delivery to Lessor, and Lessor, in such event, shall pay a part equal to the agreed share of the cost of treatment; Lessee may deduct from Lessor's royalties a part equal to the agreed share of the cost of disposing of waste water produced with said substances; (b) on gas including casinghead gas and all gaseous substances produced, saved and sold from said land, the agreed share of the net proceeds (which shall be the amount realized from such sale less compressing costs) of the gas so sold; (c) on gas not sold but used off the premises, the agreed share of the market value at the well of the gas so used. All or any part of the gas produced from said land may be transported to locations on said land or other lands and commingled with gas from other lands. Lessee shall meter such transported gas and such meter readings together with Lessee's analysis of gasoline content of gas shall furnish the basis for prorating the amount of gasoline to be credited to said land. Lessee shall not be accountable to Lessor for gas lost or used or consumed in operations hereunder. Lessee may produce gas from said land or from lands with which said land is pooled or unitized in accordance with any method of ratable taking at any time or from time to time hereafter generally in effect in any pool of which said land or any portion thereof is a part. In the absence of any such method of ratable taking, Lessee shall produce from said land or lands pooled or unitized therewith a fair and equitable proportion of the quantity of gas which it markets from lands under lease to it in the pool of which said land is a part. Lessee shall be obligated to produce only so much gas as it may be able to market at the well or wells. When there is no market for gas at the wells, Lessee's obligation to produce gas shall be suspended; (d) on gasoline extracted from gas produced on said land, the value of 48% of the agreed share of the gasoline credited to said land by Lessee. It is mutually agreed that the value shall be the price currently offered or paid by Lessee for gasoline of like specifications and quality in the same vicinity; (e) on any other substance, the agreed share of the market value at the well.

For all operations hereunder, Lessee may use, free of royalty, oil, gas or other hydrocarbons and water from said land except water from the Lessor's wells. However, if Lessee shall use in operations hereunder, fuel, power, or other substances not obtained from said land, then Lessee shall be entitled to deduct from the amount of the additional royalty accruing thereby to Lessor the agreed share of the cost of such substituted fuel, power or other substances; provided, no deduction hereunder shall exceed the amount of such additional royalty.

When any of said substances not produced from said land are injected into said land or land pooled or unitized therewith, the initial production thereafter of said substances from any such land shall be free of royalty until the amount of the said substances produced and saved therefrom shall equal that of said substances injected therein.

5. Operations as used in paragraphs 2 and 3 hereof means drilling, redrilling, deepening, any preparatory work for doing any of the foregoing if commenced in good faith and prosecuted with reasonable diligence, completion or abandonment work, testing or flowing or other work to determine productivity, secondary recovery operations or the exercise of any other right given Lessee in paragraph 1 hereof for the purpose of obtaining or resuming production in paying quantities (as defined in paragraph 2 hereof). Such operations are continuous when no more than six months elapses between the date on which production ceased or any of such operations ceased, whichever is the later, and the date on which further operations are begun or production is commenced or resumed, and this lease shall remain in full force and effect during each and every six-month period. Production in such paying quantities may be followed or preceded by continuous operations from time to time for the purpose of keeping this lease in force in accordance with paragraph 2 hereof.

6. Except as otherwise provided herein, royalty payments shall be computed and paid monthly. Lessee shall furnish to Lessor monthly written statements of the production credited or allocated to said land during the preceding calendar month. Royalties payable in money with respect to production credited or allocated to said land during any calendar month shall be paid not later than the last day of the next succeeding calendar month. If the amount estimated to be payable to any party hereto for royalties is less than ten dollars ($10), or if the amount of oil produced does not justify shipments on a monthly basis, then Lessee may, upon prior written notice to such party, make such royalty payments and written statements, on a quarterly, semi-annual or annual basis; provided, however, all sums theretofore accrued and unpaid shall be paid at least once each calendar year. Royalty payments may be made or tendered to Lessor or

to Lessor's credit in the depository named in Paragraph 3.

7. Lessee shall pay for damages caused by Lessee's operations to existing houses, barns, fences, and to growing crops and trees. Lessee shall not be liable to Lessor for damages to any oil and gas reservoir underlying said land or for the loss of said substances therein or therefrom resulting from its operations hereunder unless such damage or loss is caused by Lessee's gross negligence or willful misconduct. Lessee shall have the right at any time during the term hereof or within a reasonable time thereafter to remove all Lessee's properties and fixtures, including the right to draw and remove all casing. No wells shall be drilled closer than one hundred (100') feet to any house or barn now on said land without the consent of the owner of said house or barn. Lessee agrees to fill all sump holes and excavations made by it.

8. If, during or after the primary term hereof, a well is drilled upon adjacent property, whether by Lessee or by another party, and the Lessor has no interest in the production therefrom and the well is located within three hundred thirty feet of the exterior boundaries of the land at that time included in this lease and is completed as a producer of oil or gas in commercial quantities and causes the migration of oil or gas from said land, then Lessee shall (provided it is not then drilling or has not theretofore drilled an offset well on said land) within ninety (90) days from the date the owner of such well commences marketing production therefrom, either commence operations for the drilling of an offset well on said land or surrender and terminate this lease, in the manner provided in paragraph 15 hereof, as to a portion of said land, the dimensions of which said portion shall be equal to the distance of such well from said exterior boundary. Such surrender shall be limited to the zone or zones being drained by the well on the adjacent property. Lessee shall never be required to drill (or surrender in lieu thereof)

any offset well which, in Lessee's opinion, would be incapable of producing said substances in quantities sufficient to yield a return which, after deducting the value of all said substances to be drained into said land from such zone or zones by existing wells thereon, would exceed the drilling and operating costs of such offset well.

9. The rights of Lessor and Lessee hereunder may be transferred, in whole or in part and as to any substance or zone. No change in ownership of Lessor's interest, however accomplished, shall be binding on Lessee until Lessor has furnished Lessee with written notice of such change, and then only with respect to payments thereafter made; such notice to consist of original or certified copies of all recorded instruments, documents and other information necessary to establish a complete chain of record title from Lessor, and written instructions from Lessor and Lessor's transferee directing the disbursement of any payments which may be made thereafter. No other kind of notice, whether actual or constructive, shall be binding on Lessee, and in the absence of such notice Lessee may make payments precisely as if no change had occurred. No present or future division of Lessor's ownership as to different portions or parcels of said land shall operate to enlarge the obligations or diminish the rights of Lessee, and all Lessee's operations, particularly as to the drilling and location of wells and the measurement of production, may be conducted without regard to any such division. If all or any part of this lease is assigned, no act or omission of any leasehold owner shall affect the rights or liabilities of any other such owner, except that operations or production on any part of said land, whether assigned or not, shall serve to keep the entire lease in force as though no assignment had been made, and all payments to Lessor, except royalties on actual production, shall be apportioned between assignor and assignee in proportion to acreage.

10. If any rental or royalty is not paid when due Lessor shall notify Lessee thereof in writing and this lease shall not terminate unless the Lessee fails to make such payment within fifteen (15) days after receipt of such written notice; provided, however, that if there is a dispute as to the amount due and all undisputed amounts are paid, said 15–day period shall be extended until 5 days after such dispute is settled by final court decree, arbitration or agreement. If Lessee fails to make such payment after receipt of such notice within said period (or such extension thereof), then this lease shall terminate as to the portion or portions thereof as to which Lessee is in default.

In the event Lessor considers that Lessee has not complied with any other covenant, condition or obligation hereunder, either express or implied, Lessor shall notify Lessee, in writing, setting out specifically in what respects it is claimed that Lessee has breached this lease, and Lessee shall not be liable to Lessor for any damages caused by any breach of a covenant, condition, or obligation, express or implied, occurring more than sixty (60) days prior to the receipt by Lessee of the aforesaid written notice of such breach. The receipt of such notice by Lessee and the lapse of sixty (60) days thereafter without Lessee meeting or commencing to meet the alleged breaches shall be a condition precedent to any action by Lessor for any cause hereunder. Neither the service of said notice nor the doing of any acts by Lessee aimed to meet all or any of the alleged breaches shall be deemed an admission or presumption that Lessee has failed to perform all of its obligations hereunder. This lease shall never be forfeited or cancelled in whole or in part, either during or after the primary term hereof, for failure of Lessee to perform any of its express or implied covenants, conditions, or obligations until it shall have first been finally judicially determined that such failure exists, and any decree of termination, cancellation or forfeiture shall be in the alternative and shall provide for termination, cancellation, or forfeiture unless Lessee complies with the covenants, conditions, or obligations breached within a reasonable time to be determined by the Court. No default in the performance of any condition or obligation hereof shall affect the rights of Lessee hereunder with respect to any drilling or producing well or wells in regard to which Lessee is not in default, together with a parcel of forty acres surrounding each such oil well then completed or being drilled and a parcel of six hundred forty acres surrounding each such gas well then completed or being drilled.

11. If Lessee is prevented or hindered from drilling or conducting other operations for the purpose of obtaining or restoring production or from producing said substances by fire, flood, storm, act of God, or any cause beyond Lessee's control (including but not limited to governmental law, order or regulation, labor disputes, war, inability to secure men, materials or transportation, inability to secure a market for gas, or an adverse claim to Lessor's title when Lessor has been notified pursuant to paragraph 14 hereof), then the performance of any such operations or the production of said substances shall be suspended during the period of such prevention or hindrance. If such suspension occurs during the primary term, the payment of delay rental during such suspension shall be excused and the primary term shall be extended for a period of time equal to the period of such suspension and this lease shall remain in full force and effect during such period of suspension and any such extension of the primary term. Lessee may commence or resume the payment or tender of rentals in accordance with paragraph 3 hereof after the period of suspension by paying or tendering within 60 days after the period of suspension the proportionate part of the rental for the rental year remaining after such period of suspension. If such suspension occurs after the primary term, this lease shall remain in full force and effect during such suspension and for a reasonable time thereafter provided that within such time

following the period of suspension Lessee diligently commences or resumes operations or the production of said substances. Lessee's obligation to pay royalty on actual production shall never be suspended under this paragraph. Whenever Lessee would otherwise be required to surrender any of said land as an alternative to the performance so suspended, then so long as such performance is suspended by this paragraph Lessee shall not be required to surrender any portion of said land.

If the permission or approval of any governmental agency is necessary before drilling operations may be commenced on said land, then if such permission or approval has been applied for at least 30 days prior to the date upon which such operations must be commenced under the terms hereof, the obligation to commence such operations shall be suspended until thirty (30) days after the governmental permit is granted or approval given, or if such permit or approval is denied initially, then so long as Lessee in good faith appeals from such denial or conducts further proceedings in an attempt to secure such permit or approval and thirty days thereafter.

12. For the consideration paid at the time of execution of this agreement and without any additional consideration to be paid therefor, except as provided below, Lessor hereby grants to Lessee, its successors and assigns, the following rights, rights of way and easements in, under, upon, through and across said land which may be exercised at any time or from time to time during the duration of this lease and as long thereafter as Lessee exercises any of the rights granted in this paragraph: (a) The sole and exclusive right to locate a well or wells on the surface of said land and to slant drill said well or wells into, under, across and through said land and into and under lands other than said land together with the right to repair, redrill, deepen, maintain, rework and operate or abandon such well or wells for the production of oil, gas, hydrocarbons, and other minerals from such other lands

together with the right to develop water from said land for any of Lessee's operations pursuant to this paragraph and together with the right to construct, erect, maintain, use, operate, replace, and remove all pipelines, power lines, telephone lines, tanks, machinery, and other facilities, together with all other rights necessary or convenient for Lessee's operations under this paragraph and together with rights of way for passage over and upon and across and ingress and egress to and from said land; (b) The sole and exclusive right to drill into and through said land below a depth of five hundred feet (500') from the surface thereof, by means of a well or wells drilled from the surface of lands other than said land, and the right to abandon or repair, redrill, deepen, maintain, rework and operate such well or wells for the production of oil, gas, hydrocarbons and other minerals from lands other than said lands.

If Lessee exercises the rights granted by Lessor in Subparagraph (a) hereof, Lessee shall pay to Lessor an annual rental computed at the rate of one hundred dollars ($100) per acre for each surface acre of said lands being exclusively occupied by Lessee pursuant to such grant. If Lessee exercises the rights granted in Subparagraph (b) hereof, and thereafter completes a well capable of producing oil or gas in quantities deemed paying quantities by Lessee, then Lessee shall within sixty (60) days after such completion pay Lessor an annual rental computed at the rate of one dollar ($1) per rod of horizontal projection of the survey course of that part of the bore hole of such well traversing the subsurface of such land; provided, however, that Lessor shall not be entitled to receive any rental under the provisions of this paragraph during such times as Lessor is entitled to receive royalty or rentals under other provisions of this lease. Any such rentals shall continue until such well is abandoned. Any well drilled under the provisions of this paragraph shall be drilled so that the producing interval thereof shall lie wholly outside the boundary of said land and Lessor recognizes and agrees that Lessor has no interest in any such well or wells drilled pursuant to this paragraph or any production therefrom.

Any surrender or termination under any other provision of this lease shall be effective notwithstanding the fact that Lessee in and by such surrender or termination reserves the rights granted to Lessee under this paragraph, and regardless of such surrender or termination, the rights granted under this paragraph shall continue for the term hereinabove granted in this paragraph.

13. Lessee may at any time or times within twenty-one (21) years from the date hereof without Lessor's joinder or further consent, pool, consolidate or unitize this lease and said land in whole or in part or as to any zone, with other lands, mineral interests, and leases in the vicinity thereof so as to constitute a unit or units whenever such action in Lessee's judgment is required to comply with applicable laws or to promote or encourage the conservation of natural resources or the efficient and economical location and spacing of wells, cycling, pressure-maintenance, repressuring or secondary recovery programs, or to join in any cooperative or unit plan of development or operation approved by State or Federal authorities. The size or shape of any such unit may be changed at any time or times within twenty one (21) years from the date hereof without Lessor's joinder or further consent to permit more efficient and economical operation, to include acreage believed to be productive and to exclude acreage believed to be unproductive or which is not committed to the unit, but any increase or decrease in Lessor's royalties resulting from any such change in any such unit shall not be retroactive. Any such unit may be established or changed, and in the absence of production therefrom may be abolished and dissolved, by filing for record an instrument so declaring, a copy of which shall be delivered to Lessor or to the depository bank. Drilling or other operations (as defined in para-

graph 5 hereof) upon, or production of any one of said substances from any part of such unit shall be treated and considered for all purposes of this lease as such operations upon or such production from said land. Lessee shall allocate to the portion of said land included in any such unit a fractional part of all production from any part of such unit on the same basis as is provided in the agreement between Lessee and others whereby such unit is established or, in the absence of such an agreement or of a method of allocation therein, Lessee shall elect one of the following bases: (a) The ratio between the surface acreage in this lease included in such unit and the total of all surface acreage included in such unit; or (b) The ratio between the value, as estimated by Lessee, of recoverable production within the portion of this lease included in such unit and the total value, as estimated by Lessee, of all recoverable production within such unit. Lessee may change from one of the aforesaid bases to the other at any time or times within 21 years from the date hereof without Lessor's further joinder or consent but any increase or decrease in Lessor's royalty resulting from any such change shall not be retroactive. No offset obligation shall accrue under this lease as a result of any well drilled within any such unit.

14. Lessor warrants and agrees to defend the title to said land. The rentals and royalties hereinabove provided are determined with respect to the entire mineral estate, and if Lessor owns a lesser interest, the rentals and royalties to be paid Lessor may be reduced proportionately. If the interest of Lessor covered by this lease is subject to any outstanding royalties payable to another, such royalties shall be deducted from Lessor's royalties herein provided. Lessee shall pay all taxes levied against Lessee's plants, machinery and personal property and all taxes (except the agreed share thereof) assessed upon mineral rights or assessed upon or measured by production from or allocated to said land. Lessor shall pay all other taxes assessed against said land and the agreed share of taxes

assessed upon mineral rights and assessed upon or measured by production from or allocated to said land. Lessee may discharge in whole or in part, on behalf of Lessor, any tax, mortgage or other lien upon said land, or may redeem the same from any purchaser at any tax sale or adjudication, and may reimburse itself from any rentals and royalties accruing hereunder and shall be subrogated to such lien with the right to enforce same. Lessee shall have the right to hold or acquire mineral rights or leases from others claiming any interest in any part of said land, and to withhold from Lessor payment of rentals and royalties attributable to any interest so claimed or to any other interest which is subject to adverse claim, dispute or litigation and the same shall not be due until the ownership of such interest has been determined, and Lessee shall not thereby be held in default of any provision hereof or to have disputed Lessor's title. When Lessee becomes aware of any adverse claim to Lessor's title to said land being asserted by another, Lessee shall notify Lessor in writing and upon such notification Lessee shall be excused from drilling offset or other wells on or producing from said lands until such adverse claim has been finally determined.

15. Lessee may at any time or times surrender this lease or any zone or portion of either thereof by delivering or mailing a written notice of surrender to Lessor or to the depository bank and upon such delivery or mailing Lessee shall be relieved of all obligations as to the portion surrendered, and thereafter all payments to Lessor provided herein, except royalties on actual production, shall be reduced in the same proportion that the acreage covered hereby is reduced. If Lessee surrenders less than all horizons in any portion of this lease the rental as to such portion shall not be reduced. Within a reasonable time after any such surrender, Lessee shall file appropriate surrender instruments for record. In the event this lease is surrendered or assigned as to any zone or portion, then so long as this lease shall remain in effect as to any other

zone or portion Lessee shall have such rights of way or easements over, under, through, upon and across the surrendered or assigned zone or portion as shall be necessary or convenient for Lessee's operations on the retained portion or other lands in the vicinity thereof.

16. If any of said substances is discovered by Lessee in said land in quantities deemed paying quantities by Lessee, then Lessee shall keep one string of tools in continuous operation on said land, allowing not more than six months to elapse between completion or abandonment of the first or any succeeding well and the commencement of operations for the drilling of the next succeeding well except that if Lessee shall drill on said land a well which in Lessee's opinion is not capable of producing said substances in paying quantities, then Lessee may allow not more than one year to elapse after abandonment of each such well before commencing operations for the next succeeding well. Lessee shall be given credit for so much of the time in each six month or one year drilling interval as is not utilized and such credit may be used to extend subsequent drilling intervals in such manner as Lessee may determine. Lessee's drilling, development and offset obligations under this lease shall be fully satisfied and discharged when Lessee has drilled and completed or abandoned a total number of wells on said land, regardless of the bottomhole locations therein, equal to the nearest whole number obtained by dividing the total acreage of said land then held hereunder: (a) if oil was discovered, by 40 if no well is drilled down to a depth more than 8,500 feet below the surface, or by 80 if any well is drilled down to a depth of more than 8,500 feet but not below 13,000 feet below the surface, or by 160 if any well is drilled to a depth of more than 13,000 feet below the surface, or (b) if any of said substances other than oil was found, by 640; provided, however, that Lessee shall be required to conduct such continuous operations in the event of a discovery of gas, only if in Lessee's opinion such additional drilling is warranted by existing or antici-

pated market requirements for such gas, and in the event of a discovery of oil, only if the market price in the field for oil of like quality or gravity is more than One Dollar per barrel at the well.

If both oil and gas are discovered in said land in quantities deemed paying quantities by Lessee, then Lessee shall drill the number of wells herein provided for an oil discovery with respect to the portion of said land which in Lessee's opinion is capable of producing oil in paying quantities and Lessee shall be entitled to retain all of said lands for the term hereof.

Lessee shall not be required to but may drill more wells on said land than those herein specified.

17. This lease shall be binding upon all who execute it, whether or not they are named in the granting clause hereof and whether or not all parties named in the granting clause execute this lease. This lease may be executed in any number of counterparts and for all purposes hereof all of such counterparts shall be considered as one lease. All the provisions of this lease shall inure to the benefit of and be binding upon the heirs, executors, administrators, successors, and assigns of Lessor and Lessee.

18. The land which is subject to this lease is situated in the County of _____, State of California, and is described as follows:

including all accretions thereto and all lakes, streams, canals, waterways, dikes, roads, streets, alleys, easements and rights of way, on, within, or adjoining the lands above described and including all strips or parcels of land contiguous, adjacent to or adjoining the above-described land and owned or claimed by Lessor. For the purpose of calculating any payments based on acreage, Lessee, at Lessee's option, may act as if said land and its constituent parcels contain _____ acres, whether they actually contain more or less. This lease shall cover all the interest in said land now owned or hereafter acquired by Lessor.

IN WITNESS WHEREOF, the parties hereto have executed this agreement.

LESSEE:

CHEVRON U.S.A. INC.

> By _____
> Its Attorney–In–Fact
>
> LESSOR:

_____   _____

_____   _____

_____   _____

_____   _____

(ACKNOWLEDGMENT)

GLOSSARY OF OIL AND GAS TERMS

Acreage–Contribution Agreement A support agreement by which the contributing party agrees to contribute leases or interests in leases in the area of a test well to a drilling party in exchange for information, if the drilling party drills to an agreed depth and develops the information. See also *Support Agreements*.

Ad Coelum Doctrine The common-law doctrine that the owner of land owns everything above and below the property's boundaries from the heavens to the core of the earth—including all the elements therein. The complete maxim is cujus est solum, ejus est usque ad coelum et ad inferos [Latin "to whomsoever the soil belongs, he owns also to the sky and to the depths"] The doctrine is still accepted as the governing principle for hard minerals, but has been replaced by the rule of capture for fugacious minerals such as oil and gas.

After–Acquired Title Clause An oil and gas lease clause that extends the coverage of the lease to any interest in the described property acquired after the lease. A common formulation is "This lease covers all the interest now owned by or hereafter vested in the lessor. . . ."

Apportionment Rule The rule followed in a minority of states (including California, Mississippi, and Pennsylvania) that royalties that accrue under a lease on property that is subdivided after the lease grant are shared by the owners of the property proportionately to their interest in the property. See also *Non–Apportionment Rule.*

Area–Rate Clause An indefinite price escalation clause found in some long-term gas contracts that provides for increase of the contract price if any regulatory agency permits or prescribes a higher price for gas sold in the same area. Under the regulatory scheme of the Natural Gas Act, from 1961 to 1978, maximum prices were set on an area basis. Area-rate clauses were drafted to permit sellers to collect the highest price permitted by the regulatory authority in the relevant area.

Assignment Clause Another name for the *Change-of-Ownership Clause.*

Bonus A payment to induce a lessor to execute the lease.

Bottom–Hole Agreement A contract in which the contributing party agrees to make a cash contribution to the drilling party in exchange for geological or drilling information, if the receiving party drills to an agreed depth and conducts agreed tests. See also Support Agreements.

Capture-and-Hold Rule The conventional analysis that "production" occurs for royalty-calculation purposes when oil or gas is captured and held at the wellhead or on the lease. By this view, the costs of transporting, compressing and processing, as well as severance and gross-production taxes, are charged proportionately against the royalty interest where royalty is determined by working back from a downstream price or value. See also *Marketable–Product Rule*.

Carried Interest A fractional interest, usually in an oil and gas lease, free of some or all costs, which are borne by the remainder of the working interest owners. A common arrangement in drilling ventures is that the promoter will be "carried" to the casing point for 1/4 of the working interest; i.e., the investors will pay 100% of the drilling costs for 75% of the working interest. The promoter will bear its 25% share of completion and operating costs under such an arrangement.

Casing An industry term for pipe placed in a wellbore hole. *Surface casing* protects potable waters against pollution from drilling and producing operations. *Intermediate casing* protects deeper formations. *Production casing* is the pipe through which oil and gas is produced.

Casinghead Gas Gas produced from the casinghead (the top) of an oil well. Casinghead gas is natural gas held in solution with oil in the production formation. At production or shortly after, the gas separates from the oil.

Casing Point The point at which a well has been drilled to the desired depth and the owners must decide whether or not to place production pipe, called *casing*, in the hole and proceed to complete and equip the well for production.

Cessation-of-Production Clause An oil and gas lease savings clause that specifies what the lessee must do to maintain the lease in the event that production ceases. The purpose of the cessation-of-production clause is to make more certain the temporary-cessation-of-production doctrine. See also *Temporary–Cessation-of-Production Doctrine.*

Change-of-Ownership Clause An oil and gas lease clause specifying what notice must be given by the lessor or its assignee to the lessee of changes in ownership to bind the lessee to recognize them. The purpose of the clause is to protect a lease holder against the consequences of making an improper payment under the lease. Sometimes called an *assignment clause.*

Condensate See *Distillate.*

Continuous–Operations Clause A form of *operations clause.*

Contribution Agreement Another name for a *support agreement.*

Correlative–Rights Doctrine A corollary to the rule of capture, that the right to capture oil and gas from potentially producing formations under one's property is subject to the concomitant duty to exercise the right without negligence or waste. See also *Rule of Capture.*

Cost Depletion Recovery of one's tax basis in a producing oil or gas well by deducting basis proportionately over the producing life of the well. See also *Percentage Depletion*.

Cover–All Clause Another name for a *Mother Hubbard clause*.

Damages Clause A lease clause that imposes a duty on the lease holder to pay the lessor or the surface owner for damage, usually of a specified type, to the surface. Often damages clauses are limited to "growing crops." In the absence of a damages clause the lease holder has no legal obligation to pay for "reasonable" damage to the surface necessary to obtain oil and gas; the lessee has an implied right to use the surface for oil and gas operations.

Daywork Drilling Contract A drilling contract under which the lease operator compensates the drilling contractor on the basis of the amount of time the contractor spends conducting drilling operations. Essentially, the lease operator hires the contractor's drilling rig and staff to work under the lease operator's direction. This contract form gives broad discretion to the lease operator to give instructions to the drilling contractor how to conduct drilling operations. Courts impose broad liability upon the lease operator as a result of its broad discretion. See also *Drilling Contracts*.

Delay Rental A payment from the lease holder to the lessor to maintain the lease from period to period during the primary term without drilling. See also *Drilling–Delay Rental Clause*, *"Unless" Lease*, *"Or" Lease*, and *Paid–Up Lease*.

Deregulation Clause A gas contract provision spelling out how price is to be determined and what obligations the buyer and seller will owe one another if regulated natural gas is freed from regulation.

Distillate The "wet" element of natural gas that may be removed as a liquid. Used interchangeably with "condensate" and "natural gasoline." Also, any product of the process of distillation.

Division Order An authorization to one who has a fund for distribution from persons entitled to the fund directing how the fund is to be distributed. In the oil and gas industry, division orders are entered into by both working interest owners and royalty owners to sell oil and to give instructions for payments under a lease.

Double–Fraction Problem A common interpretative problem in conveyances that arises when one who owns a fractional interest conveys or reserves a fraction. For example, if one who owns an undivided 1/2 interest in minerals conveys "an undivided 1/2 interest in the minerals," it is uncertain whether the grantor intended to convey a half interest in 100% of the minerals or half of the grantor's half.

Drilling Contracts Agreements for the drilling of a well or wells entered into between drilling contractors, who own drilling rigs and associated equipment, and persons or entities owning or operating mineral rights or leasehold rights. Drilling contracts are generally structured to provide compensation on a daywork, footage, or turnkey basis. The compensation provision typically controls the scope of discretion given to the operator to direct the contractor and the amount of potential liability imposed on the operator, as well as method of payment. See also *Daywork Drilling Contract*, *Footage Drilling Contract*, and *Turnkey Drilling Contract*.

Drilling–Delay Rental Clause An oil and gas lease clause giving the lessee the right to maintain the lease from period to period during the primary term either by commencing drilling operations or by paying delay rentals. Leases contain drilling-delay rental clauses because courts have held that they obviate any implied covenant to drill a test well on the premises. They are accepted by lessors because they provide for periodic rental payments. See also *"Unless" Lease* and *"Or" Lease*.

Dry–Hole Agreement A contract in which the contributing party agrees to make a cash contribution to the drilling party in exchange for geological or drilling information, if the well drilled is a dry hole. See also Support Agreements.

Dry–Hole Clause A provision in an oil and gas lease specifying what a lessee must do to maintain the lease for the remainder of the primary term after drilling an unproductive well. A dry-hole clause is intended to make clear that the lease may be maintained by payment of delay rentals for the remainder of the primary term.

Duhig Rule A rule of title interpretation developed to deal with the frequent problem of overconveyances of fractional interests. The court in *Duhig v. Peavy–Moore Lumber Co., Inc.*, 135 Tex. 503, 144

S.W.2d 878 (1940), first stated the rule, which provides that where a grantor does not own enough interest to give full effect both to the granted interest and to a reserved interest, courts will give priority to the granted interest (rather than to the reserved interest) until the granted interest is fully satisfied. The *Duhig* rule is not accepted in all states and is generally limited to conveyances by warranty deed.

Economic–Out Clause Another name for a gas contract Market–Out Clause.

Entirety Clause A clause in an oil and gas lease or in a deed that states the agreement of the parties that royalties are to be apportioned in the event that the property is subdivided after the lease is granted. The purpose of the clause is to avoid the non-apportionment rule.

Escalation Clause A long-term gas contract provision providing for adjustment of the base price provided for in the agreement. Adjustment may be up or down, but the parties often refer to the provision as an "escalation clause."

Executive Right The right to lease specified land or mineral rights. The executive right is one of the incidents of the mineral interest.

Farmout Agreement An agreement by which one who owns an oil and gas lease (the farmor) agrees to assign to another (the farmee) an interest in the lease in return for drilling and testing operations on the lease or payment for them.

Fee Interest A property interest of potentially infinite duration. As used in the oil and gas industry, "fee interest" often refers to ownership of both the surface interest and the mineral interest.

FERC The Federal Energy Regulatory Commission, the successor agency to the Federal Power Commission (FPC). FERC is the agency responsible for administering the Natural Gas Act.

FERC–Out Clause A gas-contract clause that provides that the price paid to the producer shall be reduced (or the contract terminated) to the extent that the Federal Energy Regulatory Commission or other regulatory agencies will not permit it to be included in the regulated purchaser's cost of service (and, in effect, passed on to consumers).

Fixed–Term Lease An oil and gas lease for a fixed period of time–e.g., 20 years–perhaps renewable for an additional period of time, but without the indefinite "so long thereafter" provision commonly found in leases.

Footage Drilling Contract A drilling contract under which the drilling contractor is compensated on the basis of the footage drilled. The drilling contractor is hired by the lease operator to drill to a specified formation or depth and is given broad discretion to make the management decisions necessary to accomplish the task. The risk of unexpected delays, as well as most liabilities, is upon the drilling contractor rather than the lease operator.

Force–Majeure Clause A lease or contract clause that provides that the lessee will not be held to be in breach if the lessee is prevented from performing by force majeure (literally, "superior force"). Typically, force majeure clauses expressly indicate problems beyond the reasonable control of the lessee that will excuse performance.

FPC Clause Another name for an Area Rate Clause.

Free–Gas Clause An oil and gas lease clause, found commonly in leases on properties in colder states, that entitles the lessor or the surface owner to use without charge gas produced from the leased property. Free-gas clauses are usually limited either as to the uses permitted (e.g., domestic heating and light) or as to the quantity that may be taken (e.g., not more than 300 MCF per year) or both.

Freestone Rider Another name for a Pugh Clause.

Further–Exploration Covenant An implied oil and gas lease promise that, once production has been obtained from the leased premises, the lessee will continue to explore other parts of the property and other formations under it. In some jurisdictions courts have said that the covenant for further exploration does not exist independently of the implied covenant for reasonable development. See also *Reasonable–Development Covenant* and *Reasonably Prudent Operator Standard*.

Gas–Balancing Agreement A contract among owners of the production of a gas well setting forth their agreement for the balancing of production if one owner sells more of the gas stream than other owners.

Gas Contract An agreement for the sale of natural gas.

Granting Clause The clause in the oil and gas lease that spells out what rights are given by the lessor to the lessee. Typically, an oil and gas lease granting clause will specify what kinds of uses are permitted and what substances covered by the lease.

Habendum Clause The clause in an oil and gas lease that defines how long the interest granted to the lessee will extend. Modern oil and gas leases typically provide for a primary term, a fixed number of years during which the lessee has no obligation to develop the premises, and a secondary term for "so long thereafter as oil and gas produced" once development takes place.

Horsehead See *Pumping Unit*.

Implied Covenant. An implied promise, usually in an oil and gas lease, that imposes obligations on one of the parties, usually the lessee. Though courts describe lease implied covenants differently, there are at least six: (1) the covenant to test the premises, (2) the covenant to reasonably develop, (3) the covenant to further explore, (4) the covenant to protect against drainage, (5) the covenant to market, and (6) the covenant of diligent and proper operation.

> "Lease implied covenants arise from the ongoing relationship of the lessor and lessee created by the lease. The lease gives the lessee the exclusive cost-bearing right to explore and develop the leased property, poten-

tially in perpetuity. The lessor has a cost-free interest in production or revenues or value, but has given the lessee the exclusive right to drill or produce. Because the typical oil and gas lease makes the lessor's royalty—the major compensation for grant of the lease—dependent upon the quantity and quality of the lessee's actions on the property, the courts have concluded that the lessee has an obligation to perform certain unstated obligations...." John S. Lowe, Owen L. Anderson, Ernest E. Smith, and David E. Pierce, *Cases and Materials on Oil and Gas Law* 308 (West 5th ed. 2008).

Intangible Drilling Costs Costs that (1) are incurred incident to and necessary for the drilling oil and gas wells and preparing them for production, and (2) that have no salvage value. By § 612 of the Internal Revenue Code, intangible drilling costs may be deducted in the year paid rather than capitalized and depreciated.

Landman A position in the oil and gas industry responsible for acquiring oil and gas leases, curing title, negotiating arrangements for development, and managing leased properties. A landman may be either male or female.

Landowner's Royalty The share of production or production revenues or value, free of costs of production, provided for the lessor in the royalty clause of the oil and gas lease. See also *Royalty Interest*.

Leasehold Interest Another name for the Working Interest.

Leasehold Royalty Another name for the Landowner's Royalty.

Lesser–Interest Clause A lease clause that permits a lessee to reduce payments under the lease proportionately if the lessor has less than 100% of the mineral interest. Sometimes called a proportionate-reduction clause.

Marketable–Product Rule The rule that "production" for royalty-calculation purposes is not complete until a lessee has both captured and held the product and made it marketable. Until there is a "marketable product," the lessee must bear all costs associated with capturing and handling oil and gas. See also *Capture-and-Hold Rule*.

Market–Out Clause A long-term gas-contract clause that provides that if the contract price for the gas purchased (plus certain costs incurred in getting it to the purchaser's principal market) exceeds an amount that will permit the gas purchaser to resell it profitably, the contract price will be redetermined. Often market-out clauses are drafted by referring to competing fuels, e.g., fuel oil.

Marketing Covenant The promise implied in oil and gas leases that the lessee will market the production from the lease within a reasonable time and at a reasonable price. See also *Reasonably Prudent Operator Standard*.

MMBtu The abbreviation for one million British Thermal Units, one of the standard units of measurement for natural gas.

MCF The abbreviation for one thousand cubic feet, one of the standard units of measurement for natural gas.

Mineral Acre The full mineral interest in one acre of land.

Mineral Interest The right to search for, develop, and produce oil and gas (and other minerals) from land, as well as (in some states) the right to present possession of the oil and gas in place. The mineral interest is granted by an oil and gas lease. See also *Fee Interest* and *Surface Interest*.

Mineral Servitude Under the Louisiana Mineral Code, a charge upon land in favor of a person or another tract of land that creates a limited right to use of the land to explore for and produce minerals. Generally equivalent to a severed mineral interest in a common-law state.

Mother Hubbard Clause A lease clause that protects the lessee against errors in description of property by providing that the lease covers all the land owned by the lessor in the area. Sometimes called a *cover-all clause*. Sometimes combined with an after-acquired title clause.

Natural Gasoline See *Distillate*.

Net–Profits Interest A share of production or production revenues or value free of the costs of production, to the extent that there is a net profit. The methodology of defining *net profits* is crucial to a net-profits interest.

Non–Apportionment Rule The rule—followed in the majority of states—that royalties accruing under a lease on property that has been subdivided after the lease grant are not to be shared by the owners of the various subdivisions but belong exclusively to the owner of the subdivision where the producing well is located. The non-apportionment rule may be modified in an oil and gas lease by an *Entirety Clause*. See also *Apportionment Rule*.

Non-Executive Right An oil and gas interest that does not possess the right to lease; e.g., a royalty interest, a non-executive mineral interest.

Non–Ownership Theory The characterization of oil and gas rights that a severed mineral interest owner has merely a right to search, develop and produce oil and gas from land, but not a present right to possess the oil and gas in place. Because there is no right to present possession, the interest of a severed mineral interest owner in a non-ownership theory state is akin to a *profit a prendre*, a right to use the land and remove items of value from it. Adopted in California, Louisiana and Oklahoma, as well as various other producing states. See also *Ownership–In–Place Theory*.

Nonparticipating Royalty A share of production, or the value or proceeds of production, free of the costs of production, carved out of the mineral interest. A nonparticipating-royalty owner is entitled to the stated share of production or cash without regard to the terms of any lease. Nonparticipating royalties are often retained by fee-simple owners or mineral-interest owners who sell their rights. See also *Royalty* and *Overriding Royalty*.

No–Term Lease A lease with a drilling-delay rental clause that allows a lessee to extend the primary term indefinitely by paying delay rentals. No-term leases were common at the end of the 19th Century. Some courts refused to enforce them on the ground that they created an estate terminable at the will of either the lessor or the lessee. Other courts upheld them, but with the stipulation that the lessee had an obligation to test or release the lease within a reasonable time.

Obstruction An equitable doctrine that suspends the running of time under a lease or extends the lease for a reasonable time if the lessor or one claiming through the lessor interferes with rights granted by the lease. Some courts apply the obstruction doctrine to interference by a severed surface owner.

Operating Agreement A contract among owners of the working interest in a producing oil or gas well or wells setting forth the parties' agreement about drilling, development, operations and accounting.

Operations Clause A clause frequently found in oil and gas leases providing that the lease will continue so long as operations for oil and gas development continue on the premises. There are numerous variations. Two common ones are the well-completion clause and the continuous-operations clause. A *well-completion clause* provides that a lessee who starts drilling before the lease terminates has the right to complete the well and to maintain the lease if the drilling achieves production. A *continuous-operations clause* gives a lessee the right not only to continue drilling a well begun before termination but also to commence additional wells.

"Or" Lease An oil and gas lease with a drilling-delay rental clause structured so that the lessee promises to commence drilling operations or to pay delay rentals from time to time during the primary term. If the lessee fails to do one or the other, the lease does not automatically terminate; instead the lessee is liable to pay the delay rental.

Overriding Royalty A share of production, or the value or proceeds of production, free of the costs of production, carved out of a lessee's interest under an oil and gas lease. Overriding-royalty interests are frequently used to compensate those who have helped to structure a drilling venture. An over-riding-royalty interest terminates when the under-lying lease terminates. See also *Royalty* and *Non–Participating Royalty*.

Ownership-in-Place Theory The characterization of oil and gas rights that a fee-simple or mineral-interest owner owns the right to present possession of the oil and gas in place as well as the right to use the land surface to search, develop and produce from the property. Adopted in Texas, New Mexico, Kansas, Mississippi, and other major producing states. The rights of a severed mineral-interest own-er to oil and gas in these states are often described as an estate in fee simple absolute, but ownership of specific oil and gas molecules is subject to the rule of capture even in ownership-in-place theory states. See also *Non–Ownership Theory*.

Paid–Up Lease An oil and gas lease that does not provide for delay-rental payment. The lease is effective for the whole period of the primary term.

Partition The division of undivided interests, in kind or by sale, by voluntary agreement or judicial action.

Percentage Depletion A provision of § 611 of the Internal Revenue Code that permits a taxpayer who owns an economic interest in a producing oil or gas well to deduct a specified percentage of the gross income from the well in lieu of depleting the actual basis. See also *Cost Depletion*.

Petroleum Conservation Law A state law that limits the rule of capture and defines the correlative-rights doctrine by regulating the drilling and operation of oil and gas wells. Petroleum conservation laws are intended to prevent waste and protect correlative rights.

Pooling Bringing together, either by voluntary agreement (voluntary pooling) or by order of an administrative agency (compulsory or forced pooling), small tracts or fractional interests to drill a well. Pooling is usually undertaken to comply with well spacing requirements established by state law or regulation. Pooling is usually associated with drilling a single well and operating that well by primary-production techniques. In the oil and gas industry, the term is sometimes used interchangeably with *unitization*.

Pooling Clause A clause found in most leases that grants the lessee the power to combine part or all of the leased acreage with other properties for exploration, development, or operation.

Prescription A Louisiana doctrine that extinguishes unused mineral servitudes after 10 years. To interrupt the running of the prescription period, there must be operations to discover or produce on the land or land pooled with it.

Price–Renegotiation Clause A clause in a gas contract providing for price renegotiation from time to time or upon election of one of the parties.

Primary Recovery Oil or gas production that occurs because of the pressure differential between the formation where the oil or gas is located and the borehole, though the primary recovery includes oil produced using pumping units or other artificial-lift mechanisms. See also *Secondary Recovery* and *Tertiary Recovery*.

Primary Term The option period—set by the oil and gas lease habendum clause—during which the lessee retains the right to search, develop and produce from the premises without having any obligation to do so. The primary term should be sufficiently long to permit the lessee to evaluate the property and make arrangements to drill it. In practice, the primary term may extend for 24 hours or 25 years, depending upon how much competition there is for leases in the area. See also *Habendum Clause* and *Secondary Term*.

Production Payment A share of production value or proceeds from property, free of the costs of production, that terminates when an agreed sum has been paid; e.g., "1/5 of all oil and gas produced and saved from said land until the market value at the well of such production shall aggregate One Million Dollars...."

Profit a Prendre At common law, the right to enter the land of another and take away some fruit of the soil. In many states mineral rights or oil and gas leases are classified as profits a prendre.

Proportionate–Reduction Clause Another name for the *Lesser–Interest Clause*.

Protection Covenant The promise implied in an oil and gas lease that the lessee will protect the premises against drainage by drilling a producing well to the reservoir that is subject to drainage, if a reasonably prudent operator would do so. See also *Reasonably Prudent Operator Standard*.

Pugh Clause A lease clause (called a Freestone Rider in Texas) modifying the effect of most lease pooling clauses by severing pooled portions of the lease from unpooled portions of the lease so that drilling or production on a pooled portion will not maintain the lease as to unpooled portions.

Pumping Unit Equipment used to pump oil to the surface when the pressure differential between the pressure in the formation and in the borehole is insufficient to cause oil to rise up the borehole to the surface. Sometimes called a *pumpjack* or *horsehead*.

Pumpjack Another term for a *pumping unit*.

Reasonable–Development Covenant The promise implied in oil and gas leases that, once a lessee obtains production, the lessee will continue to develop the premises as would a reasonably prudent operator rather than merely holding the lease by the production already obtained. See also *Further–Exploration Covenant*.

Reasonably Prudent Operator Standard The test generally applied to determine a lessee's compliance with implied lease covenants. Also called the "reasonable prudent operator" standard and the "prudent operator" standard. The term refers to what a reasonable, competent operator in the oil and gas industry, acting in good faith and with economic motivation, and taking into account the lessor's interests as well as its own, would do under the circumstances. Also called the *reasonable prudent operator standard* and the *prudent operator standard*.

Regulatory–Out Clause Another name for a FERC–Out Clause.

Rental Division Order A stipulation signed by those entitled to delay rentals stipulating their interests and how much rental each is to receive.

Royalty Interest A share of production, or the value or proceeds of production, free of the costs of production, when and if there is production. Royalty is usually expressed as a fraction; e.g., 1/6. A royalty-interest owner has no right to operate the property, and therefore no right to lease or to share in bonus or delay rentals. In some states a royalty owner has the right of access and egress to take the royalty production. There are several different, but related, kinds of royalty interests. See e.g., *Landowner's Royalty*, *Non–Participating Royalty*, and *Overriding Royalty*.

Rule of Capture The fundamental principle of oil and gas law that there is no liability for capturing oil and gas that drains from another's lands. The owner of mineral rights in a tract of land acquires title to the oil and gas produced from wells drilled on the land, though part of the oil and gas may have migrated from adjoining lands.

Secondary Recovery The second stage of oil or gas production, typically involving injection of water or gas or both to maintain the pressure differential between the formation where the oil or gas is located and the borehole. See also *Primary Recovery* and *Tertiary Recovery*.

Secondary Term The term of the oil and gas lease after production has been established, typically "as long thereafter as oil and gas is produced from the premises." See also *Habendum Clause* and *Primary Term*.

Separator Equipment used at the well site to separate oil, water, and gas produced in solution with oil. Basic separators simply heat oil to speed the natural separation process. More complex separators may use chemicals.

Severance A transfer or reservation of a part of the "bundle of rights" that make up property ownership. Mineral rights are frequently "severed" from surface rights in property that may contain oil and gas or other minerals.

Shut-in Royalty Clause A lease provision permitting the lessee to maintain the lease while there is no production from the premises because wells capable of production are not producing. The lessee pays the lessor a "shut-in royalty" in lieu of production.

Subrogation Clause A lease provision permitting the lessee to pay taxes, mortgages, or other encumbrances on the leased property and to recover those payments out of future proceeds from the lease.

Support Agreements Contracts between people or entities in the oil and gas industry that encourage and "support" exploratory operations. Generally, one party agrees to contribute money or property to another if the other will drill a well on leases that it holds and provide the contributing party with information from tests conducted. For the contributing party, a support agreement is a purchase of geological or technological information. For the party receiving the support, the contribution lessens the cost or the risk of drilling operations. For further discussion, see *Dry–Hole Agreement*, *Bottom–Hole Agreement*, and *Acreage–Contribution Agreement*.

Surface Interest All rights to property other than the mineral interest. The surface interest has the right to the surface subject to the right of the mineral-interest owner to use the surface. The surface interest is entitled to all substances found in or under the soil that are not defined as *minerals*.

Surrender Clause A clause commonly found in an oil and gas lease authorizing a lessee to release its rights to all or any portion of the leased premises at any time and be relieved of further obligations relating to the acreage surrendered.

Temporary–Cessation-of-Production Doctrine The rule that an oil and gas lease term "for so long thereafter as oil and gas are produced" will not terminate once the lease owner attains production unless the cessation of production is for an "unreasonable" length of time, taking into account all of the facts and circumstances. See also *Cessation-of-Production Clause*.

Term Clause Another name for the *Habendum Clause*.

Term Interest A mineral interest or royalty interest that is not perpetual. A term interest may be for a fixed term (e.g., for 25 years) or a defeasible term (e.g., for 25 years and so long thereafter as there is production from the premises).

Tertiary Recovery The third stage of oil or gas production, involving injection of chemicals, hydrocarbons, carbon dioxide, or steam to maintain formation pressure and to improve the flow of oil and gas through the formation to the borehole. Sometimes called *enhanced recovery*. See also *Primary Recovery* and *Secondary Recovery*.

Top Lease A lease granted on property already subject to an oil and gas lease. Generally, a top lease grants rights if and when the existing lease expires.

Turnkey Drilling Contract A drilling contract under which the drilling contractor agrees to perform stated functions for an agreed price. The lease operator has little or no discretion to instruct the drilling contractor and little or no liability exposure for the contractor's actions.

Unitization Bringing together some or all of the well spacing units over a producing reservoir for joint operations, either by agreement of the owners (voluntary unitization) or by order of an administrative agency (compulsory or "forced" unitization). Unitization is usually undertaken after primary production has begun to fall off substantially to permit efficient secondary or tertiary-recovery operations. In the oil and gas industry, the term is sometimes used interchangeably with *Pooling*.

Unitization Clause A lease provision granting the lessee the right to unitize the leased premises, generally for secondary or tertiary-recovery operations. It is somewhat unusual to see "true" unitization clauses; generally the pooling clause addresses the right to unitize tangentially and subject to acreage limitations that make unitized operations difficult.

"Unless" Lease An oil and gas lease with a drilling-delay rental clause structured as a special limitation to the primary term. The lease automatically terminates, though the lessee has no liability for its failure to perform, "unless" delay rentals are paid or drilling operations are commenced.

Warranty Clause A deed or lease clause by which the grantor guarantees that title is without defect and agrees to defend it. If the warranty is breached, the grantor may be liable to the grantee to the extent that the grantor has received payments. Presence of a warranty clause in a mineral deed or oil and gas lease may also cause after-acquired interests to pass from the grantor to the grantee by application of estoppel by deed.

Well–Completion Clause See *Operations Clause*.

Working Interest The rights to the mineral interest granted by an oil and gas lease, so-called because the lessee acquires the right to work on the leased property to search, develop and produce oil and gas (and the obligation to pay all costs). Sometimes used to describe the mineral interest itself.

INDEX

References are to Pages

467

476 *INDEX*
References are to Pages

†

DATE DUE